NA7574 .B76 2005
Broto, Eduard.

Resort houses

2005.

resort houses

Edition 2005

Author: Eduard Broto
Publisher: Carles Broto
Editorial Coordinator: Jacobo Krauel
Graphic designer & production: Pilar Chueca
Text: contributed by the architects,
edited by Amber Ockrassa and Marta Rojals

© Carles Broto i Comerma
Jonqueres, 10, 1-5
08003 Barcelona, Spain
Tel.: +34 93 301 21 99
Fax: +34-93-301 00 21
E-mail: info@linksbooks.net
www. linksbooks.net

All rights reserved. No part of this book may be used or reproduced in any manner whatsoever without written permission except in the case of brief quotations embodied in critical articles and reviews.

resort houses

Introduction — 7

Strindberg Arkitekter AB
Villa Näckros — 8

Pierre Thibault, architecte
Beaver's Lake Refuge — 22

Boije Design AB
Stem to Stern Perfection — 36

JAHN Associates
Kutti Beach House — 50

Wortmann & Bañares Arquitectos
House in La Cerdanya — 60

JAHN Associates
Pearl Beach House — 72

Wingårdh Arkitektkontor AB
Villa Astrid   82

E. Cobb Architects
Lakeshore in the Cascade Mountain Range   96

Bellemo & Cat
Cocoon House   110

Carl-Viggo Hølmebakk
Mountain Cottage in Sollia   122

Denton & Corker & Marshall
Marshall House   136

Peter Hulting Architect
Meter Arkitektur
Guest Appearance   144

Jarmund-Vigsnæs
Villa Bjørnsen / Sund   154

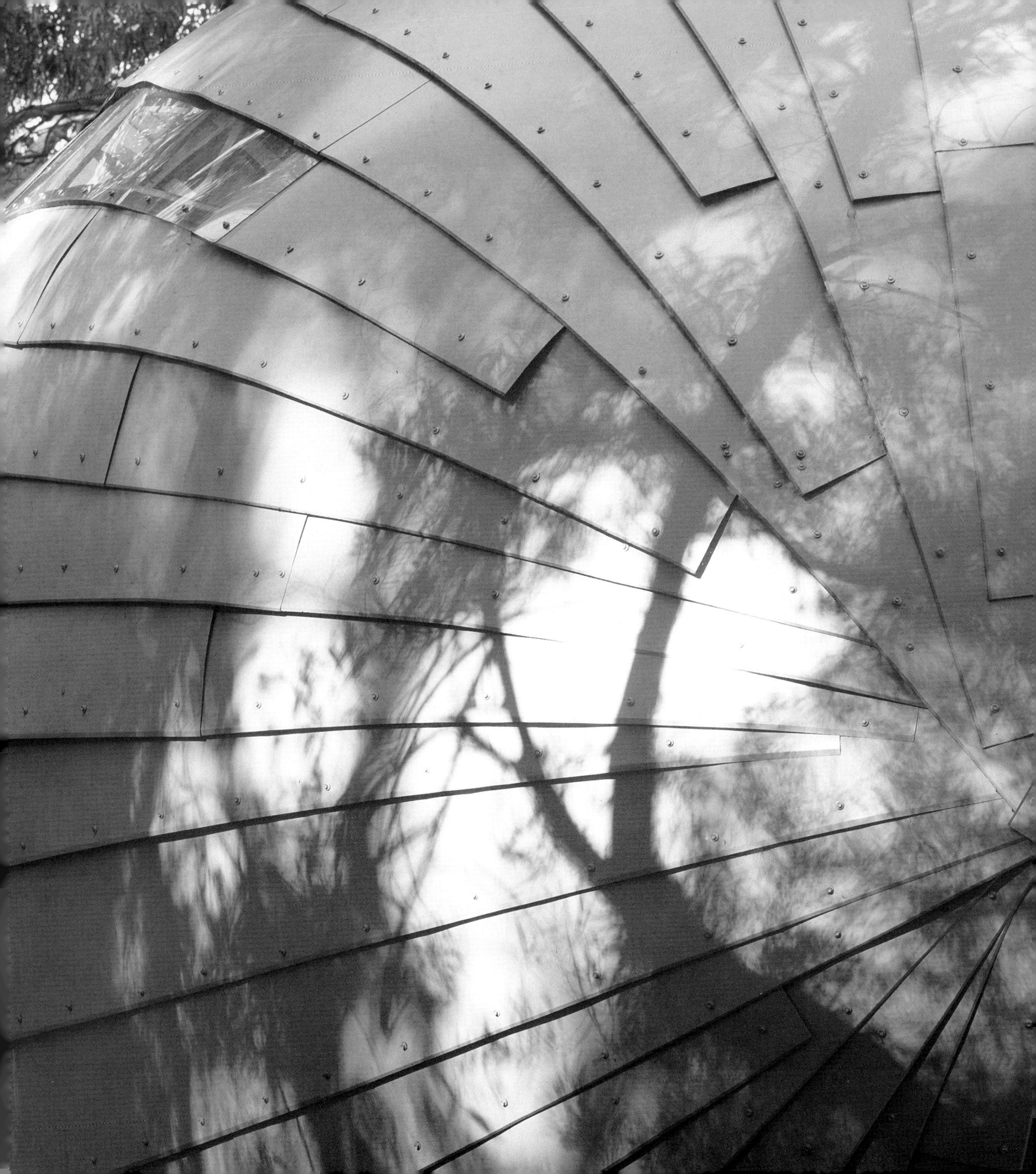

INTRODUCTION

Cities are centers of wealth, culture and trade. They are also the places where dwellings and workplaces are most densely concentrated; thus, it is in cities where most architecture has traditionally developed. With increasing transport and communications infrastructure however, more and more people are deciding to move to the country in search of contact with nature and the tranquility of a life far from the bustle of the city. In rejection of a life lived among the urban masses, there is a growing tendency to return to a more traditional way of life by renovating isolated buildings in rural areas, paying greater attention to the environment surrounding the dwelling and seeking privileged views that can be enjoyed from any part of the house. This residential unit par excellence is the architectural form that most lends itself to creative approaches - it is the basis on which privacy was built and invented. Despite the invasion of the media and pervasive stereotyped behaviors and fashions, the home is still the only place that is designed and decorated in privacy, the place that reflects the individual's resistance to normalization and standardization and an outlet to express difference and identity. The house is a place of rest - and nowadays it can also be a place of work, as home offices and workshops start to replace the idea of the workplace that developed with the industrial revolution.

This volume offers a representative selection of country houses by some of the most prestigious contemporary architects. They all show a respect for nature - some even introduce ecological innovations into the design - and pay great attention to the treatment of natural light and views. They also show a desire for the dwellings to dialogue with the landscape through the materials and colors used. Though they consistently seek a relationship with the landscape, all the projects presented here show different solutions that respond to the different needs and preferences of their inhabitants, their culture, values and beliefs, and to the physical and climatic context of the location. Through close attention to the client brief, the composition and the construction, these proposals renew the relationship between the dwelling and the surrounding environment.

Strindberg Arkitekter AB
Villa Näckros

Photographs: James Silverman

Kalmar, Sweden

Situated on the east coast of Sweden, Villa Näckros is a world away from the traditional 'houseboats' of the past. Where floating homes have always been restricted in terms of both space and comfort, this one offers a spacious, contemporary living environment that combines all the luxuries of the modern day home with the spatial freedom and unrivalled views that only waterfront living can provide. One of Strindberg's key design solutions was to use repetition where possible. This worked to both simplify the construction process and help keep costs down. A spacious, light-filled home was achieved, in part, by dividing the space into a number of split-levels.

Encompassing 1916 square feet (178 square meters) of living space, set over three half levels, as well as a roof garden and terrace, the Villa's square shape evolved from the need to create a structure that would be as stable as possible. "We had to create something that would float, but designing a portable home was not the main objective in this case," explains Strindberg. "There was no need to assume the traditional shape of a boat."

The hull is constructed from reinforced concrete, which has been externally isolated to eliminate moisture on the inside. The weight of the concrete, combined with the shape of the hull, provides optimum stability. This method of construction has now been patented by the company. "Everything is glued together; there are no mechanical fastenings."

The main living area is characterized by large floor-to-ceiling windows, again overlooking the water. Oak flooring and neutral walls provide a blank canvas upon which to showcase the room's almost sculptural furnishings. Swathes of light also enable innovative pieces, such as the large white sculpture by Swedish sculptor Eva Hild and Olga Thorson's handmade ceramic 'Woman' lamp to create their own playful shadows across the floor. In the corner, a fireplace draws the eye upwards, emphasizing the room's double ceiling height. Carpeting has been used to subtly sub-divide and define the open plan living space, while Mats Theselius's Ambassad chairs, with their coppered steel frames upholstered in rivet prime leather, provide the perfect accompaniment to Mats Lindehoff's Kub tables. Downstairs, the bedrooms have been designed with simplicity in mind. Built-in wardrobes create a clean line around the room's perimeter while the blind provides privacy without restricting the room's primary light source. A second of Olga Thorson's limited edition ceramic lamps - this time, 'Man' - provides an element of continuity whilst retaining its unique individuality.

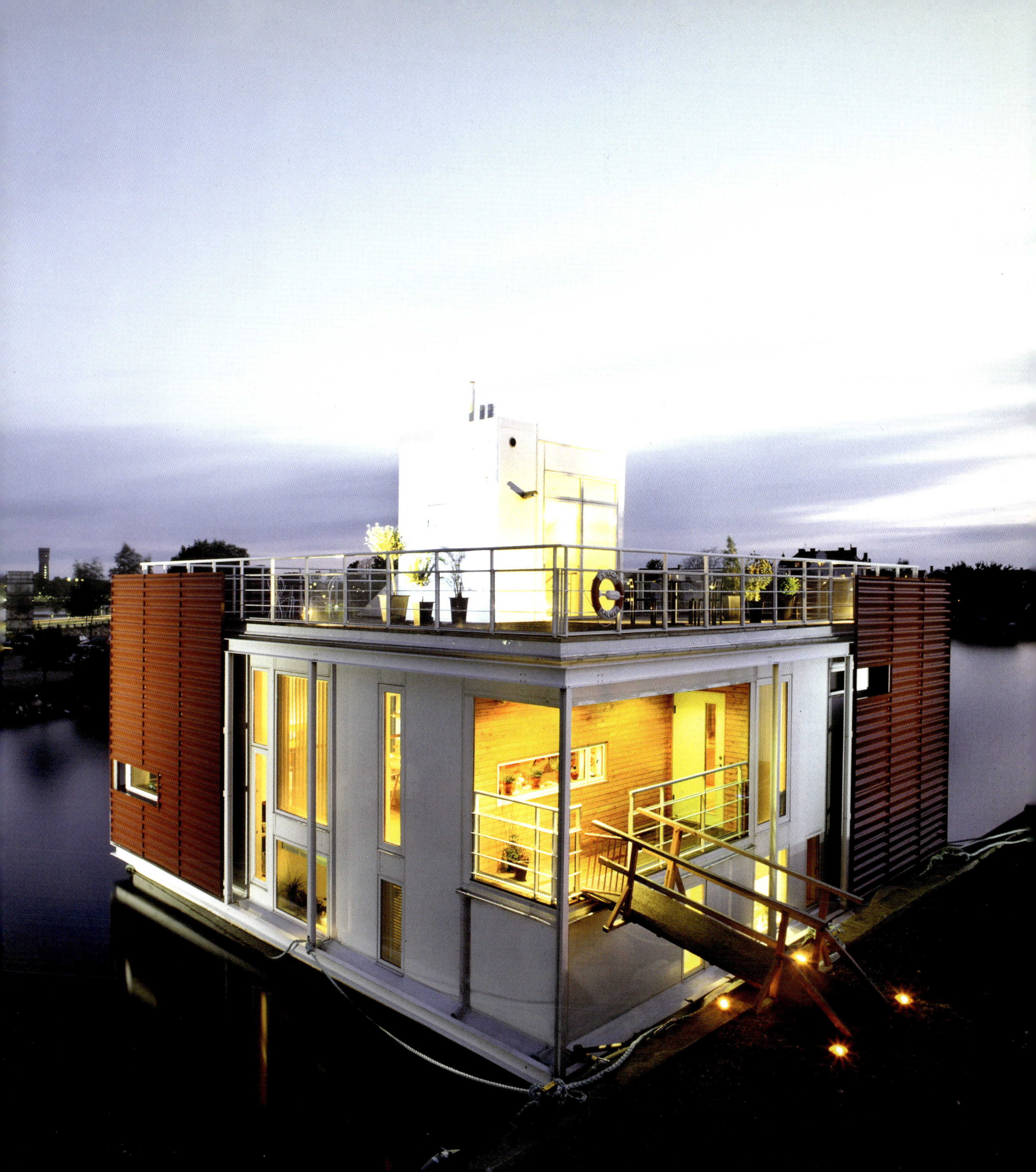

The red corrugated aluminum exterior and aluminum structure of the Villa provide a striking silhouette. Night façade lighting was designed by Andrew Gauld of gaulddesign.

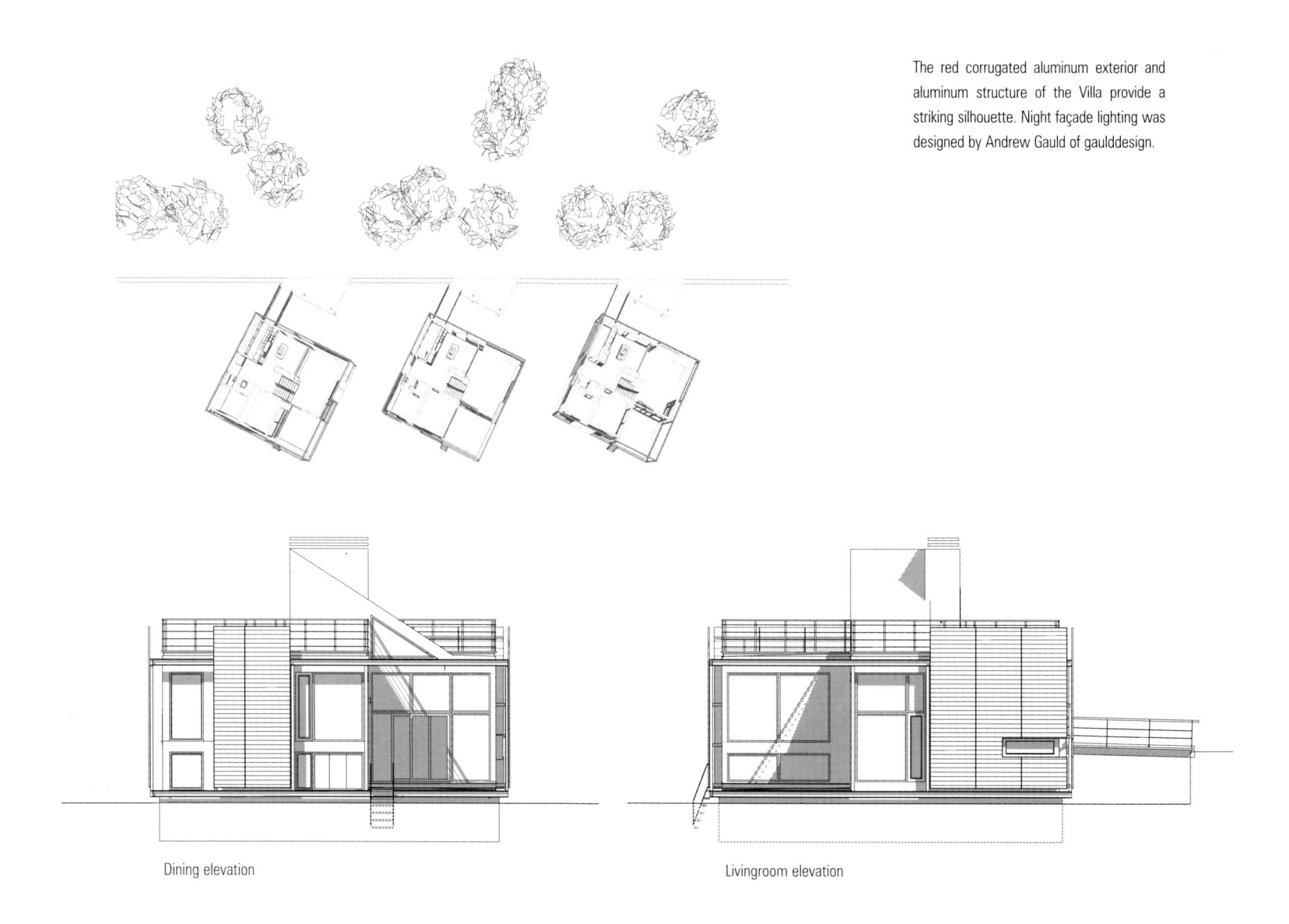

Dining elevation

Livingroom elevation

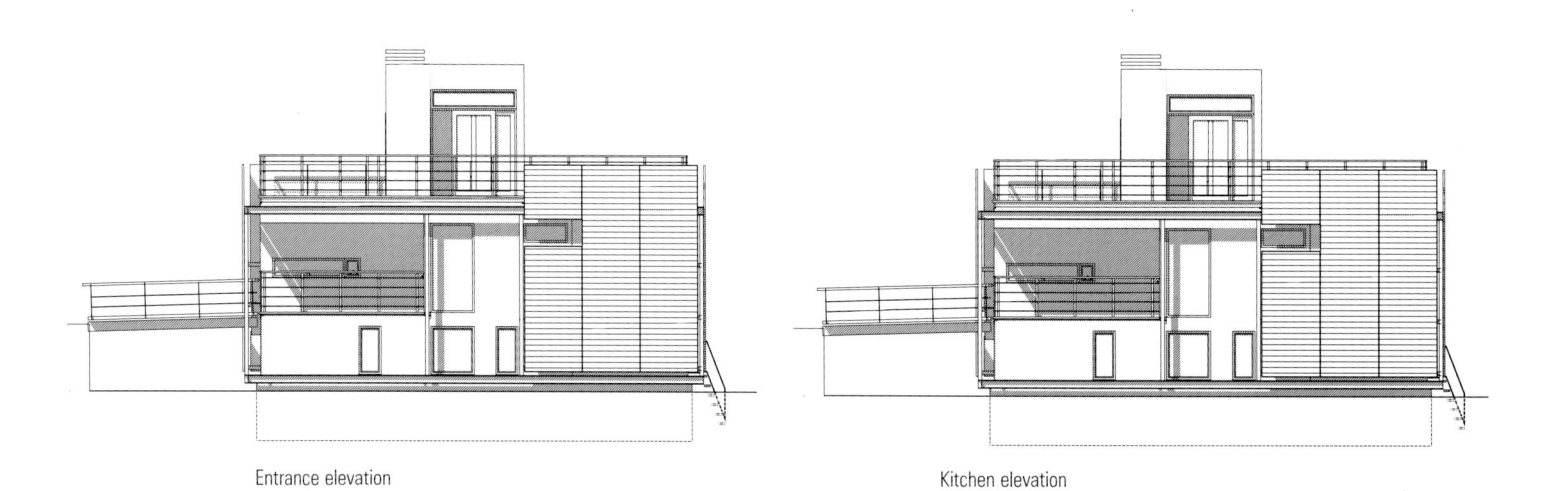

Entrance elevation

Kitchen elevation

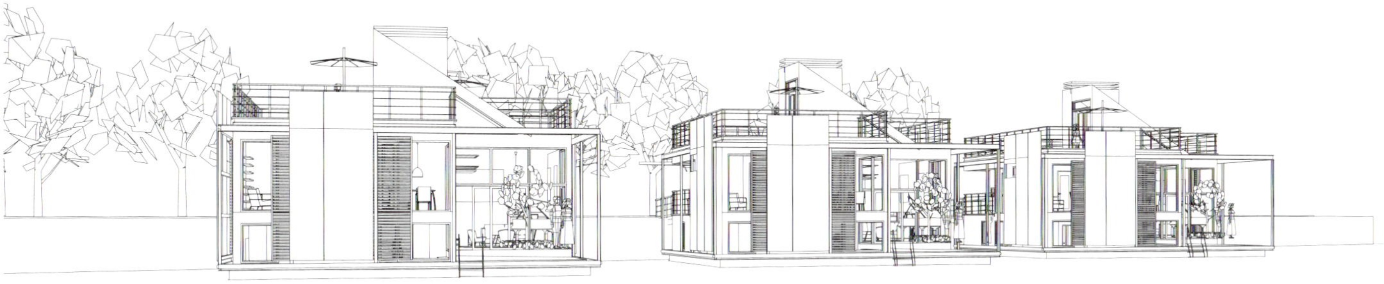

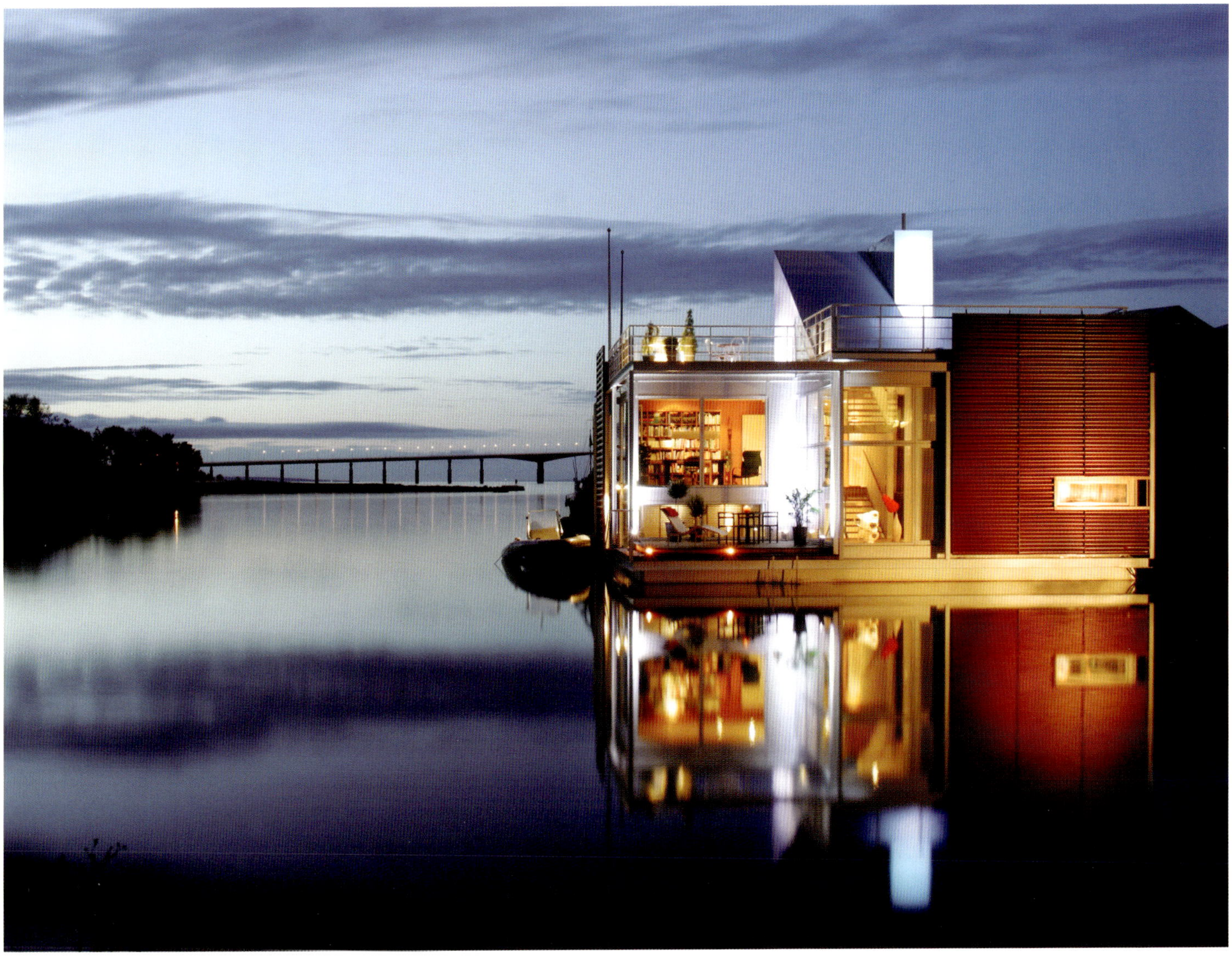

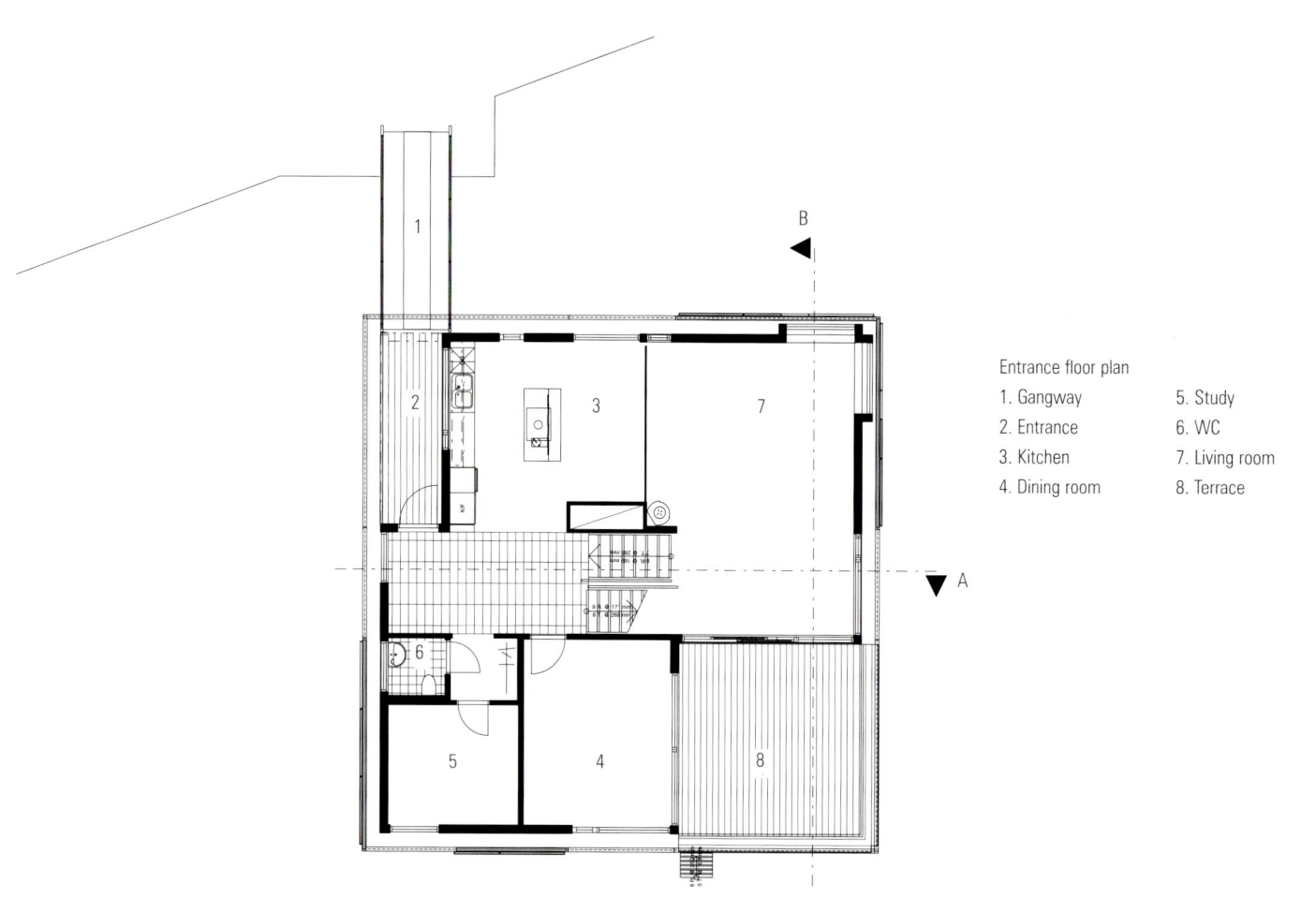

Entrance floor plan
1. Gangway 5. Study
2. Entrance 6. WC
3. Kitchen   7. Living room
4. Dining room 8. Terrace

13

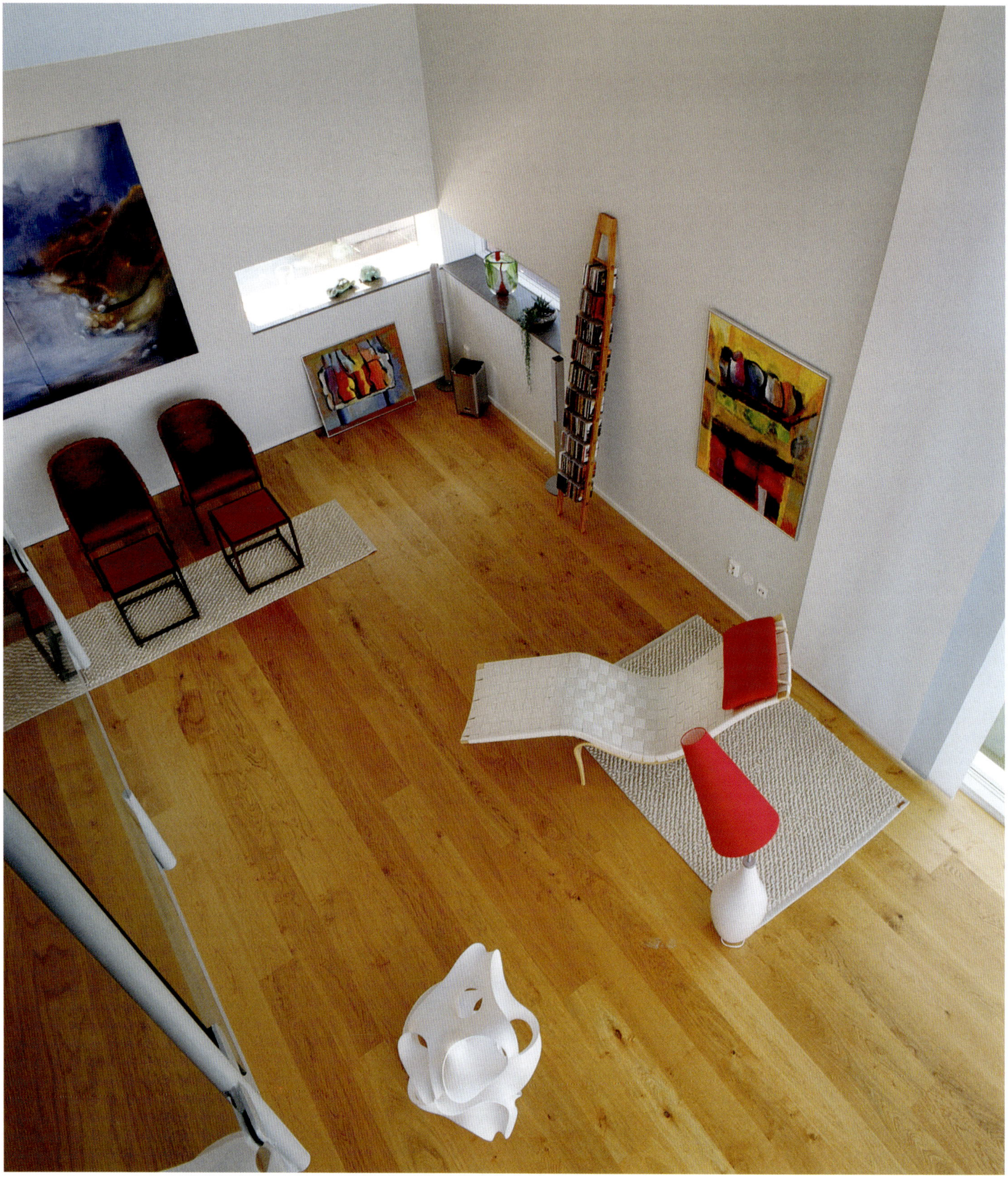

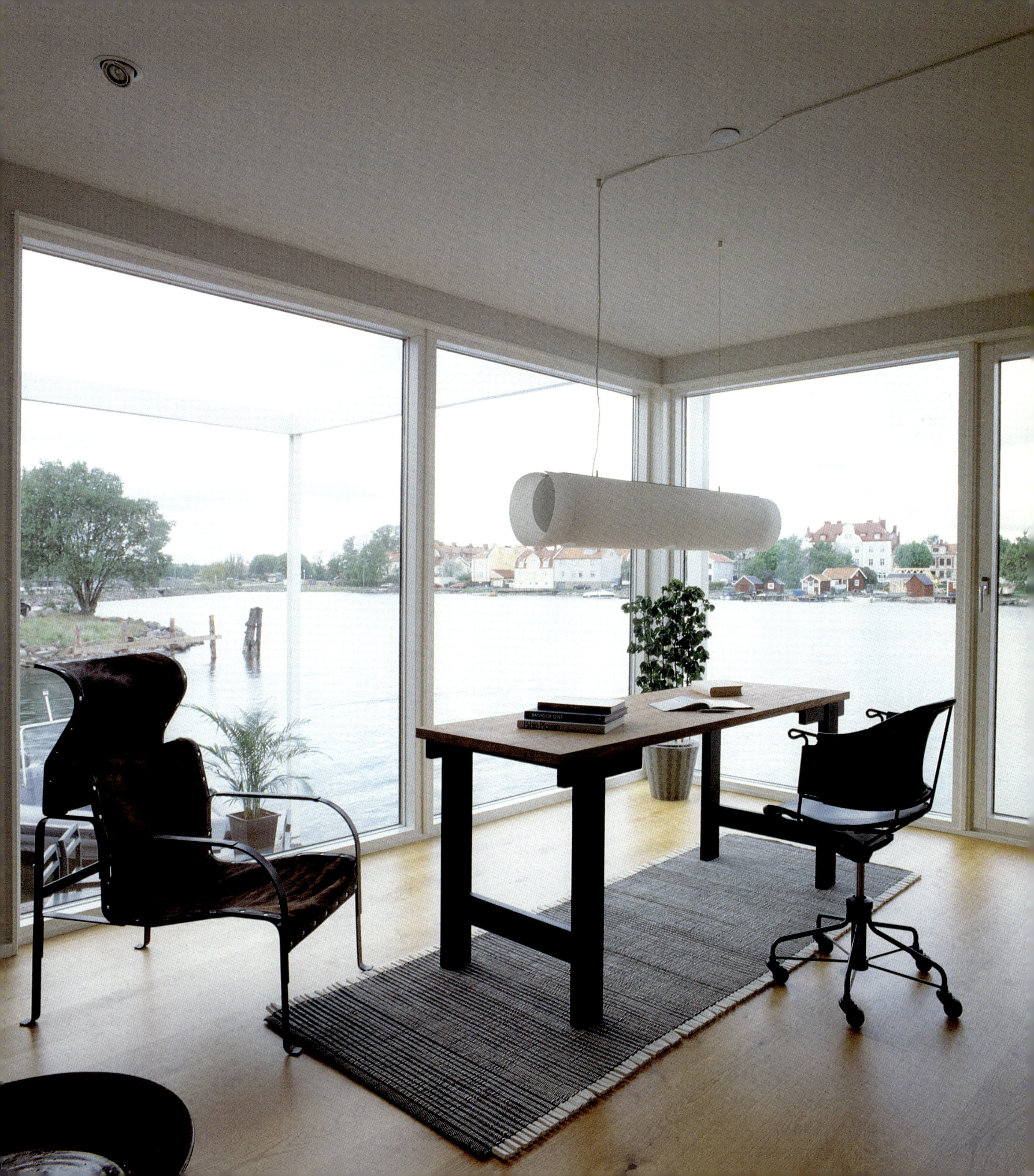

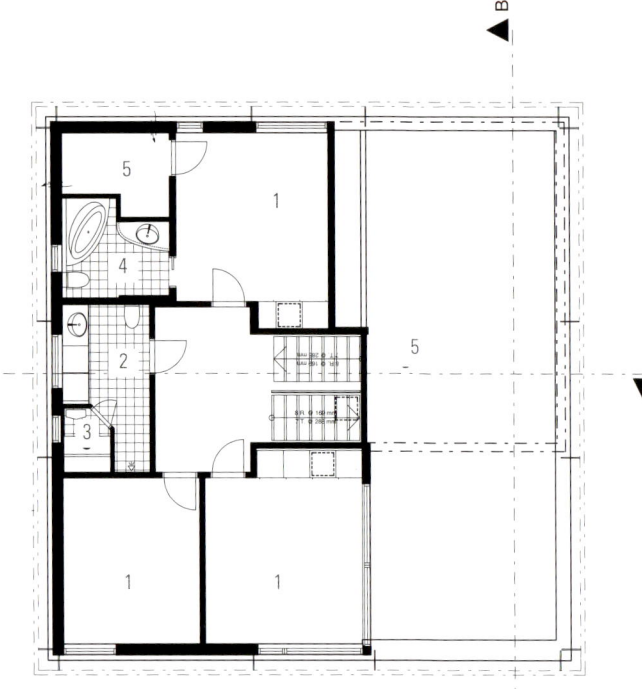

Ground floor plan
1. Bedroom
2. Bathroom / Laundry
3. Sauna
4. Bathroom
5. Mechanical equipment room
6. Store

Roof plan
1. Terrace
2. Kitchenette

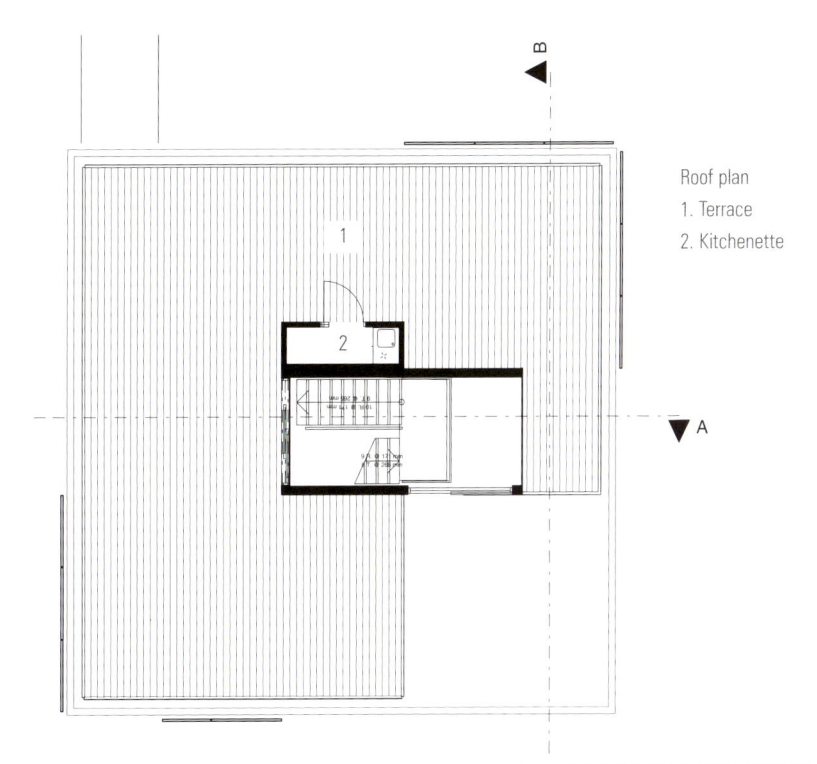

Section AA

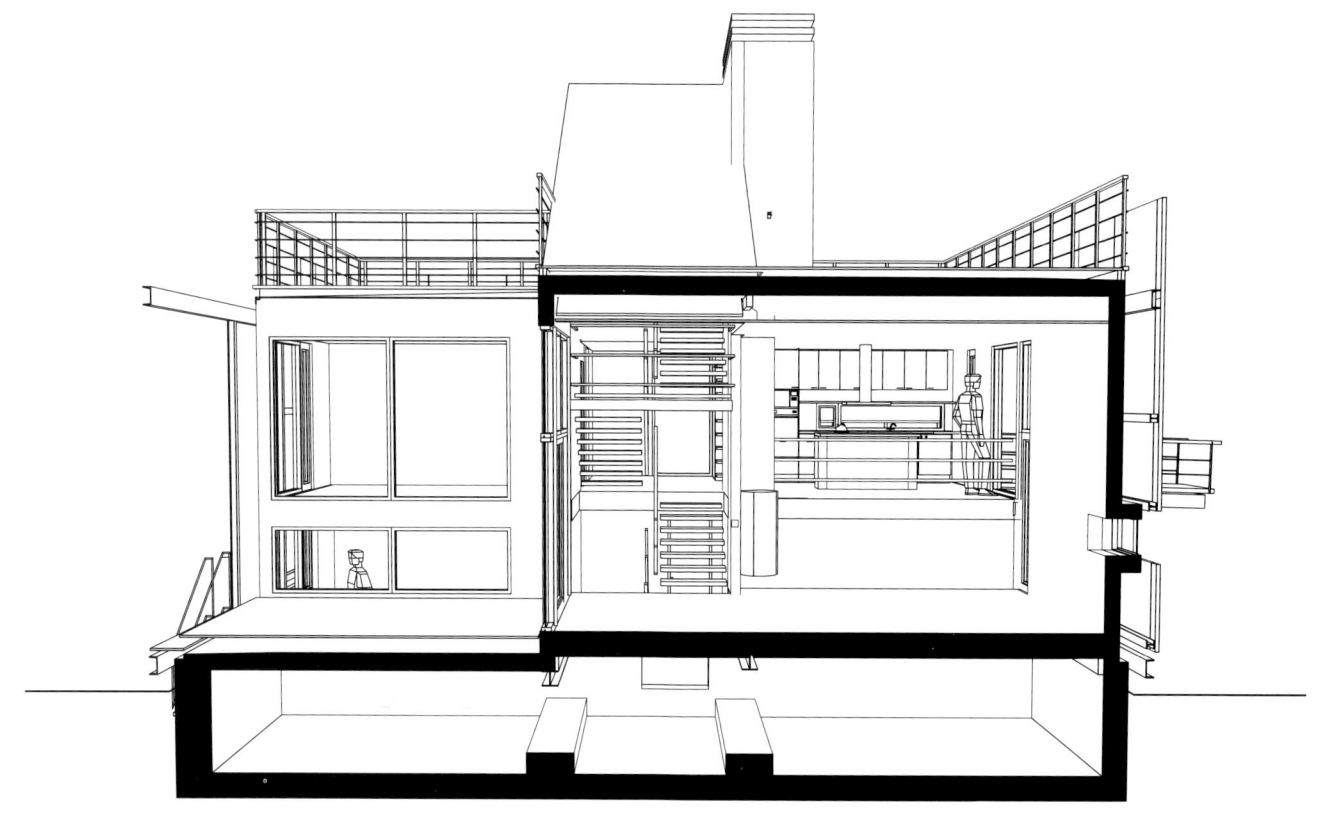

Section BB

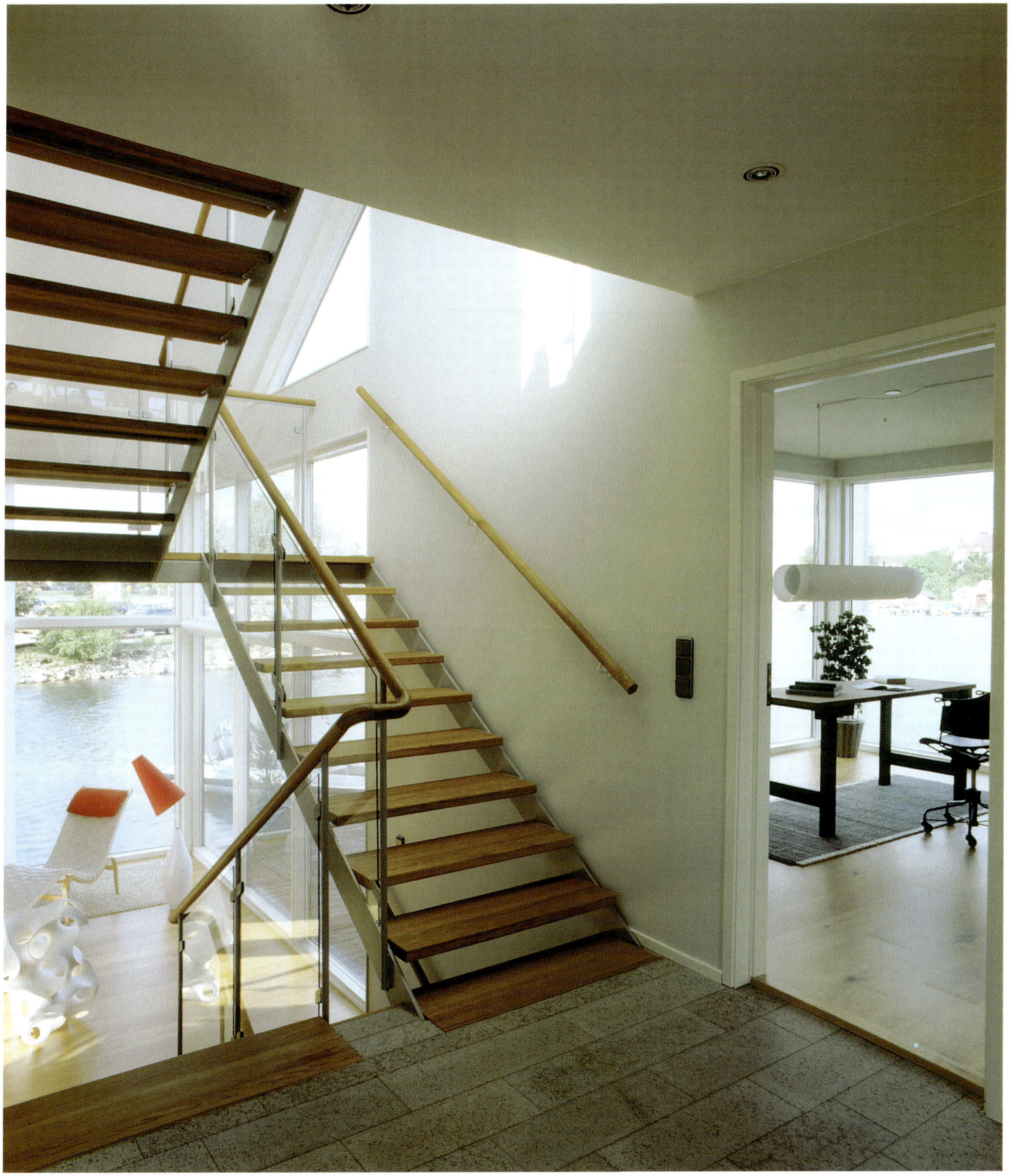

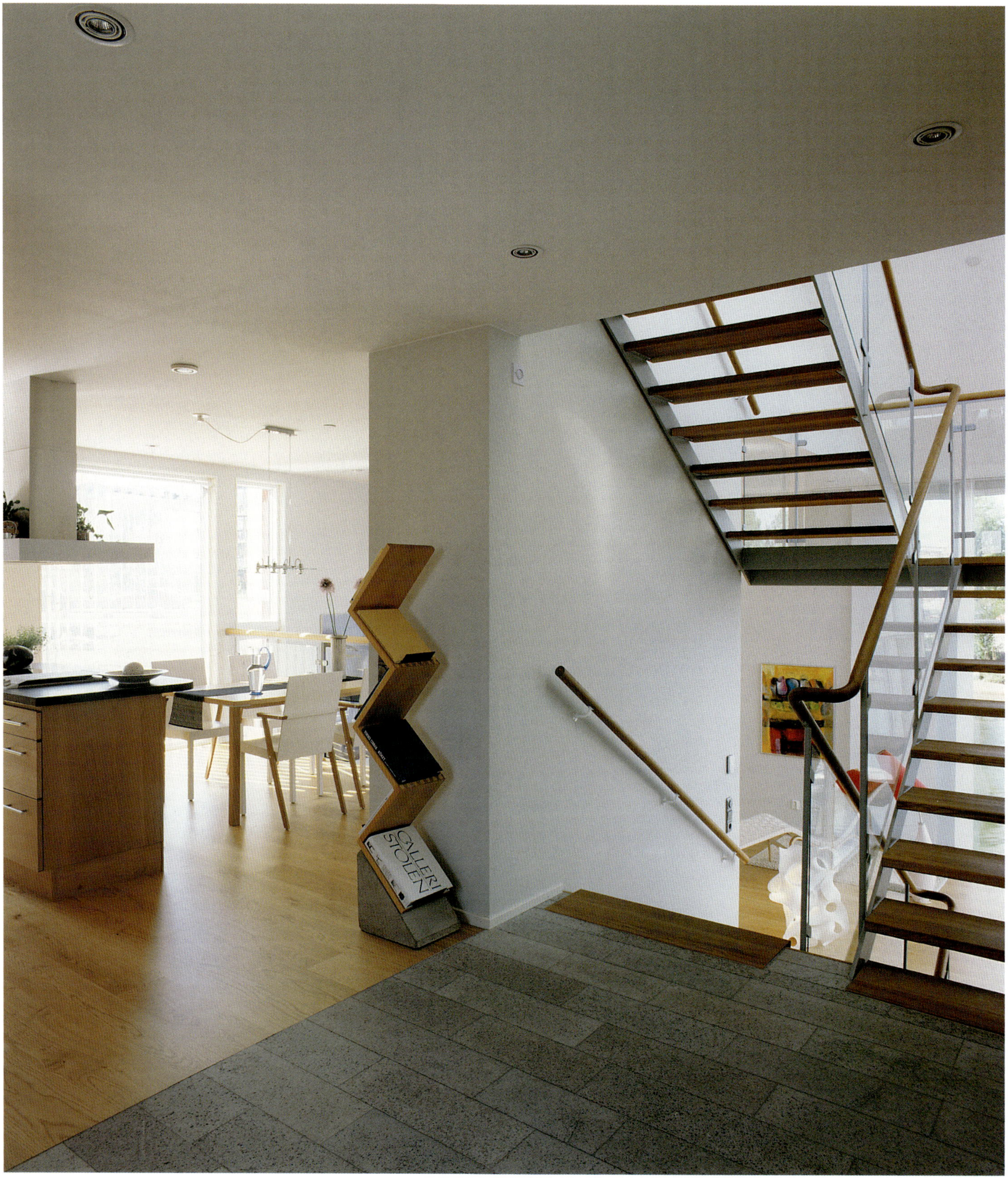
GALLERI
STOLEN

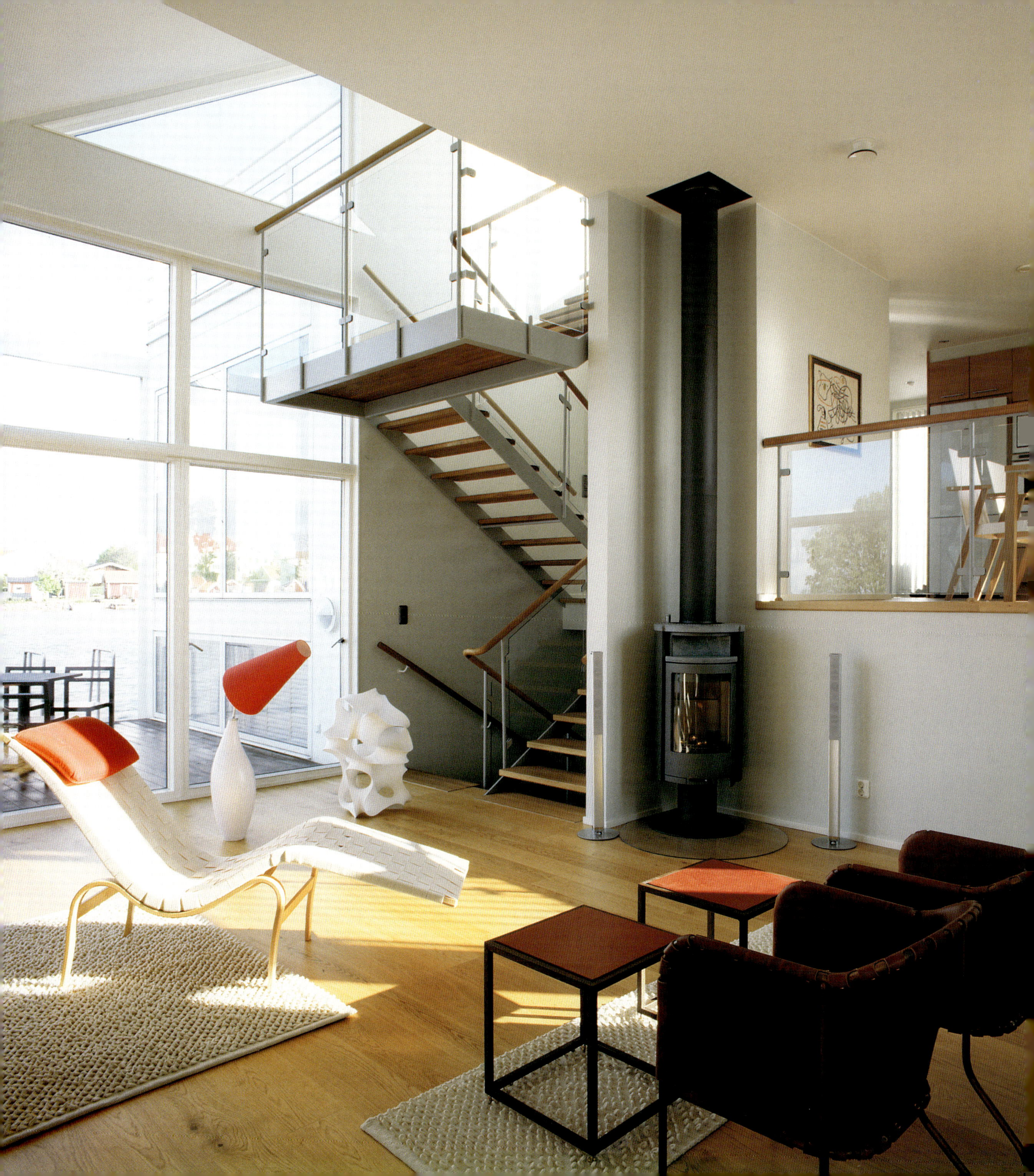

Pierre Thibault, architecte
Beaver's Lake Refuge

Photographs: Alain Laforest

Grandes-Piles, Québec, Canada

The program was for a four-season refuge large enough to accommodate family and friends and serve as a permanent residence. The 4000-square-foot (371.61 sq m) project had to contain three bedrooms and facilities, a workroom, an office and large living spaces.

The site, Beaver Lake, is an entrancing environment located in the heart of a forest that features no visible trace of man's presence. The lake, surrounded by a soothing but penetrating landscape, is dotted with beaver dams. Dark trunks float on the surface of the water. Around the lake, trees are gnawed and stripped; unadorned silhouettes of trees emit a forceful presence that cannot be overlooked. Moss covers giant boulders and branches strewn over the forest floor seem like part of an unfinished painting. The environmental after effects of the natural 'builders' for whom the lake was named became the model behind the design concept, guiding the project's development.

The organizational design logically followed the shoreline and the living spaces were integrated accordingly. Made up of four distinct blocks, the house is linked by a wall of logs delineating a corridor - a backbone, or ballast - to the villa. Four roofs appear to float over these blocks like giant parasols, held in place by slanted wooden poles that echo and meld into the surrounding landscape.

Fragmenting the volume made it possible to size each block for height, width and depth according to the function it would house and the desired spatial sequence. Scrupulously studied in this way, these elements were thereby able to afford majestic heights in the main living area and to provide intimate bedrooms and a warm kitchen with cubic proportions.

Fragmentation also allowed orienting each block for the appropriate natural lighting and for specific visual pleasure. This flexibility allowed for the creation of a wide variety of spaces perfectly adapted to their use.

Permeability between the interior and the exterior rapidly became an important part of the project. Inside, trees become columns that vertically intersect both living spaces and corridor, giving rise to a dialogue between the rational logic of the villa and nature's organic counterpart. Outside, wooden floors reach out to the lake and become a terrace, met by the outer columns, which mirror the surrounding trees. Roofs angle toward the sky.

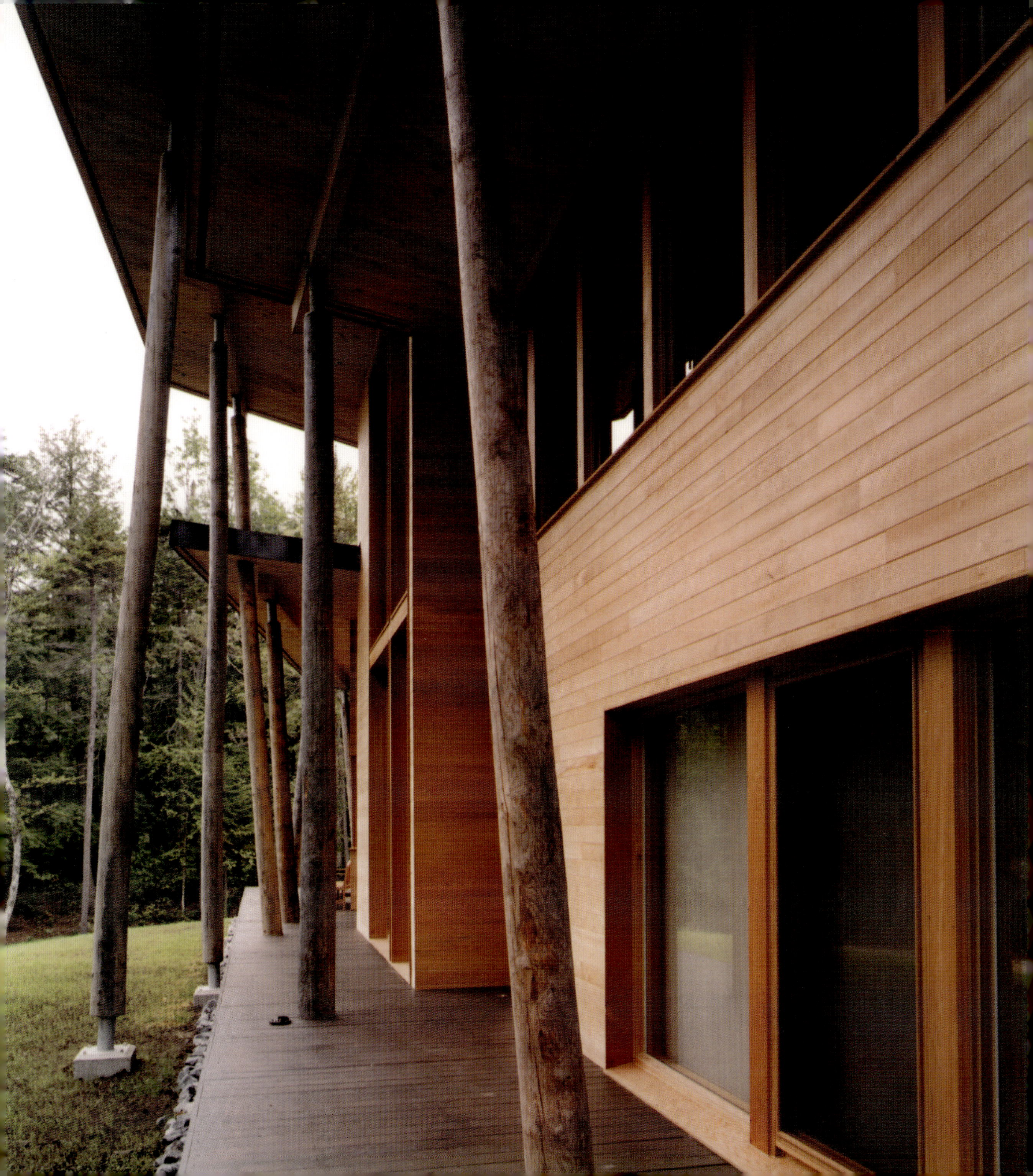

The organizational design logically followed the shoreline and the living spaces were integrated accordingly. Made up of four distinct blocks, the house is linked by a wall of logs delineating a corridor - a backbone, or ballast - to the villa.

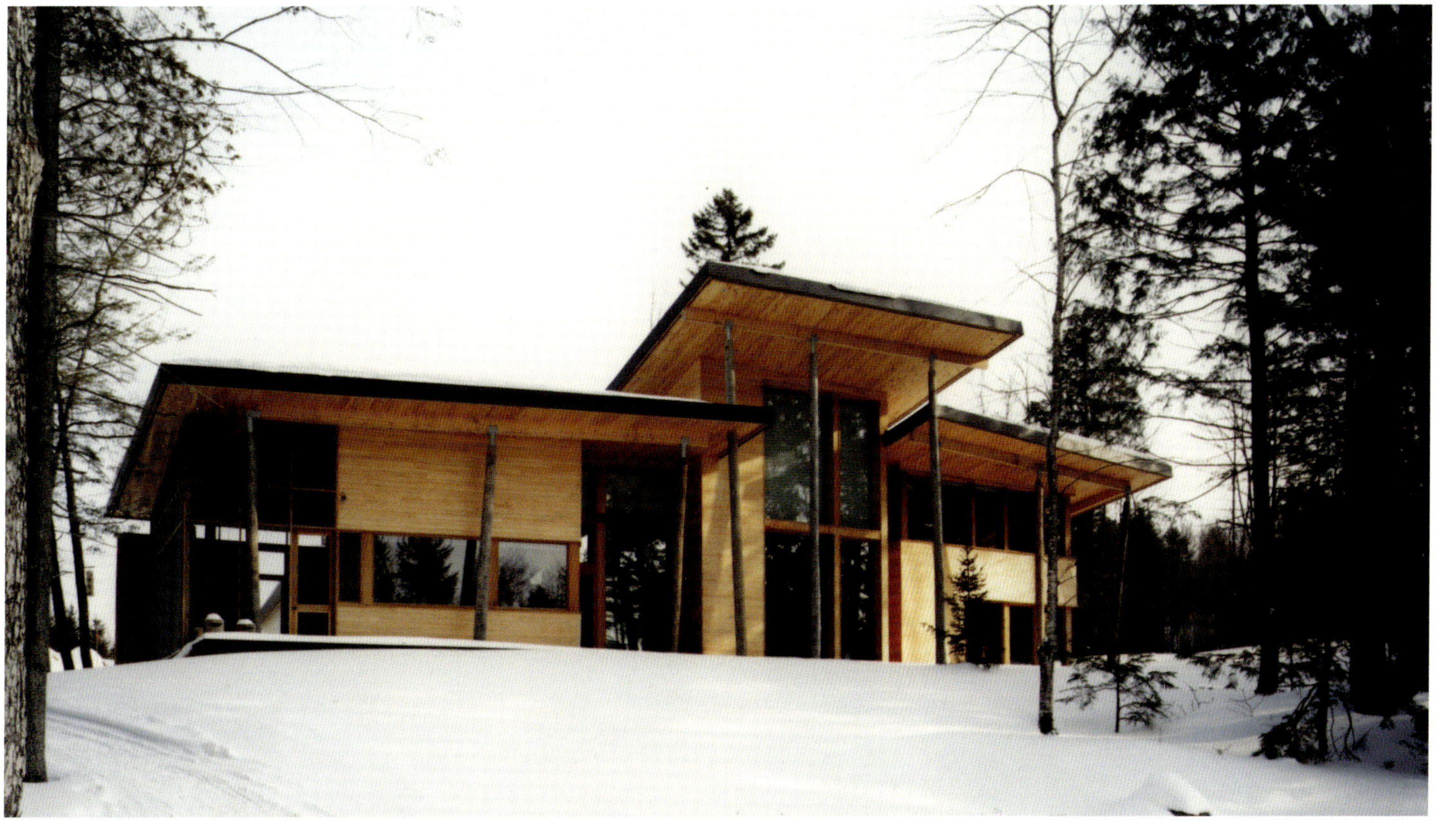

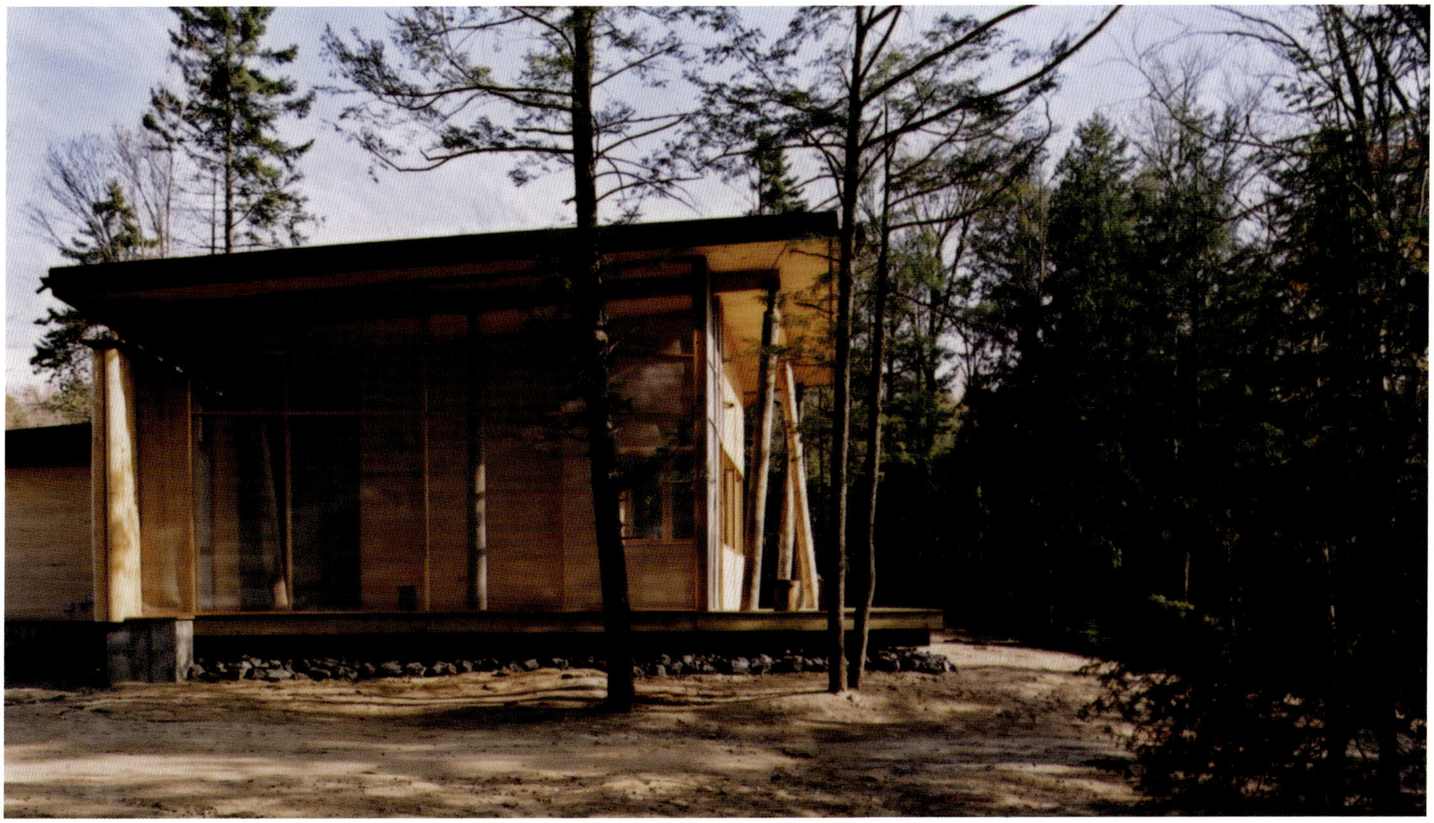

Basement floor plan

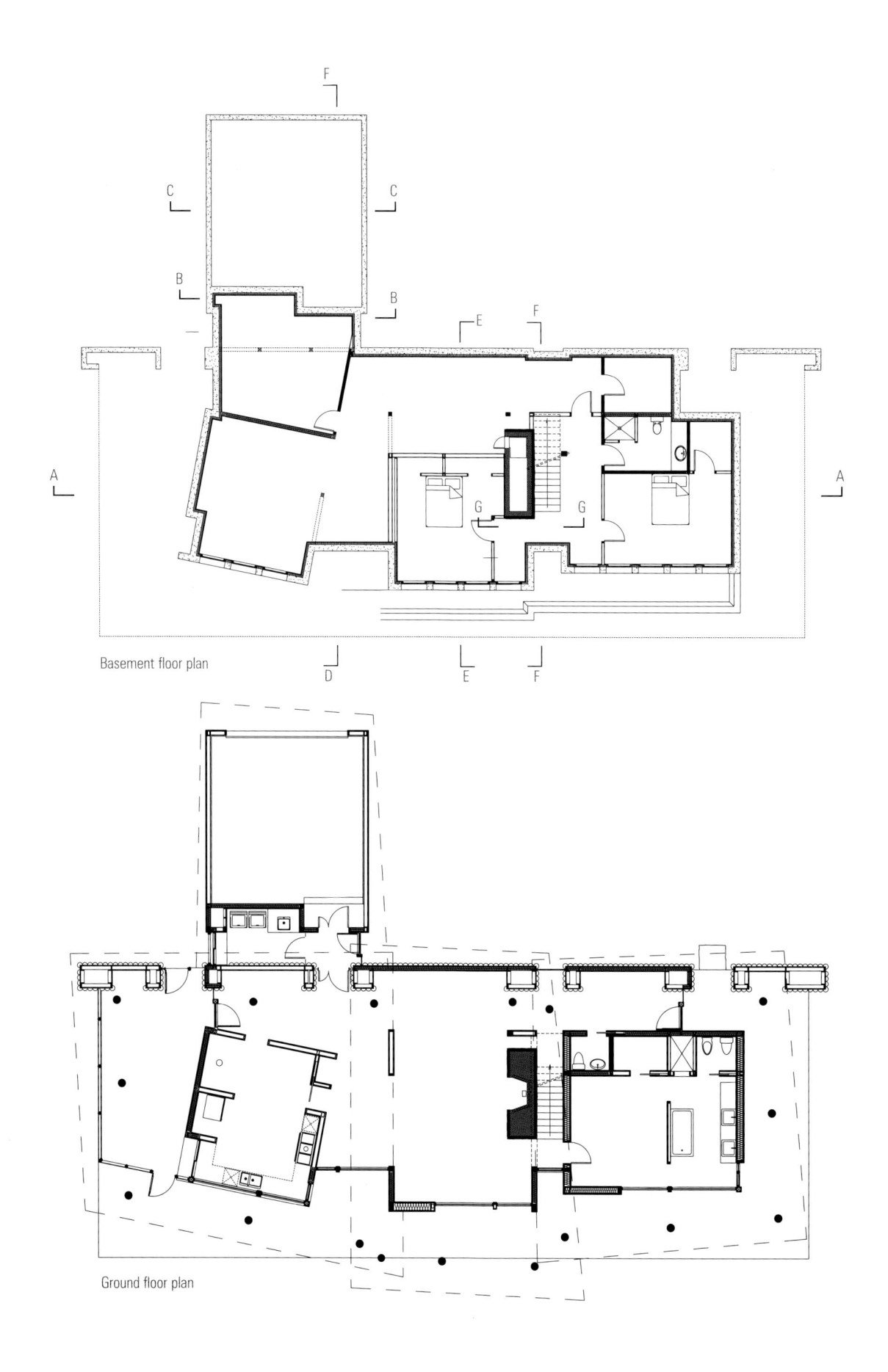

Ground floor plan

27

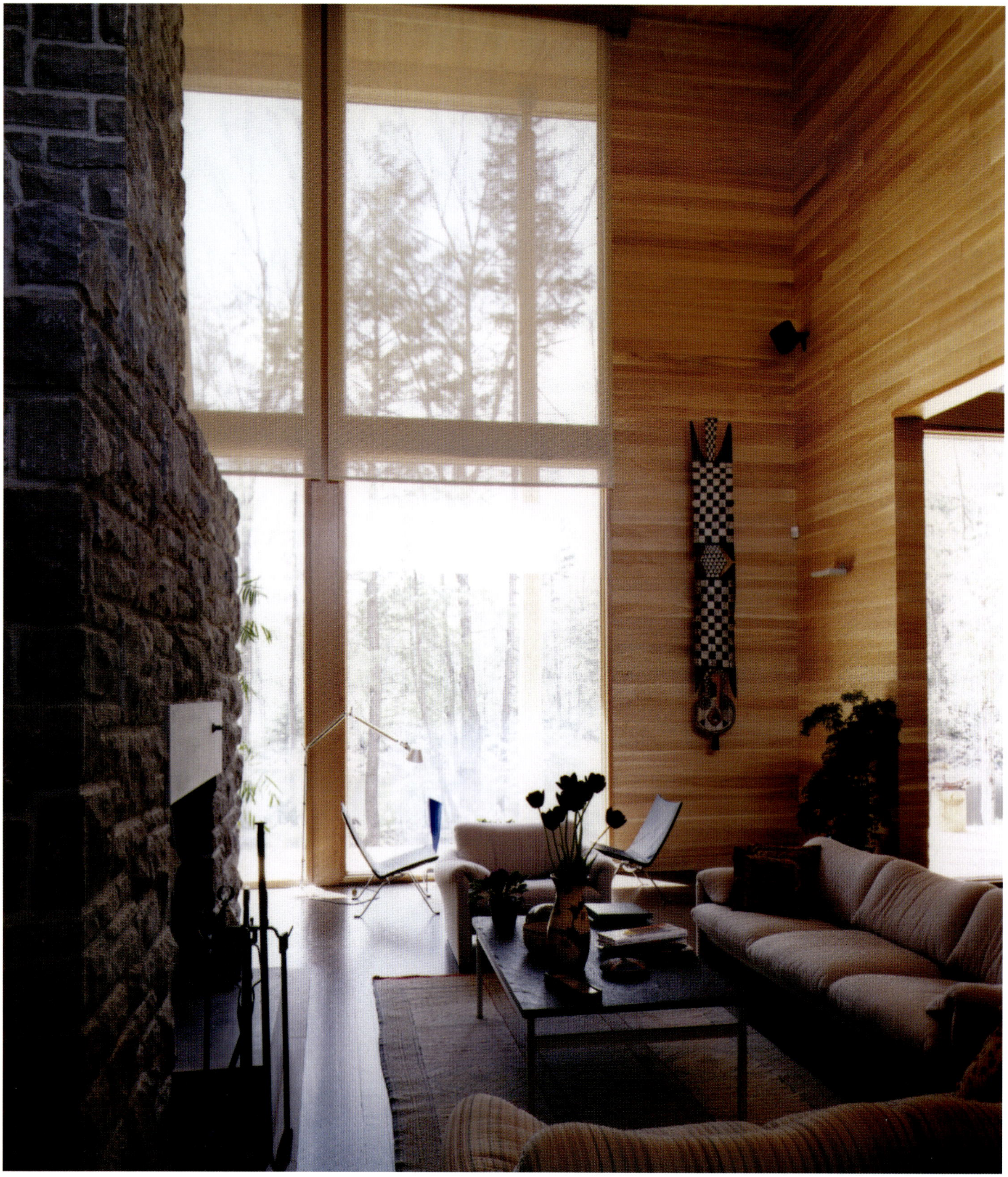

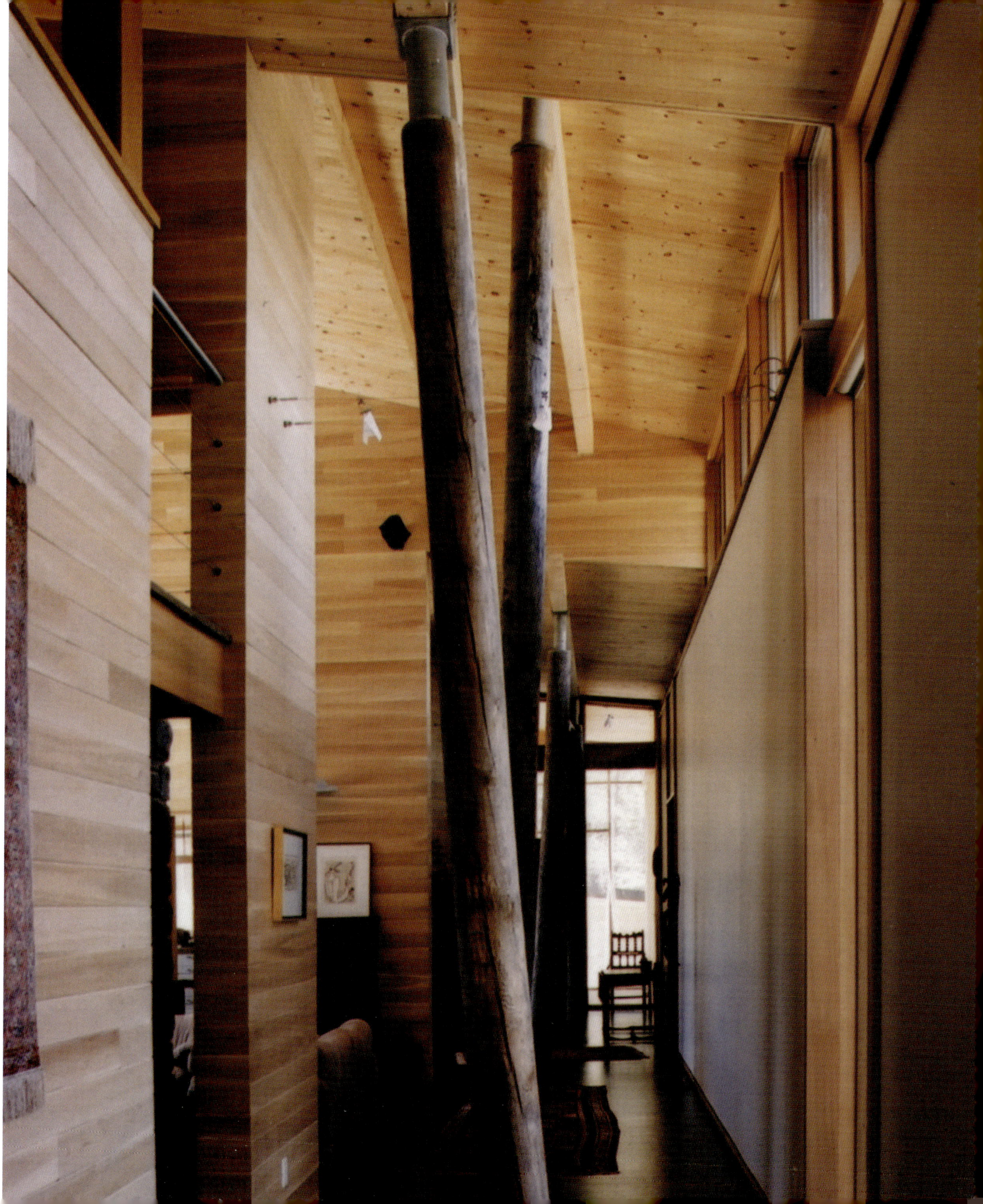

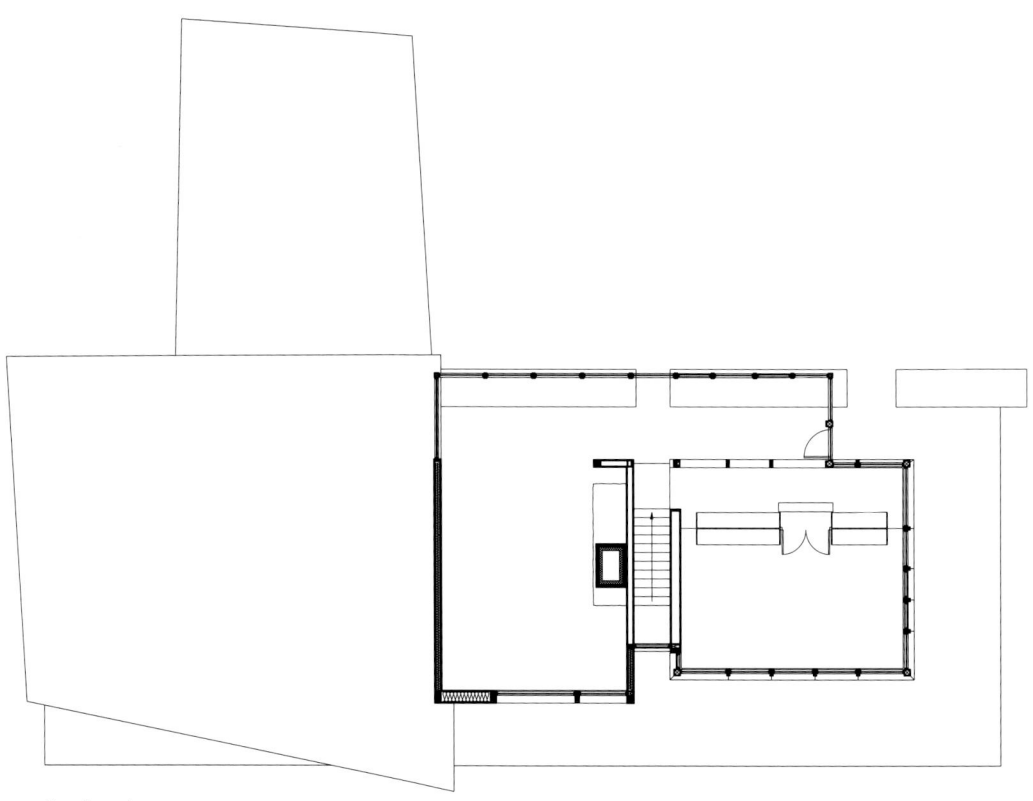

First floor plan

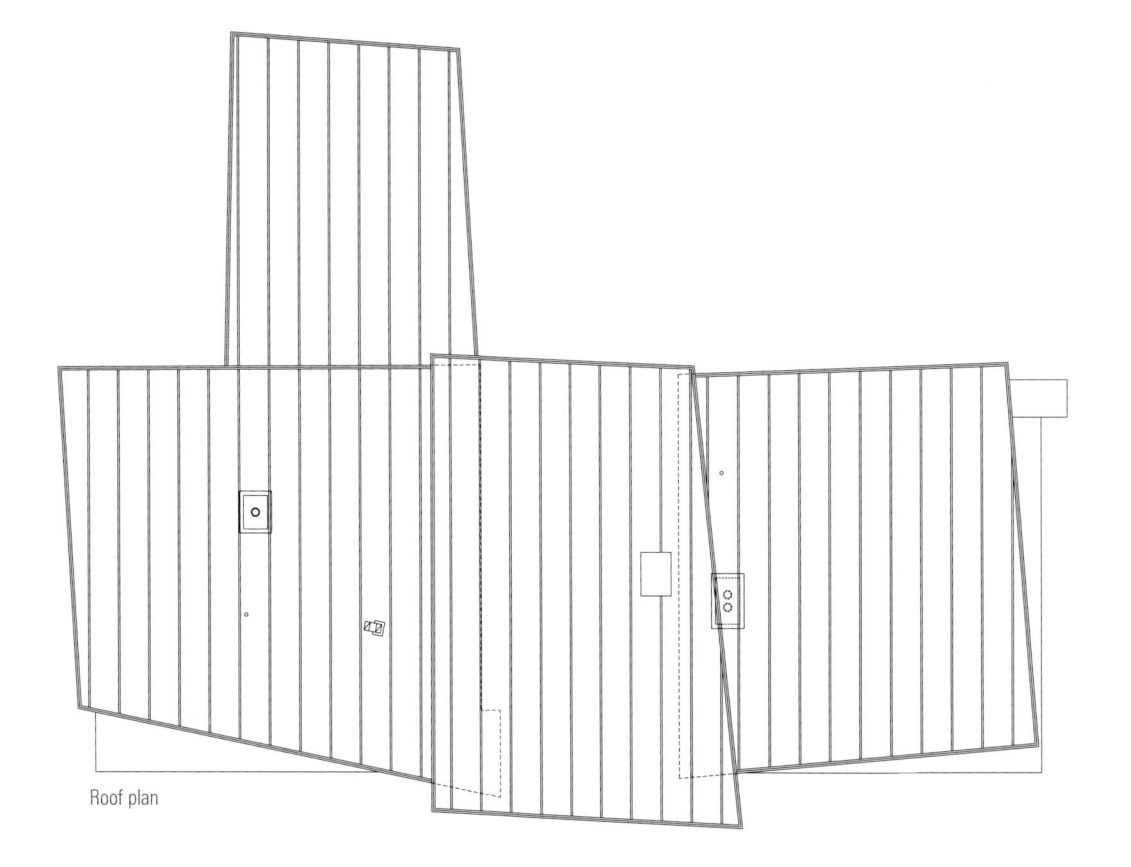

Roof plan

The villa is an extension of its environment, wide and generous at times, closed and careful at others, offering a lifestyle that incorporates nature in its very essence, melding the inside and the outside into one.

North elevation

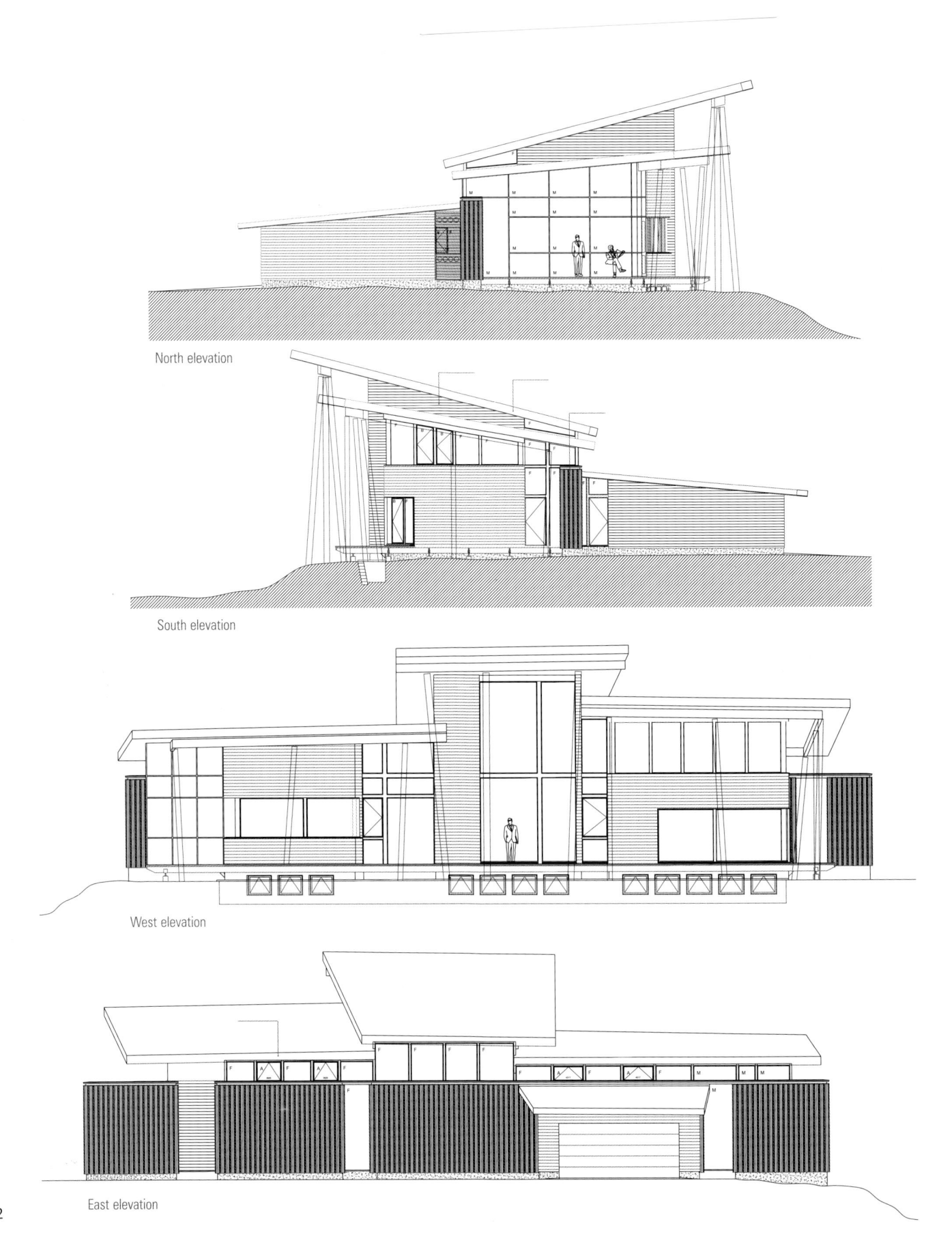

South elevation

West elevation

East elevation

33

Section AA

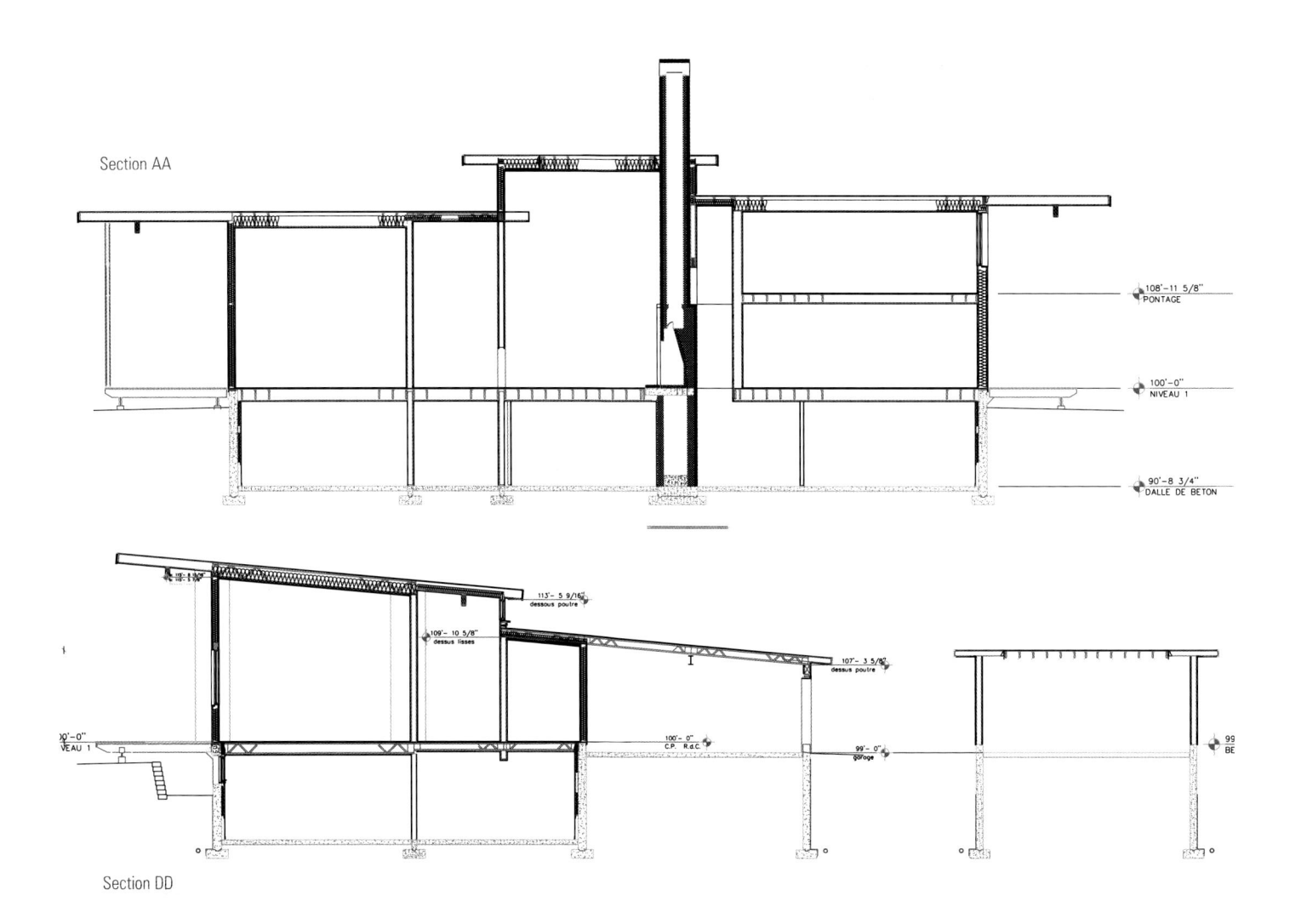

Section DD

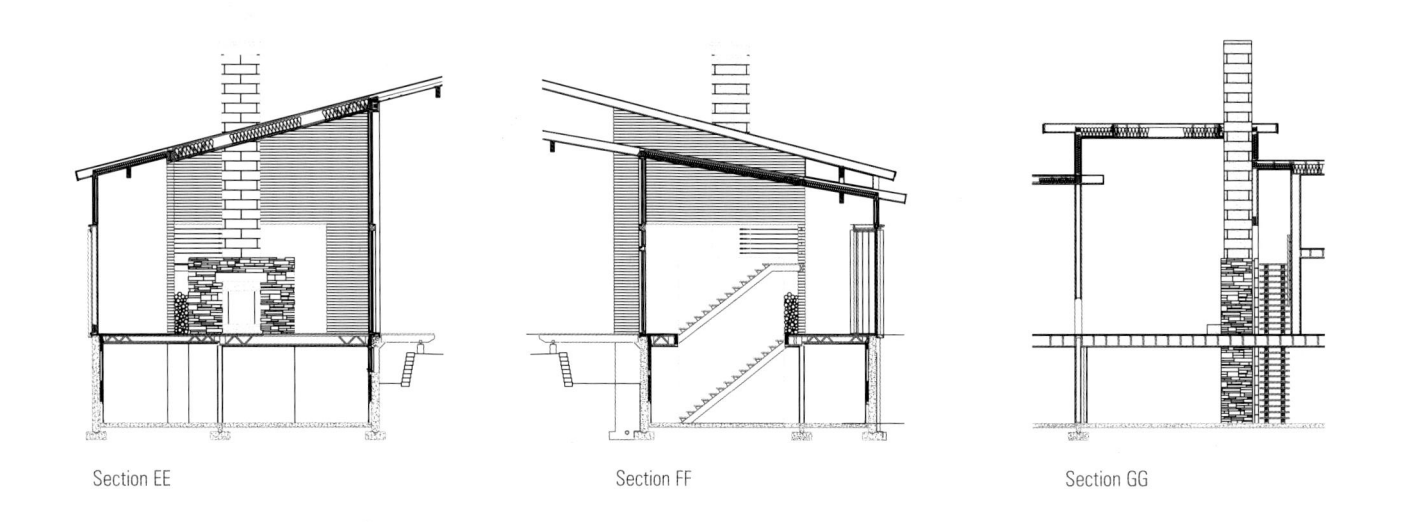

Section EE

Section FF

Section GG

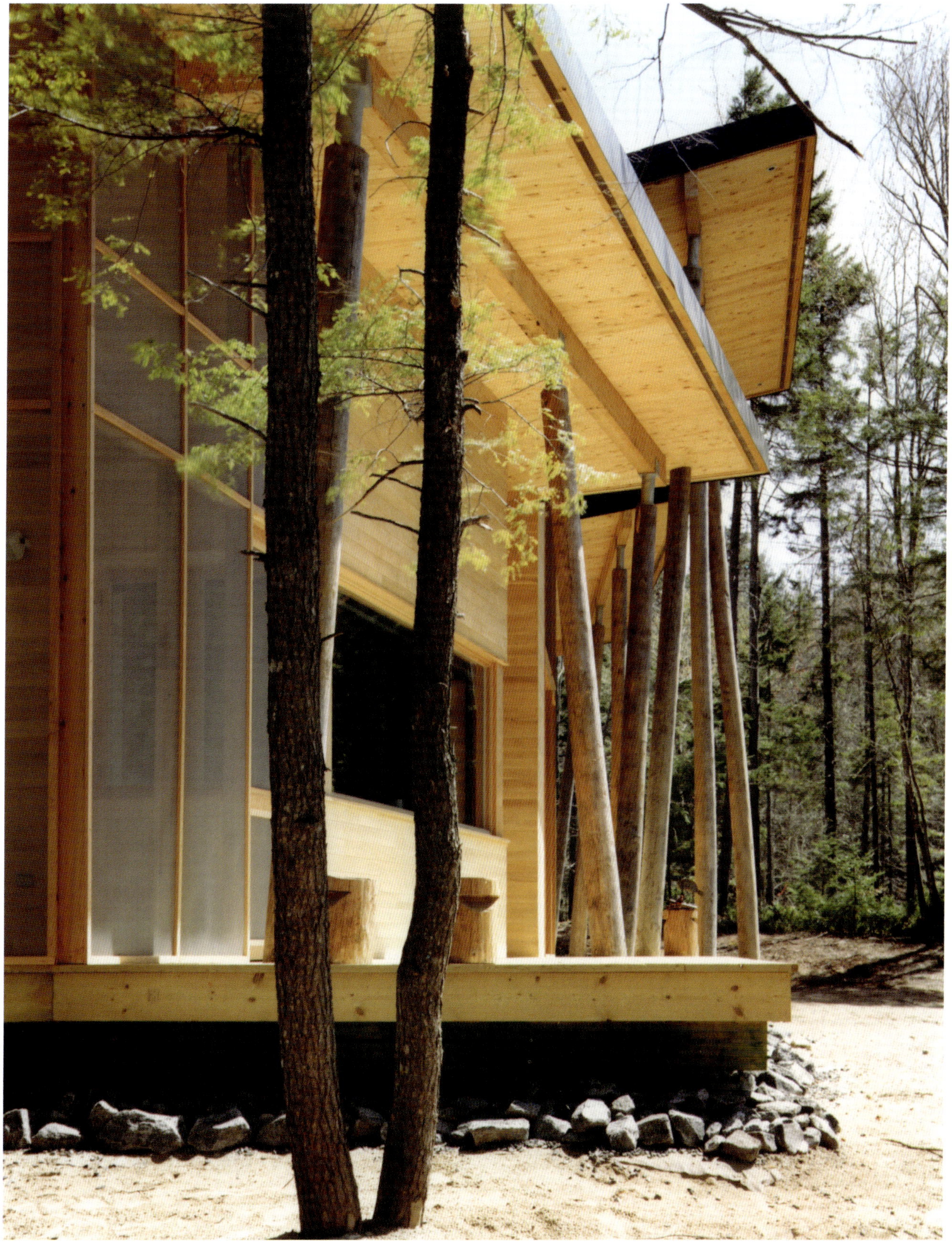

Boije Design AB
Stem to Stern Perfection

Photographs: James Silverman
Styling: Pernilla Åsberg

Skåne, Sweden

Architect and furniture designer Bror Boije's love of sailing is reflected in this custom designed H-shaped home consisting of two naves. Port holes, wooden decks, and high gabled ceilings giving the feel of unfurled sails set the nautical motif of the design, accentuated by small recessed lights on the ceilings glowing like little stars. The floors throughout are of varnished fiber concrete and the wood detailing is mahogany. Open railings in metal and wood emulate those used on the deck of a boat.

In the foyer, a beautiful Art Deco-inspired armoire in cherry wood (there are only ten in existence) provides a place for keys and spare glasses. Adjacent to this space is a stunning two-story library and seating area, with furniture designed by Bror.

The two naves were designed with a view to pragmatism, with the areas for socializing, relaxing and dining set in the front sea-facing volume and the more functional spaces all housed in the further nave. All sections can be closed off from the others with teakwood pocket doors, making each area as intimate as needed. The traffic flow of the house was designed for ease of access and use despite age or disability.

The kitchen is truly the heart of this home, with a large mahogany table and chairs designed by Bror. The table, which can be expanded to accommodate more guests or folded down when not in use, features electrical height adjustment and a marble strip in the center for hot dishes. The 'Linette' chairs can be reclined back to provide for relaxed dining. The skylight is an integral part of the space, providing a sense of openness by bringing in ample natural light. The fireplace in the kitchen also serves the outer courtyard space for summertime barbecues. A cutting board is built into the workspace, and a ceramic stovetop sits on a grey marble counter.

The functional areas of the house occupy two floors. On the first level is the master suite with a view of the garden and the sea. The elegantly-crafted platform bed has a mahogany headboard with built-in end tables. The finishes used in the master bathroom replicate those used in the kitchen: stainless steel hand basins are recessed into the mahogany vanity, providing a natural contrast to the modern high-gloss cabinetry. The toilet and shower area are concealed by frameless opaque glass doors that separate it from the bathing area.

On the upper level, two bedrooms reminiscent of cabins on a ship, are accessible from below by a classic, space-efficient, spiral stairway. Skylights are incorporated into the rooms for natural lighting or for stargazing before sleep. All rooms are fitted with sliding teakwood doors that make efficient use of space.

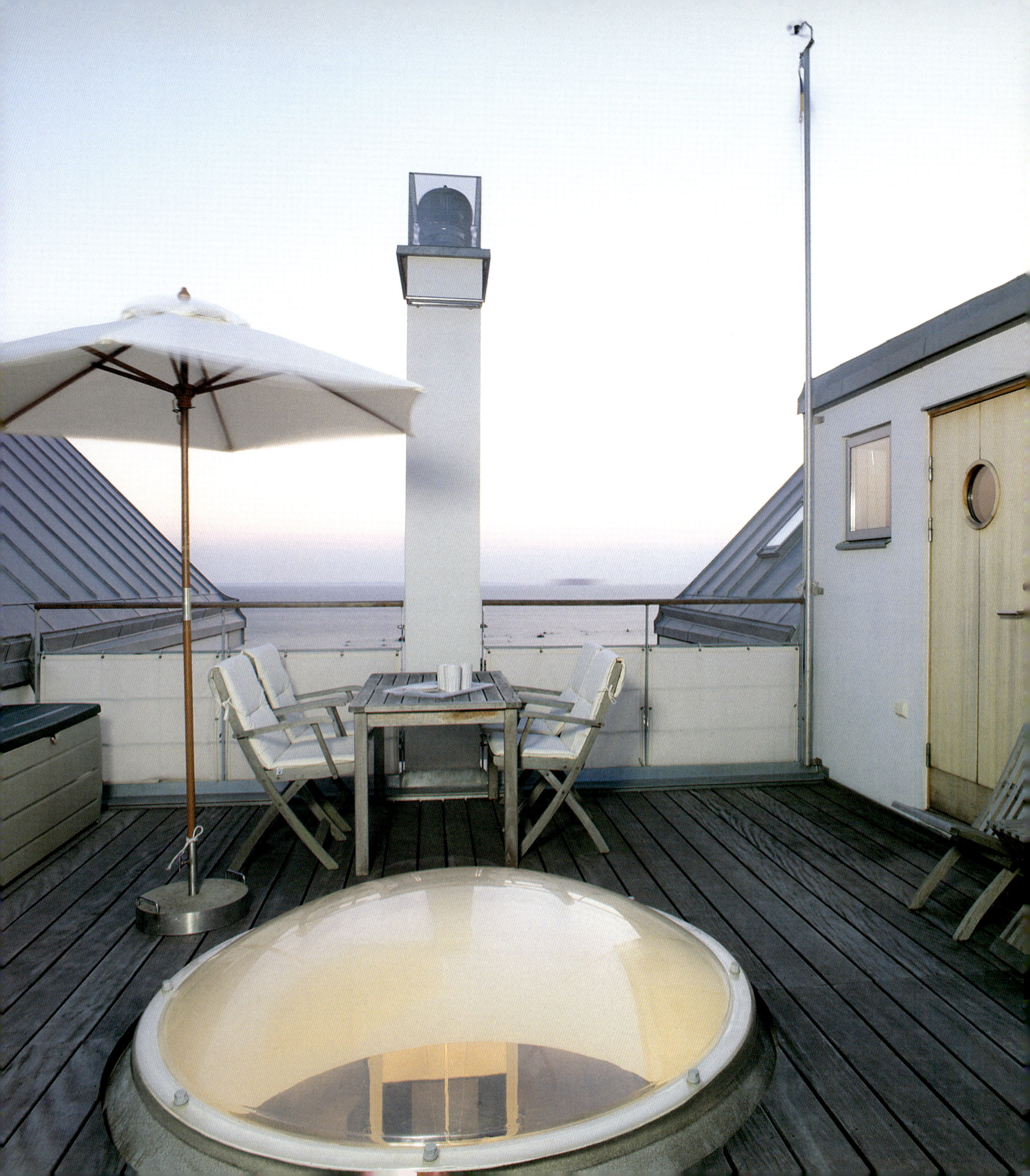

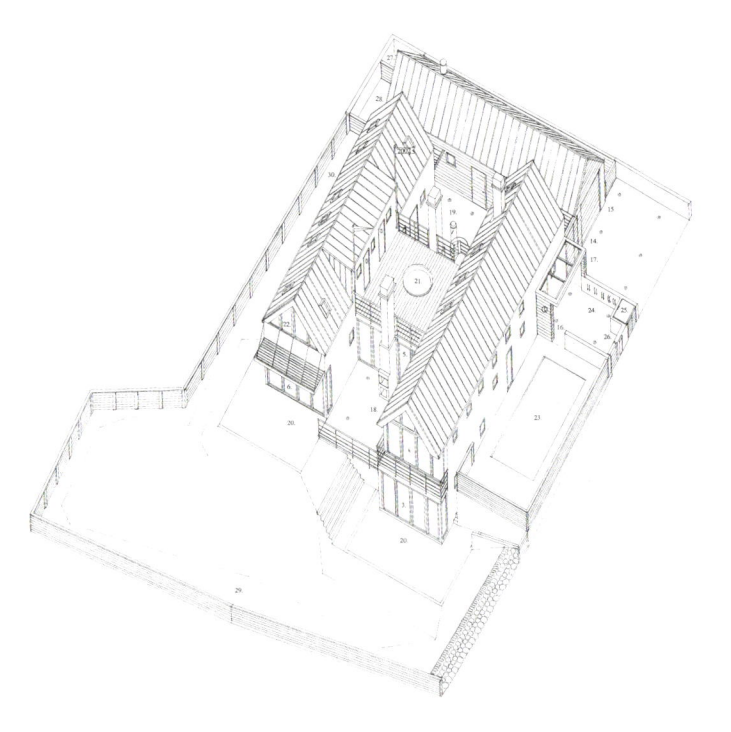

All the large windows face west, overlooking the sea. The longer sides of the house are designed with smaller windows to ensure privacy, while this side is open to the sea view from many perspectives inside and out.

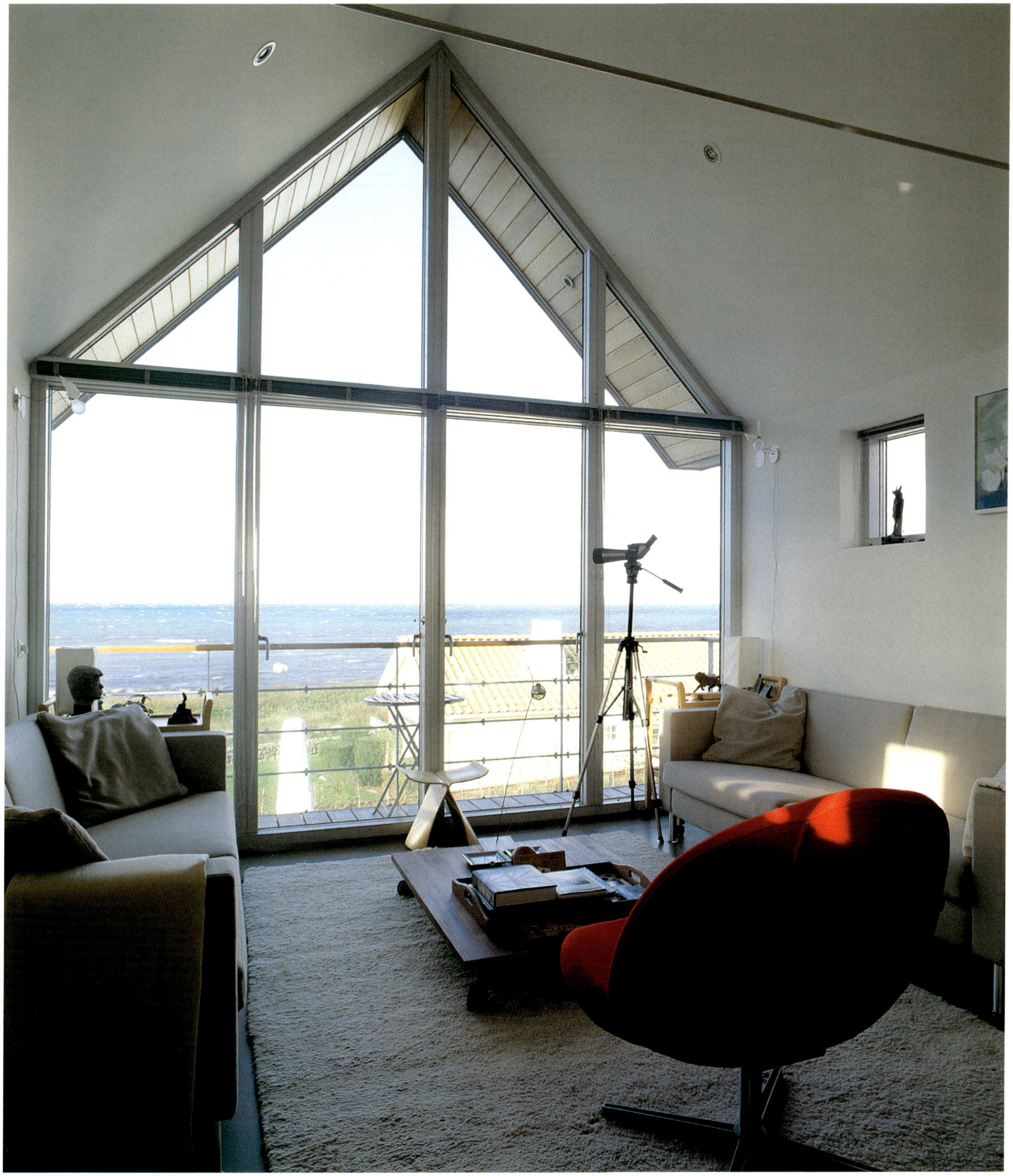

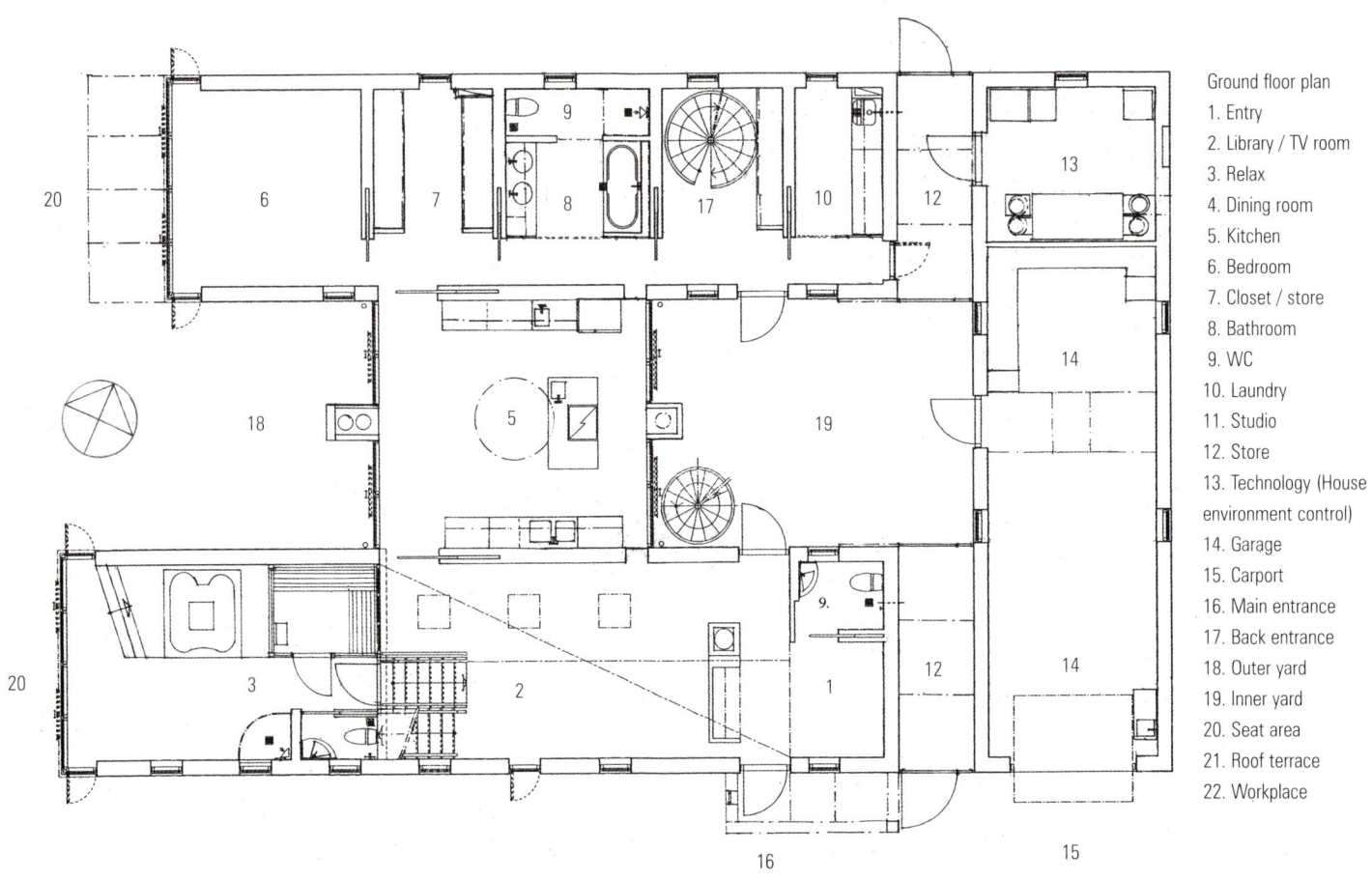

Ground floor plan
1. Entry
2. Library / TV room
3. Relax
4. Dining room
5. Kitchen
6. Bedroom
7. Closet / store
8. Bathroom
9. WC
10. Laundry
11. Studio
12. Store
13. Technology (House environment control)
14. Garage
15. Carport
16. Main entrance
17. Back entrance
18. Outer yard
19. Inner yard
20. Seat area
21. Roof terrace
22. Workplace

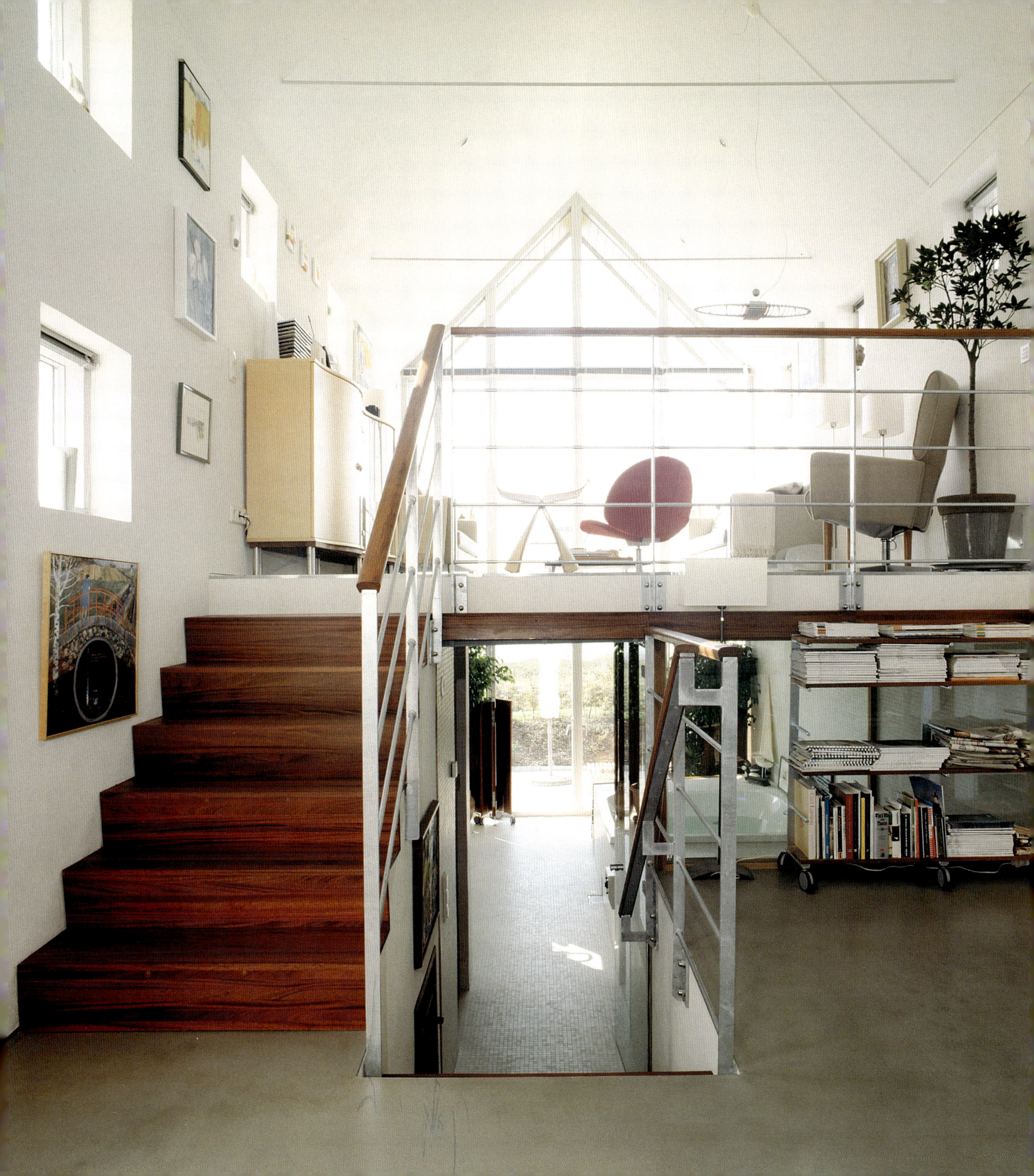

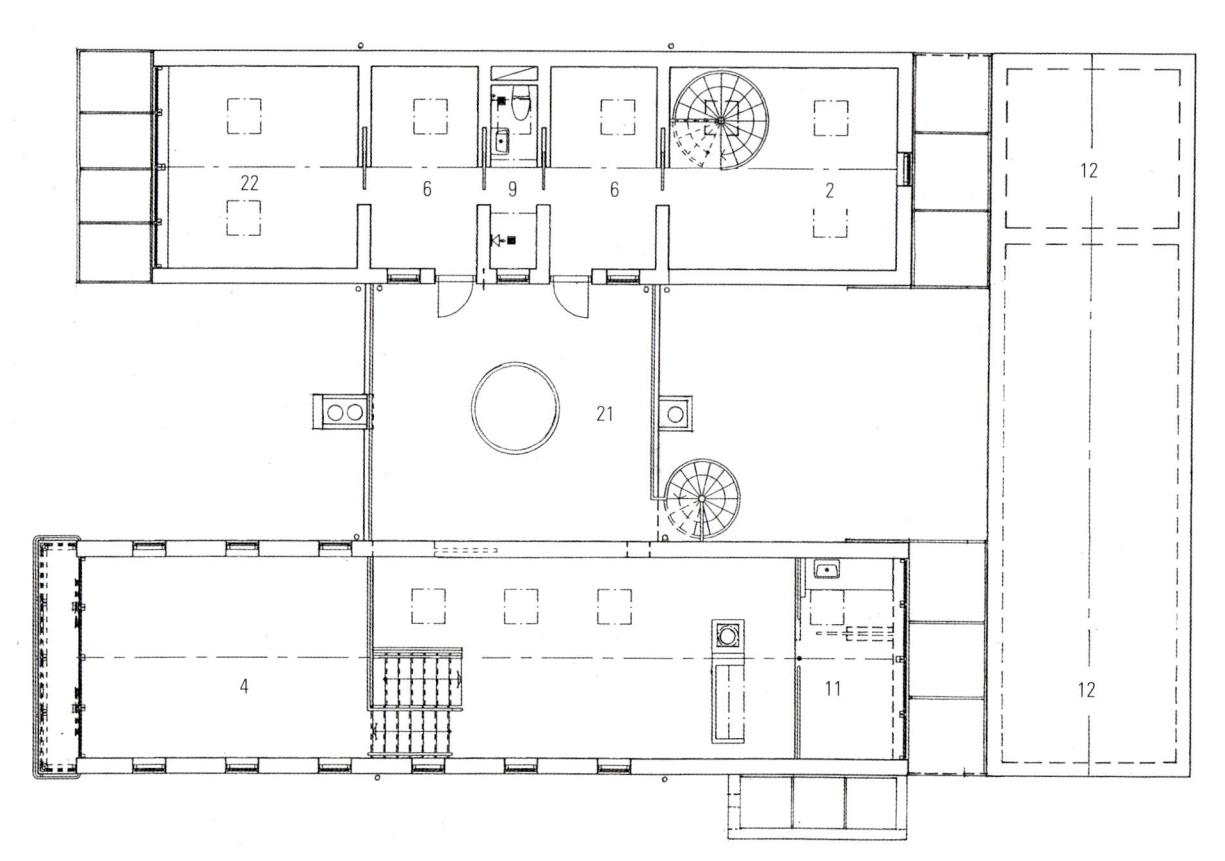

First floor plan
1. Entry
2. Library / TV room
3. Relax
4. Dining room
5. Kitchen
6. Bedroom
7. Closet / store
8. Bathroom
9. WC
10. Laundry
11. Studio
12. Store
13. Technology (House environment control)
14. Garage
15. Carport
16. Main entrance
17. Back entrance
18. Outer yard
19. Inner yard
20. Seat area
21. Roof terrace
22. Workplace

43

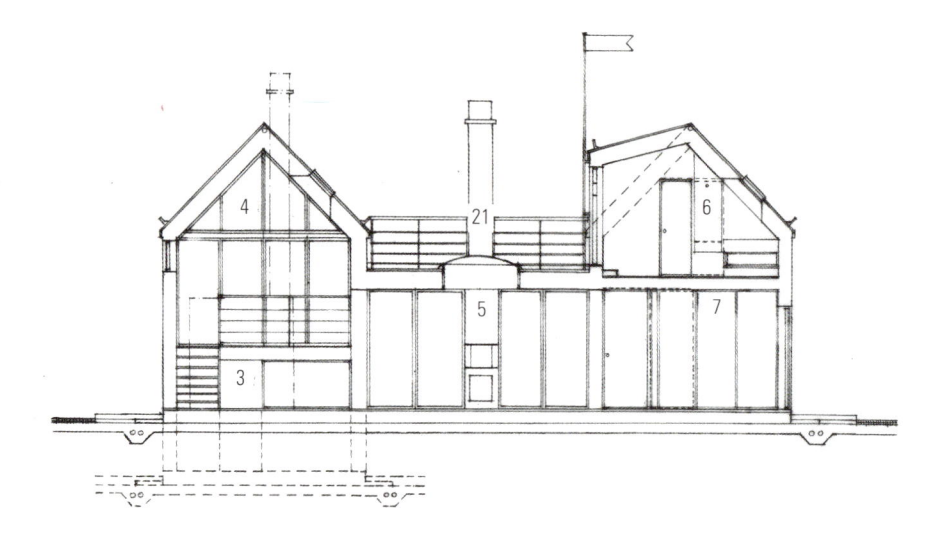

Cross section
1. Entry
2. Library / TV room
3. Relax
4. Dining room
5. Kitchen
6. Bedroom
7. Closet / store
8. Bathroom
9. WC
10. Laundry
11. Studio
12. Store
13. Technology (House environment control)
14. Garage
15. Carport
16. Main entrance
17. Back entrance
18. Outer yard
19. Inner yard
20. Seat area
21. Roof terrace
22. Workplace

Longitudinal section

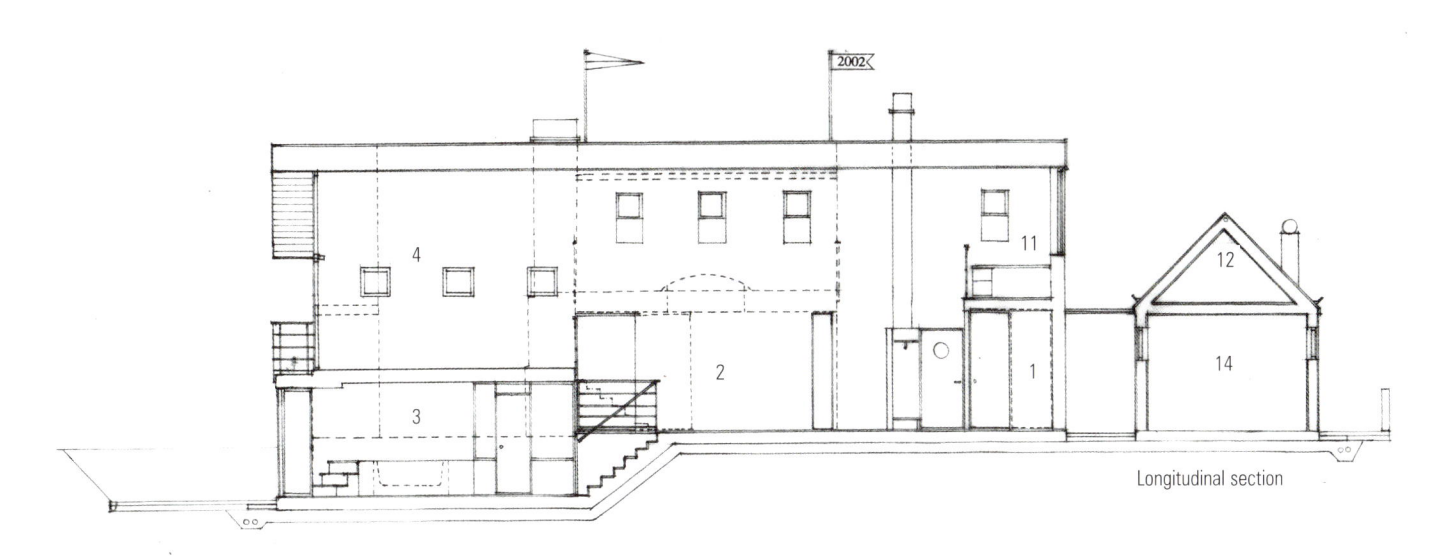

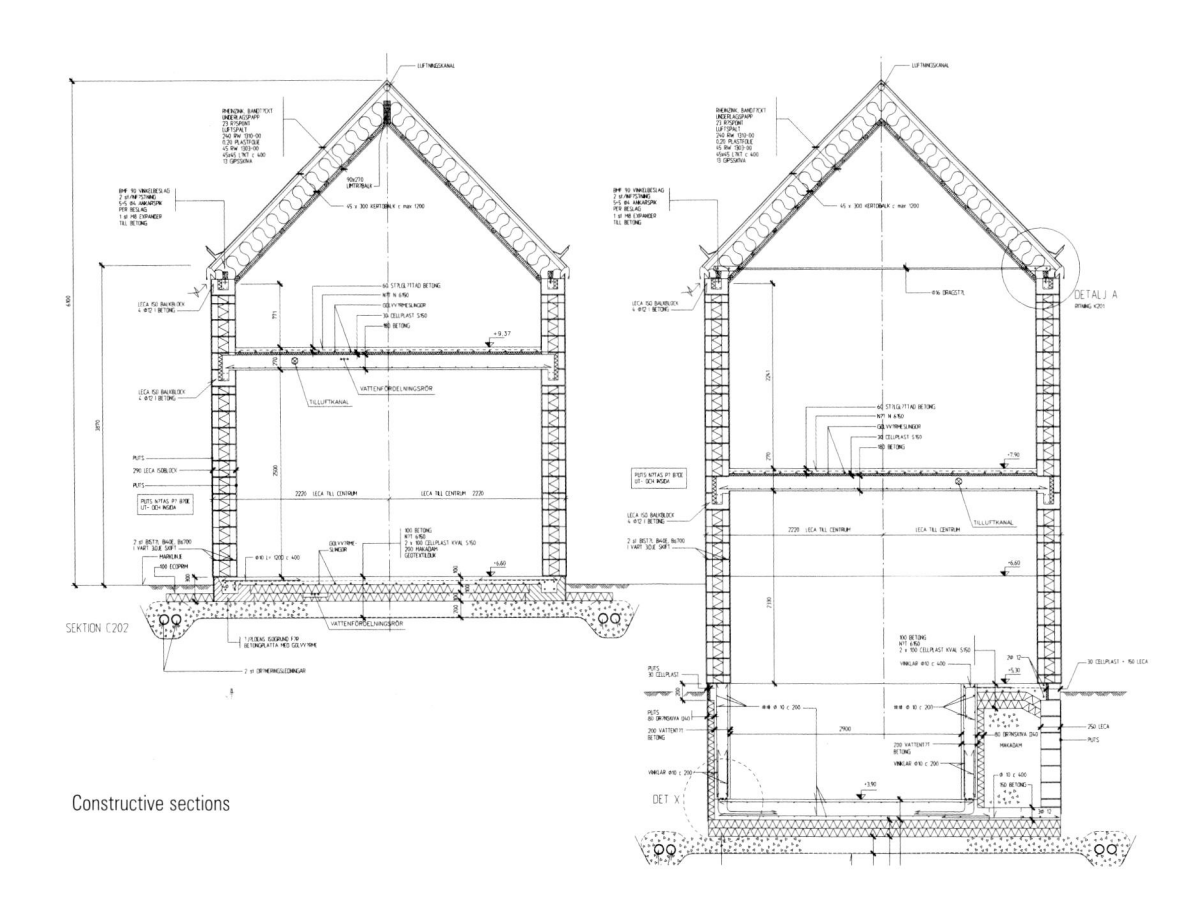

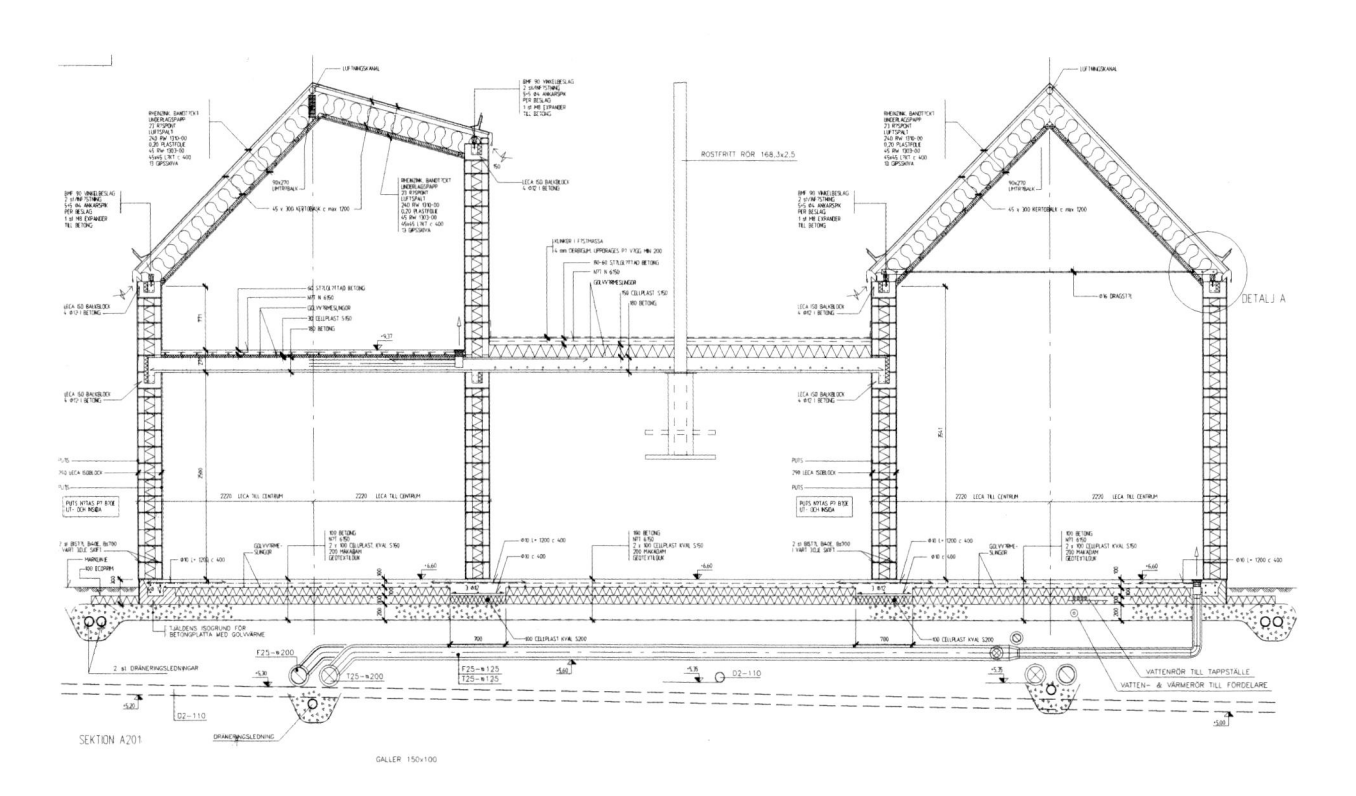

Constructive sections

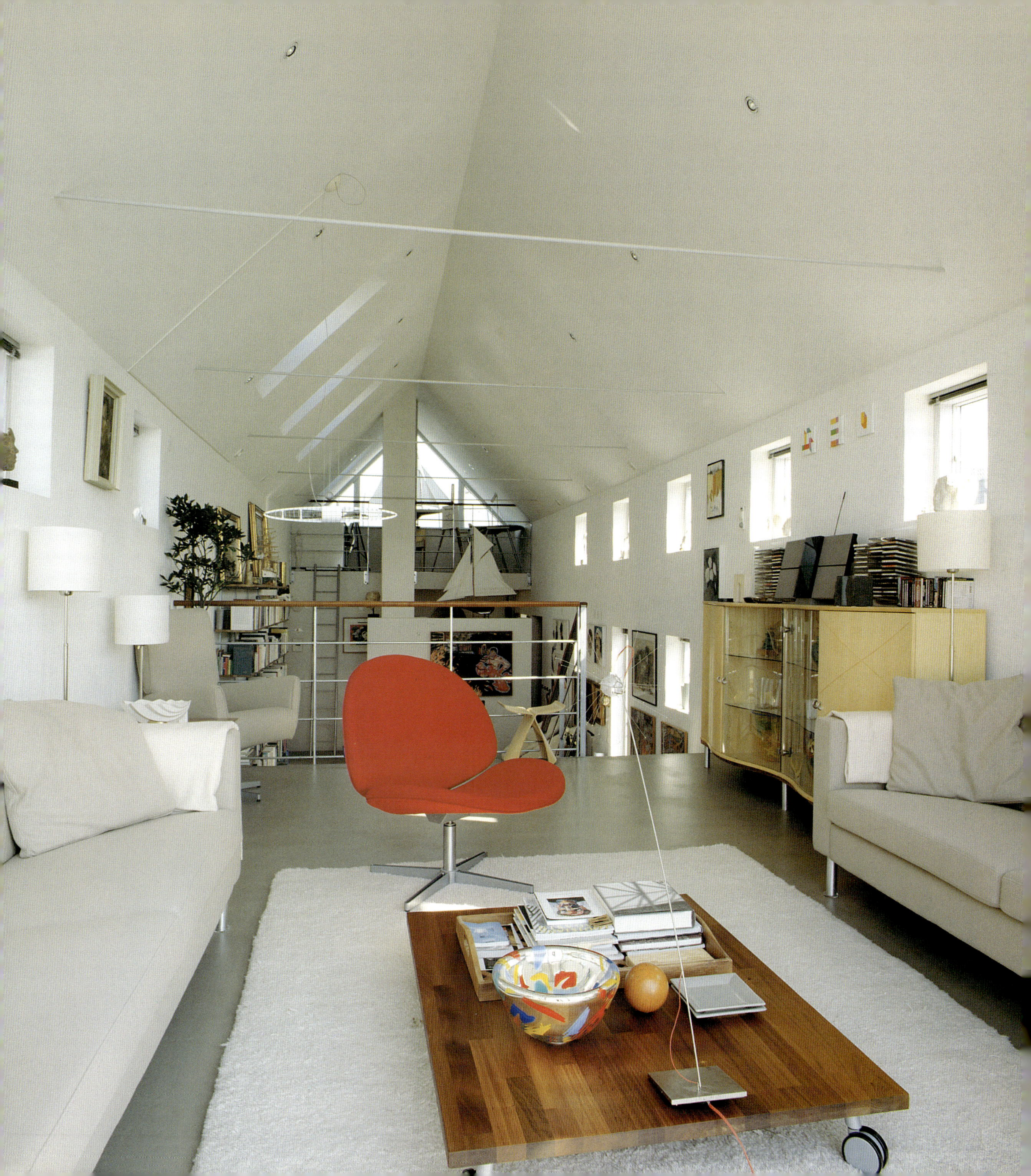

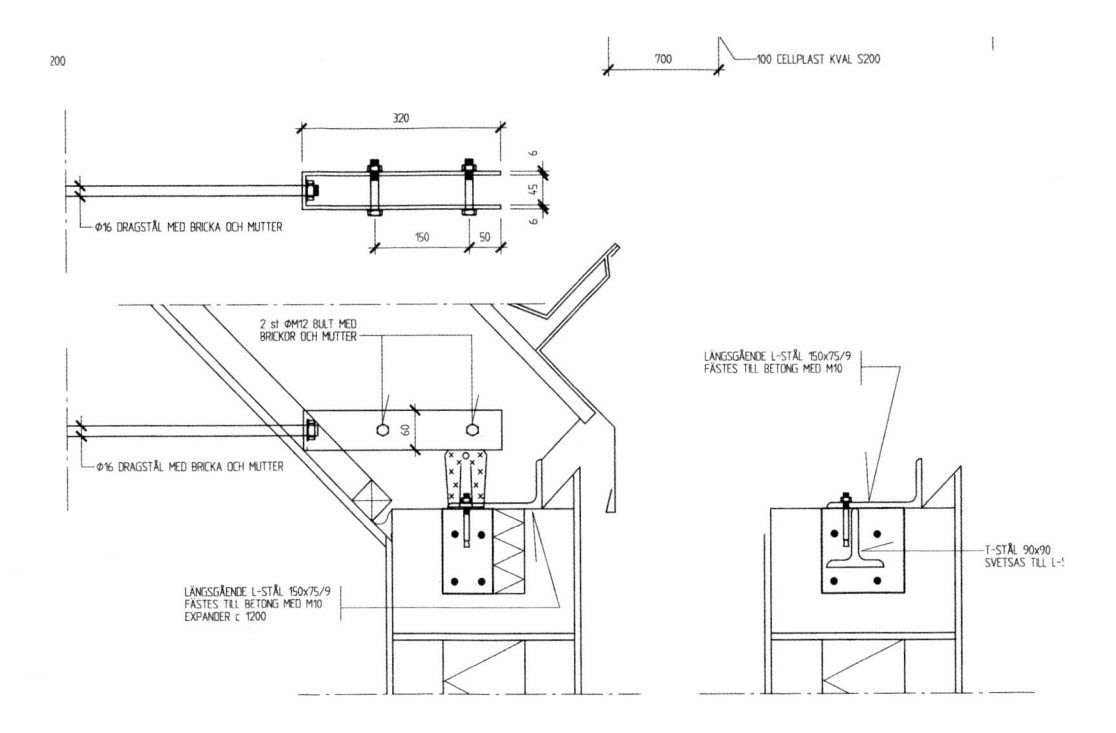

Constructive details

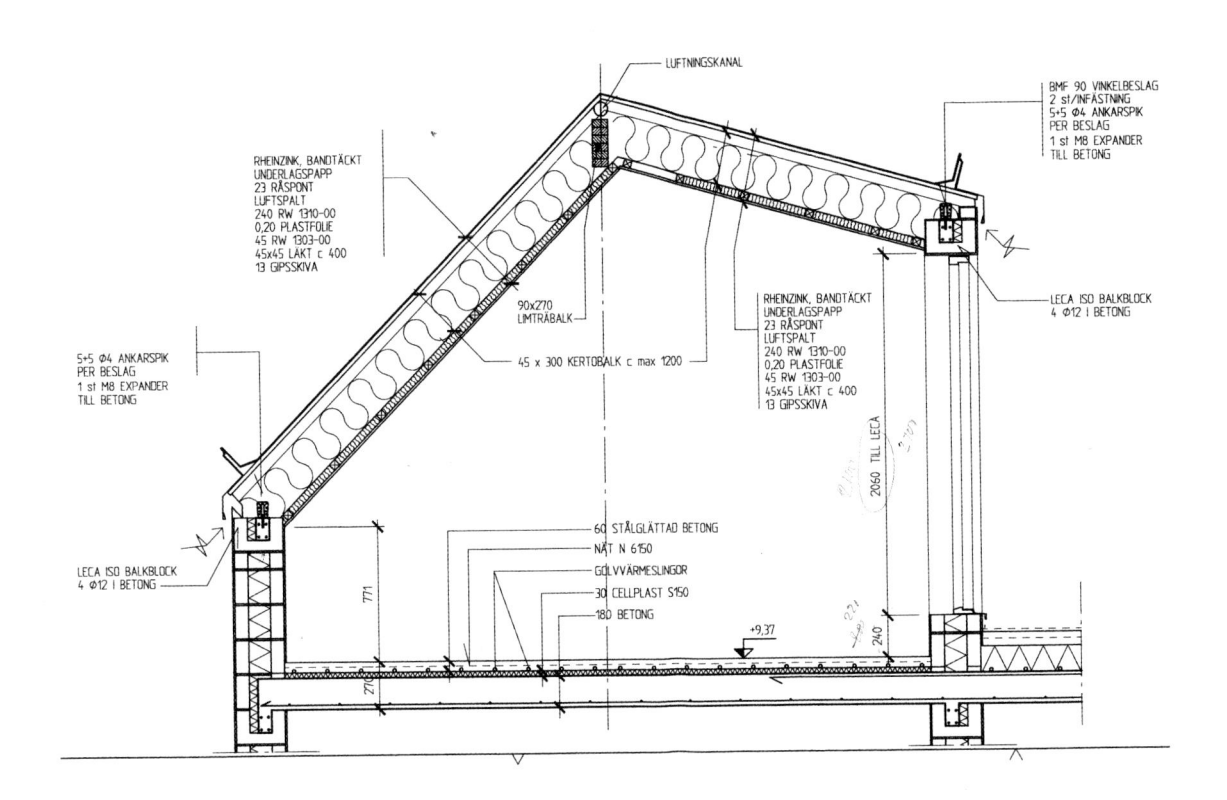

With exact attention to the function of the room, and serious consideration to aesthetics, the studio obtains plenty of natural light from the west and north, and has a soothing view of the sea and sky.

JAHN Associates
Kutti Beach House

Photographs: John Gollings

Vaucluse, Australia

Recently moved to Australia from England, the clients commissioned the design and construction of their new family home. It was designed to enhance the quality of life of its occupants, paying particular attention to the amenities of the surroundings, the idea being to establish distinctive ties between the building and streetscape, and between the building and harbor.

On a conceptual level, the project avoids the usual typology of a single mass in the center of the site with minimal setbacks to side boundaries. Instead, the plan is split, with a timber-framed harbor pavilion on the north and a load-bearing masonry street-side wing on the south, creating a courtyard in the center of the program. This provides greater capacity for ventilation, natural light and views to all the rooms from multiple perspectives.

Each component has its own individual architectonic character, while at the same time sitting in harmony with the other aspects of the program. The harbor (summer) pavilion is designed to capture the atmosphere of a beach house, while the stone-clad street (winter) wing provides enclosure and warmth and is more urban. The design creates a choice of internal and external living areas that are responsive to climate and that maximize access to harbor views, sunlight and ventilation. In planning terms, it is a model solution for large sites.

The rich palette of materials creates an organic interplay of textures and tones. The exterior walls are clad in Western red cedar weatherboards, the warmth of which perfectly complements the colder tones of the rendered masonry and split face Mintaro slate placed at seemingly random heights and thicknesses. Inside, Western red cedar weatherboards also line the walls as well as rendered and set plaster masonry. The floor finishes consist of recycled blackbutt from Queensland, 600X600mm lineal-cut travertine with off-white sand/cement slurry fill and Vietnamese bluestone, the latter gracing the entry level. In concert with the wall cladding, both inside and out, the window and door frames are also in Western red cedar, except for those with 'frameless' glazing.

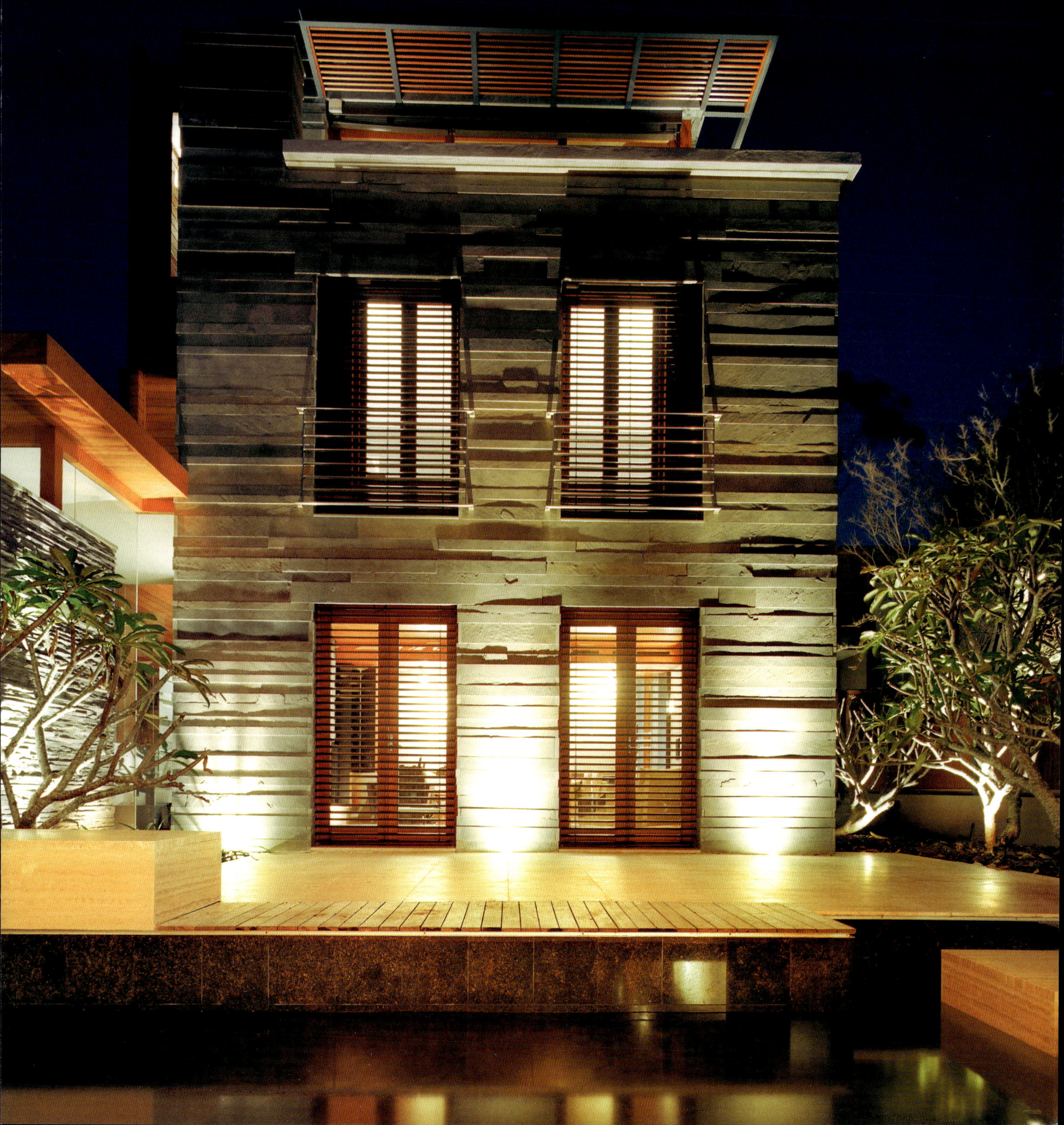

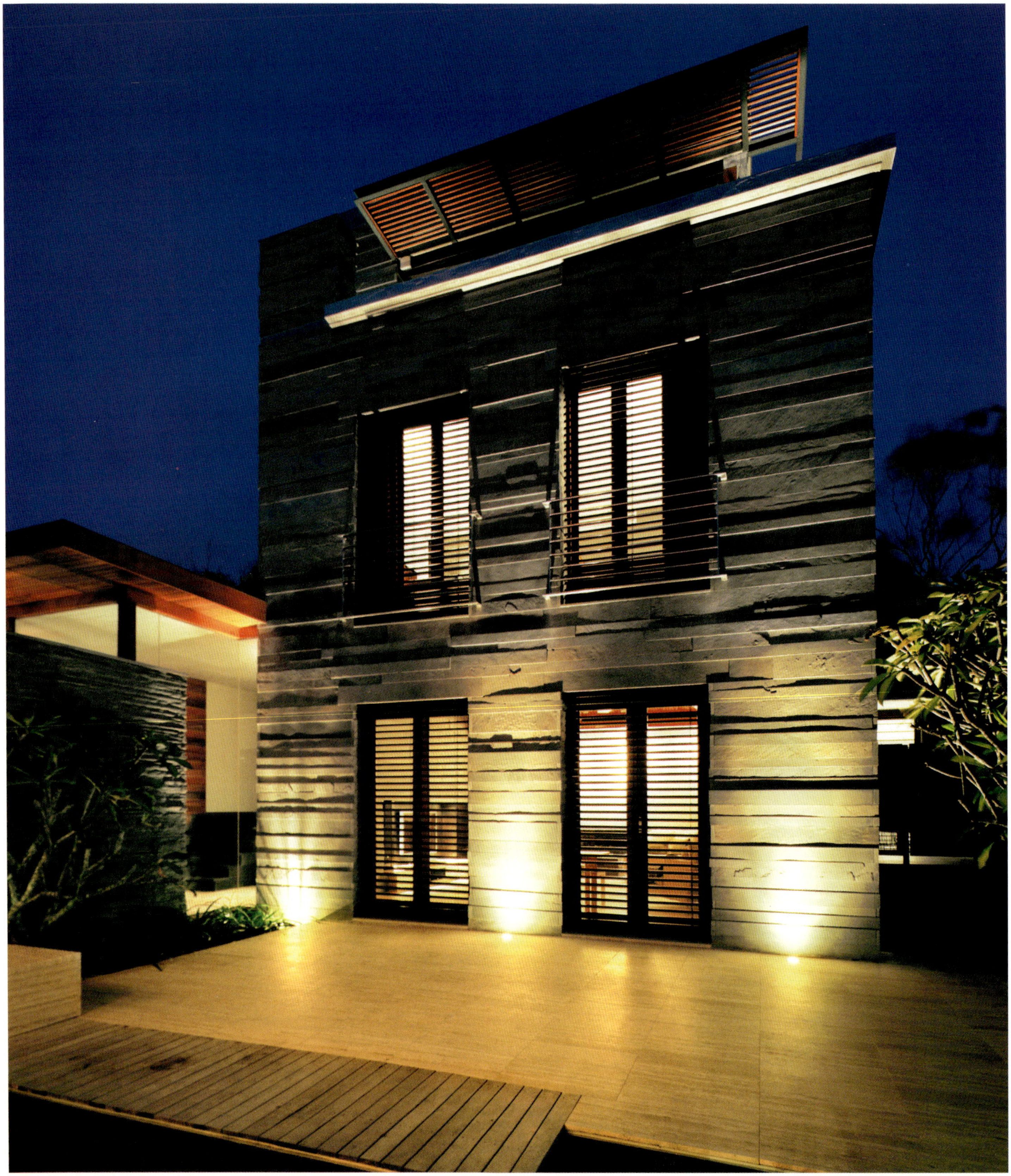

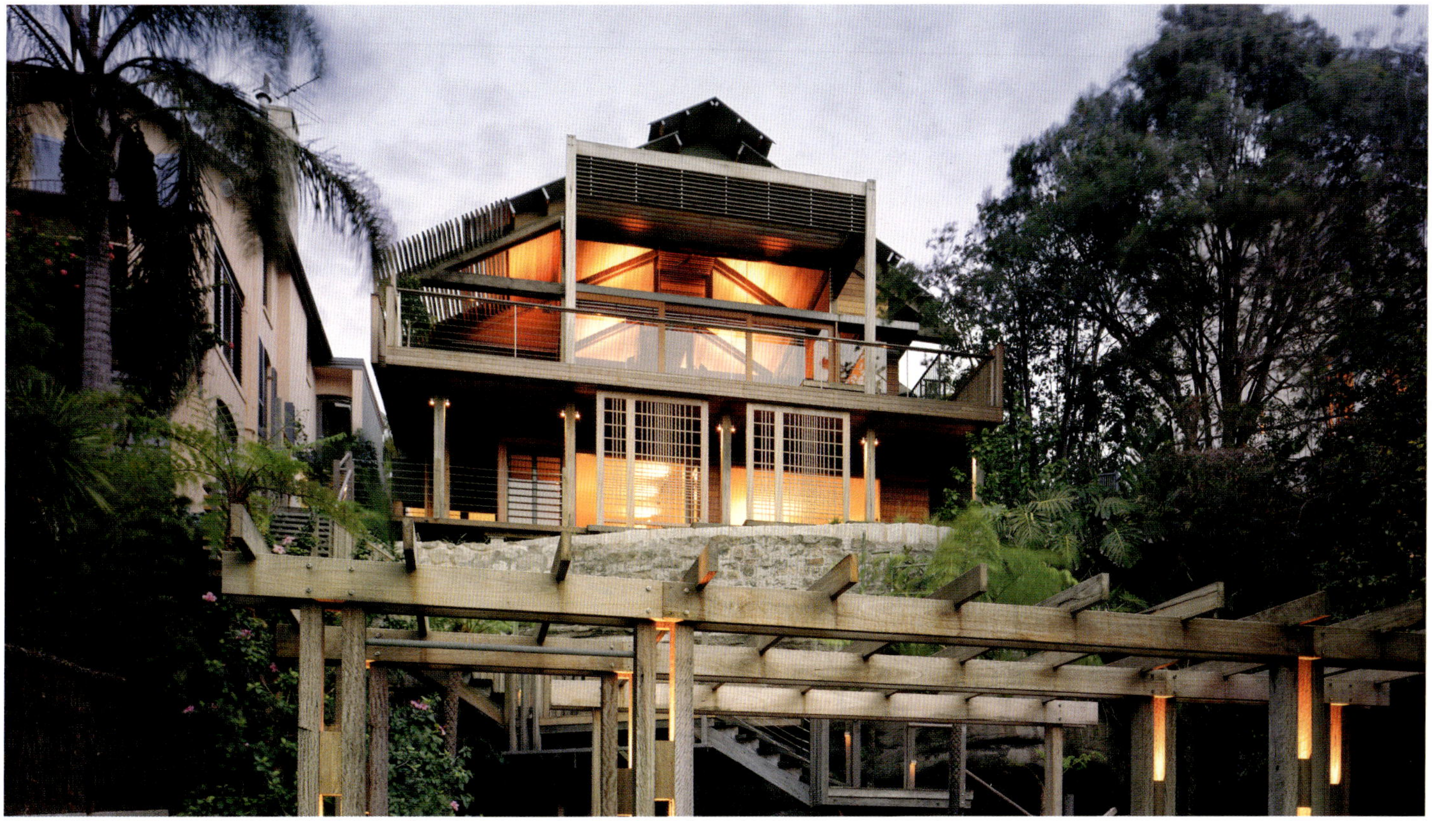

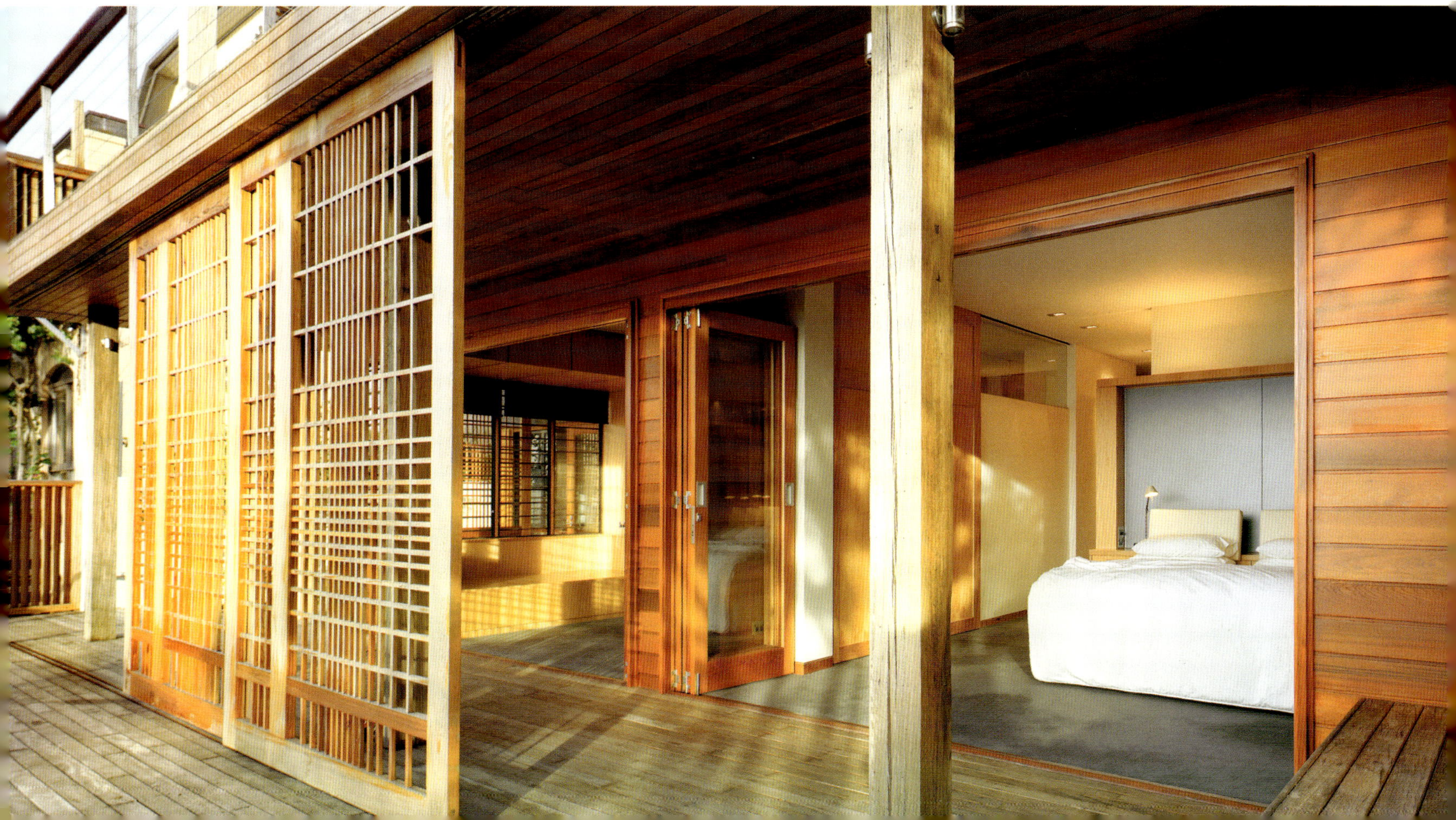

Basement floor plan

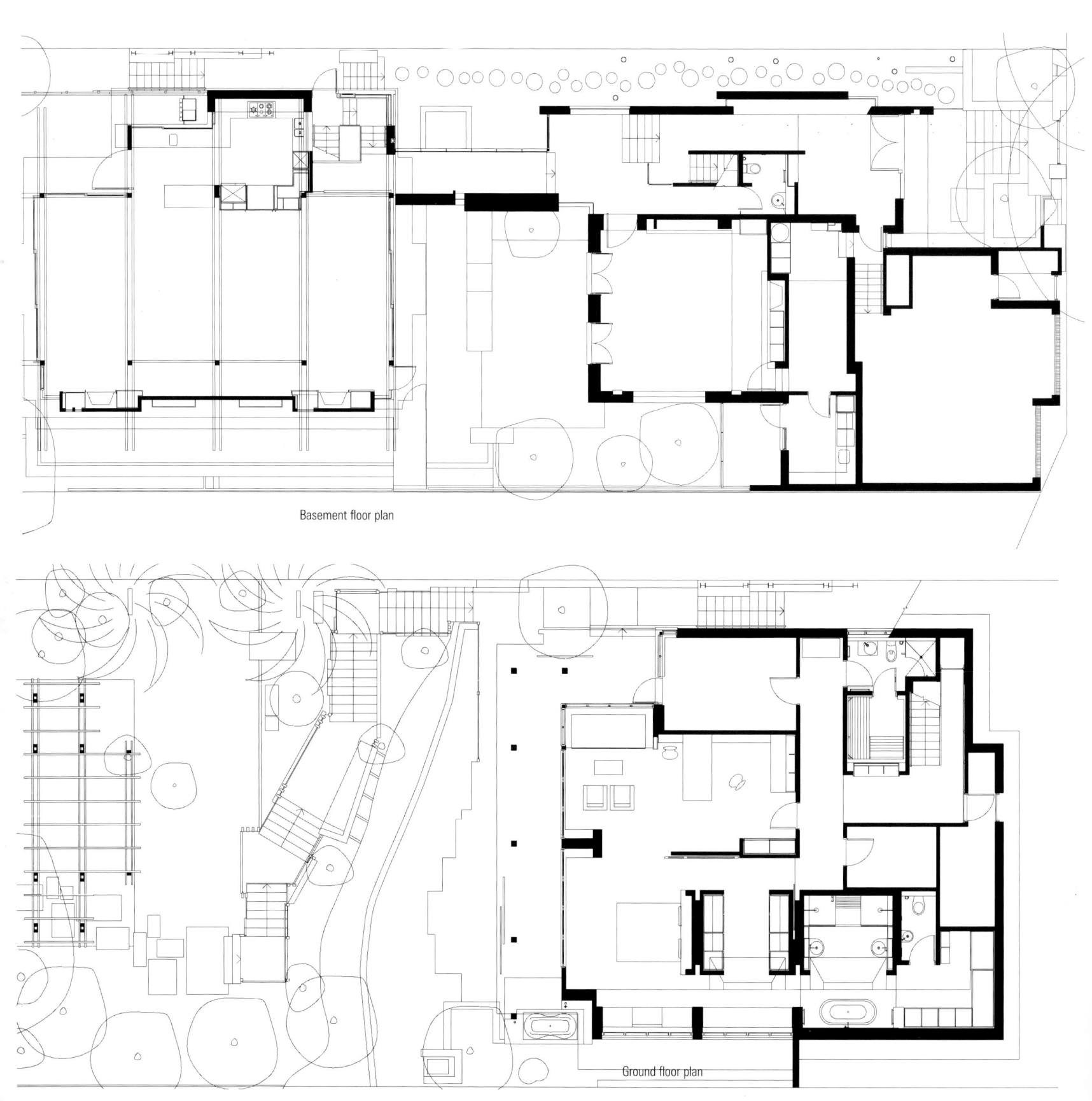

Ground floor plan

54

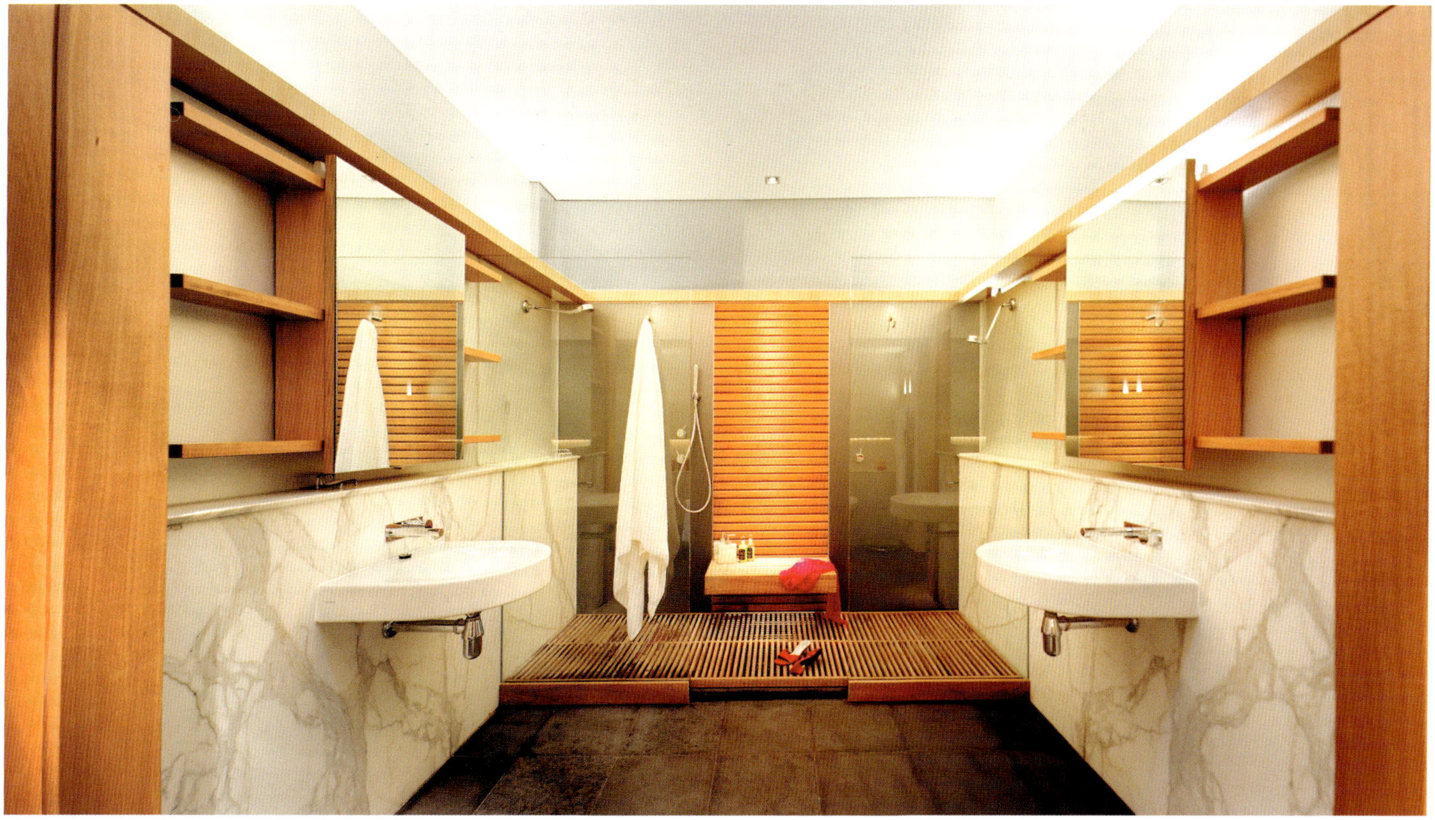

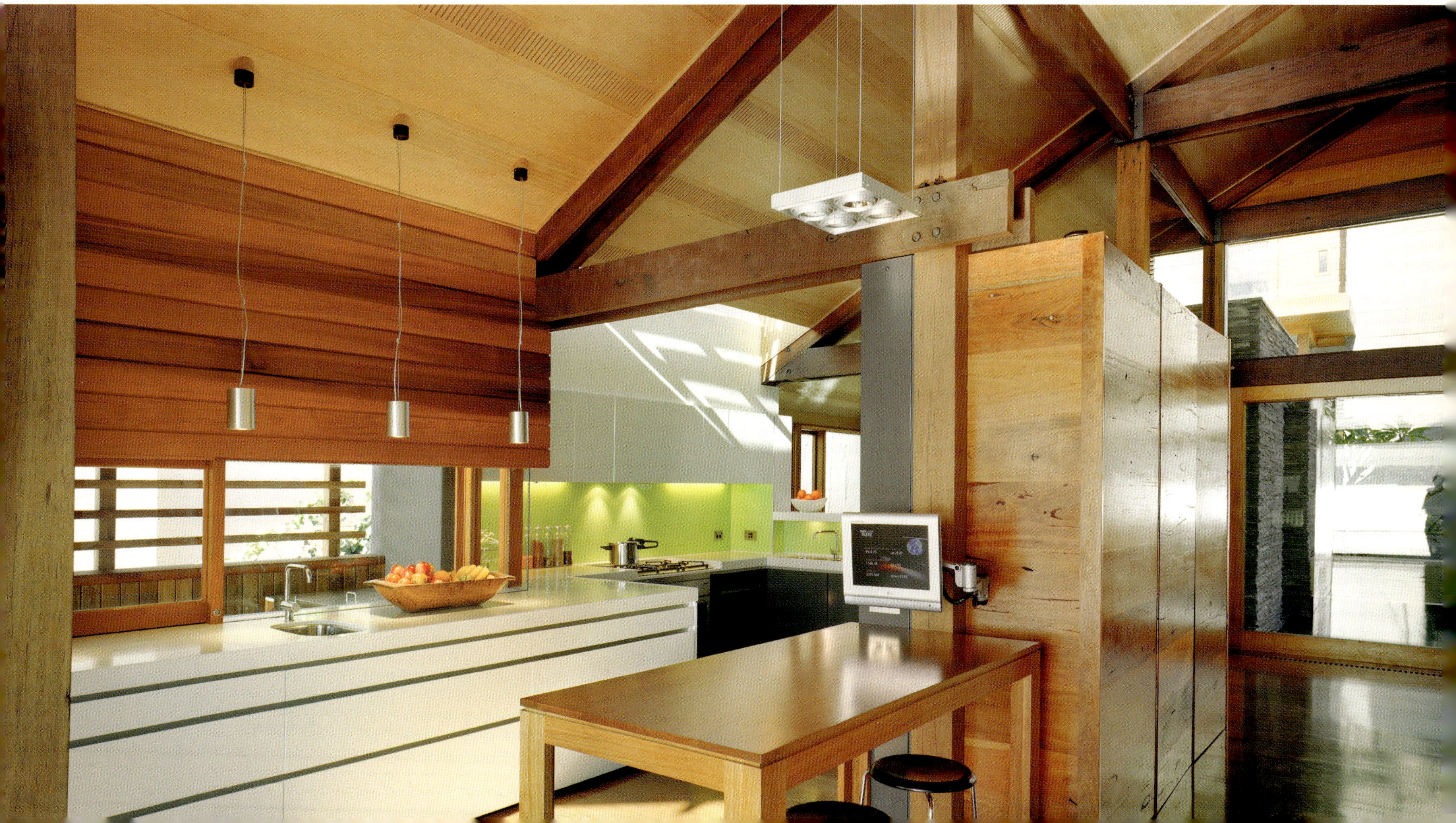

First floor plan

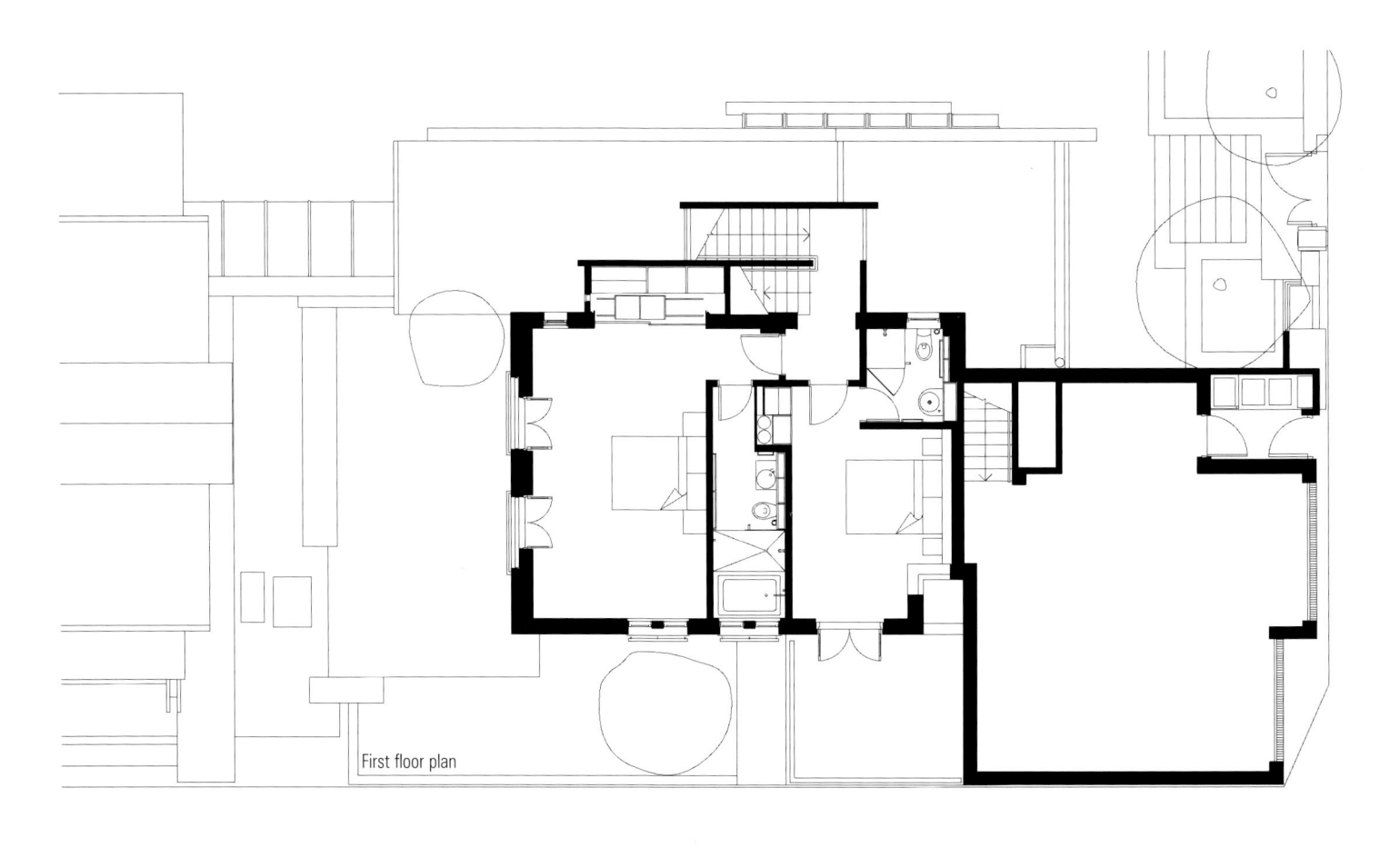

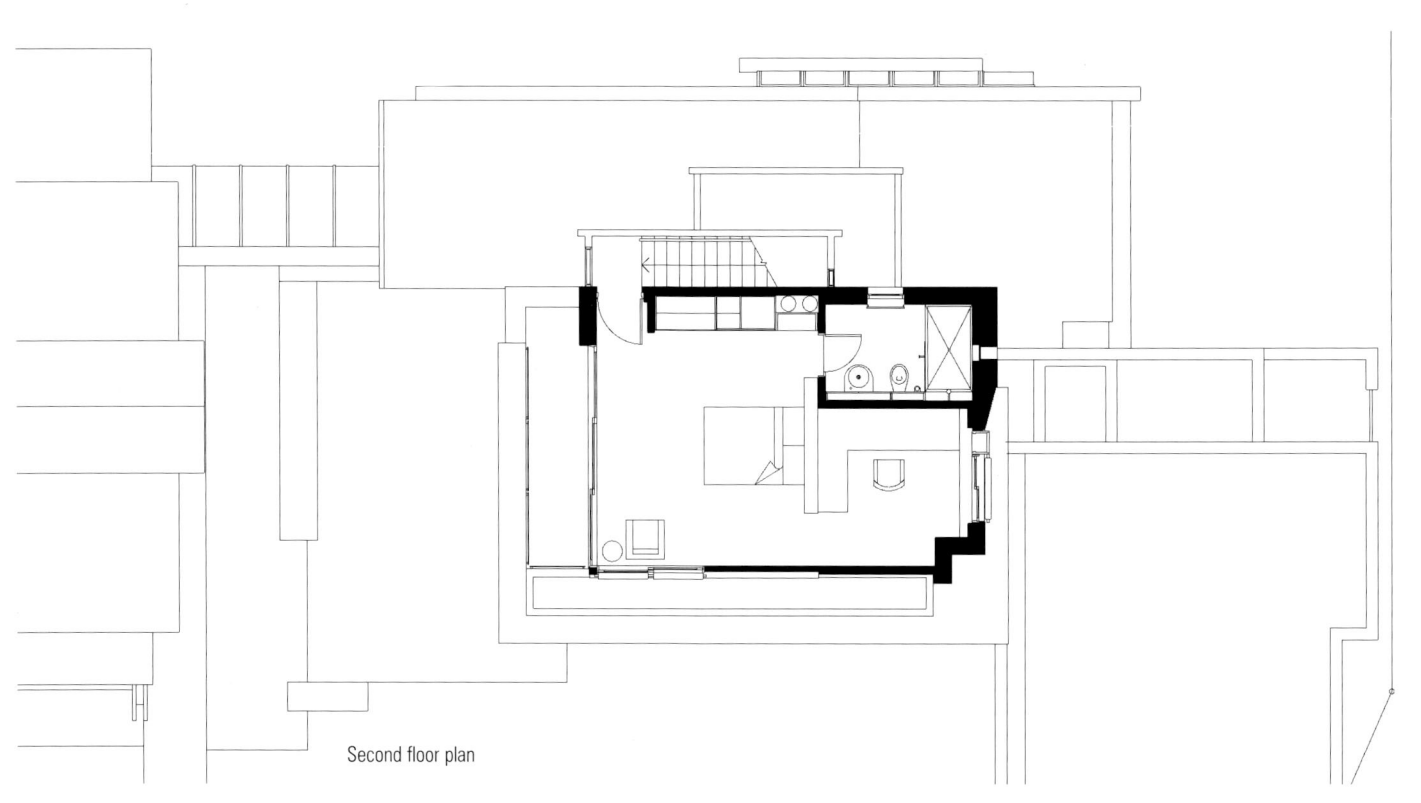

Second floor plan

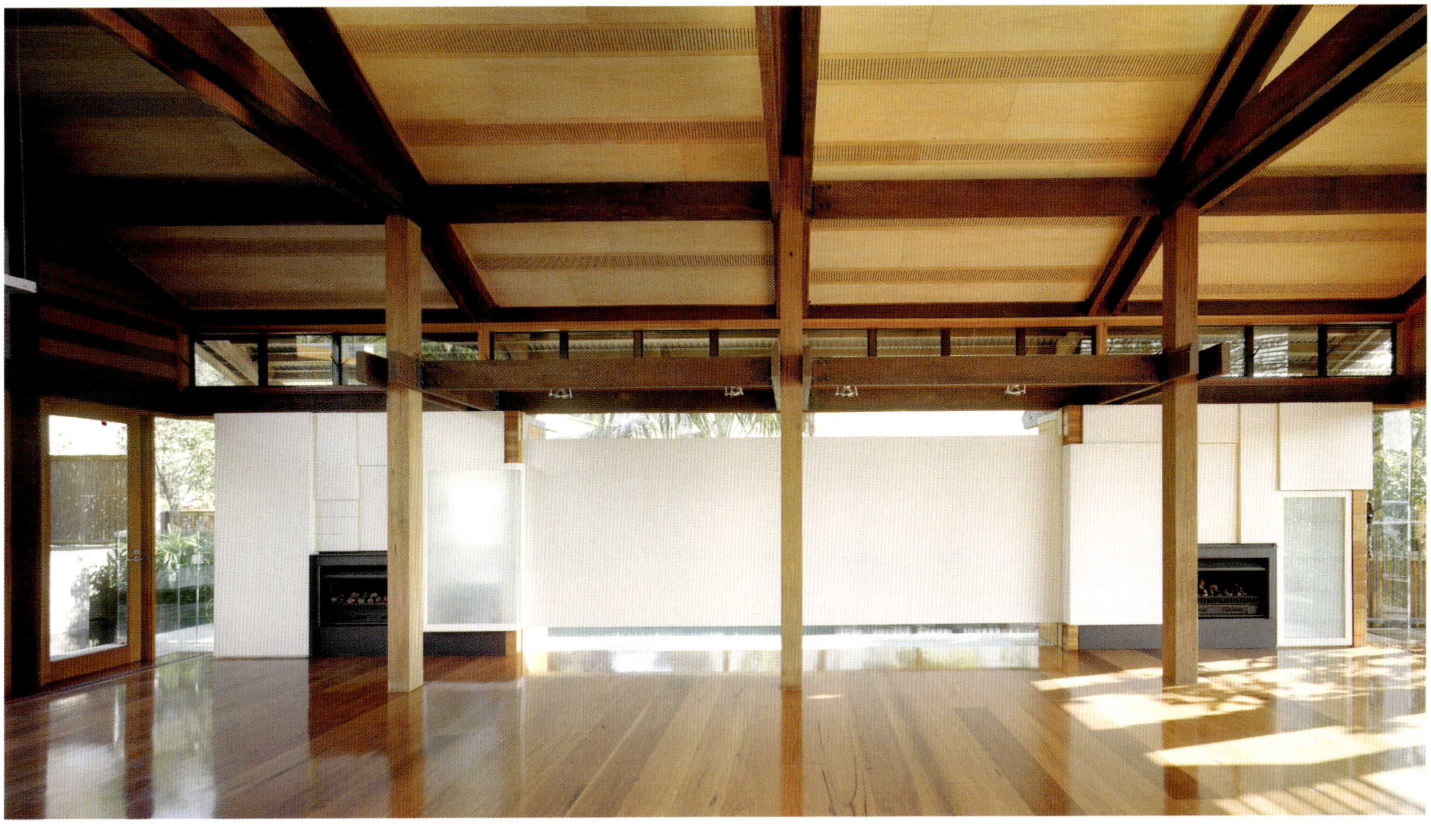

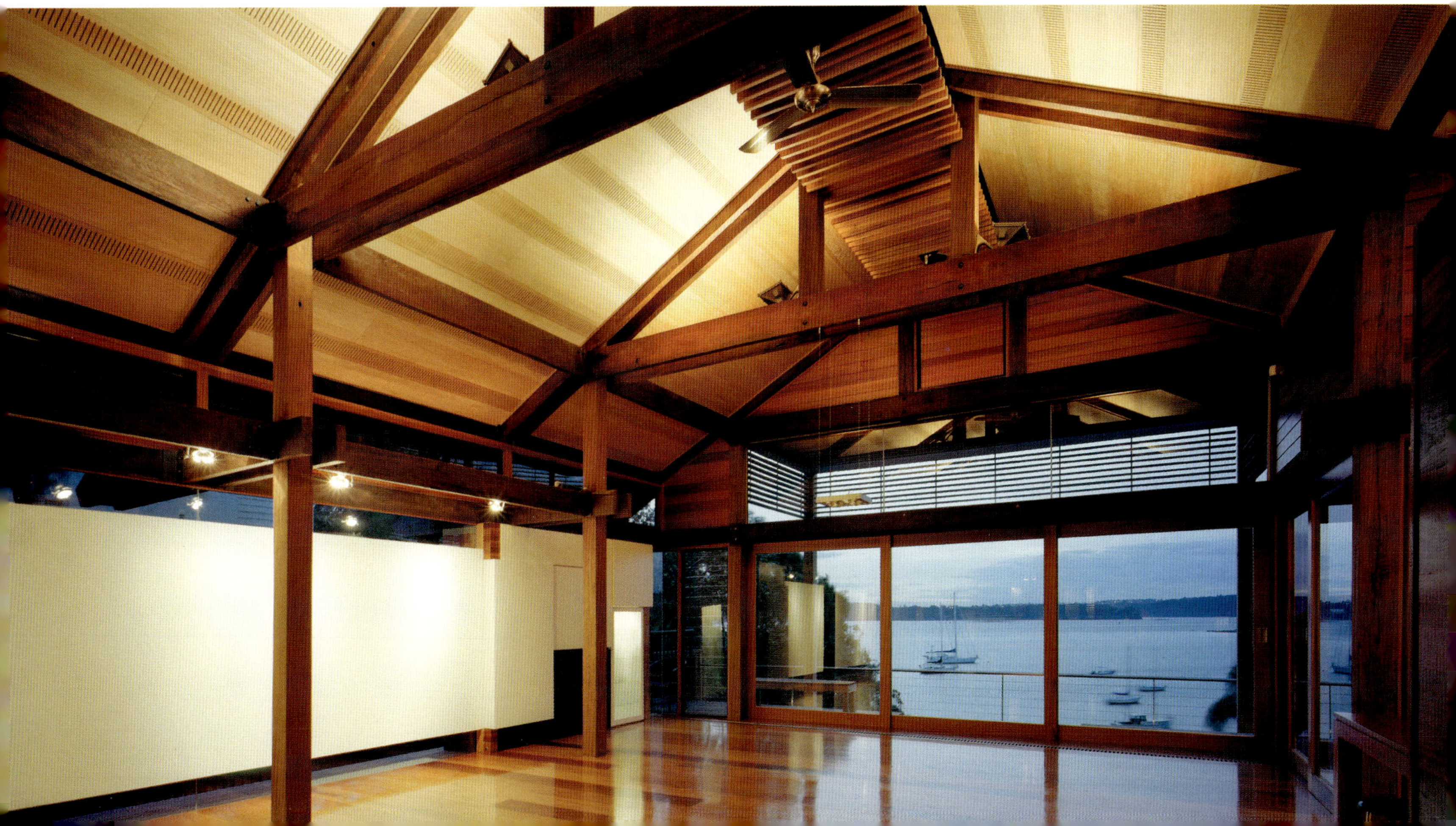

The plan is split, with a timber-framed harbor pavilion on the north and a load-bearing masonry street-side wing on the south, creating a courtyard in the center of the program. This provides greater capacity for ventilation, natural light and views to all the rooms from multiple perspectives.

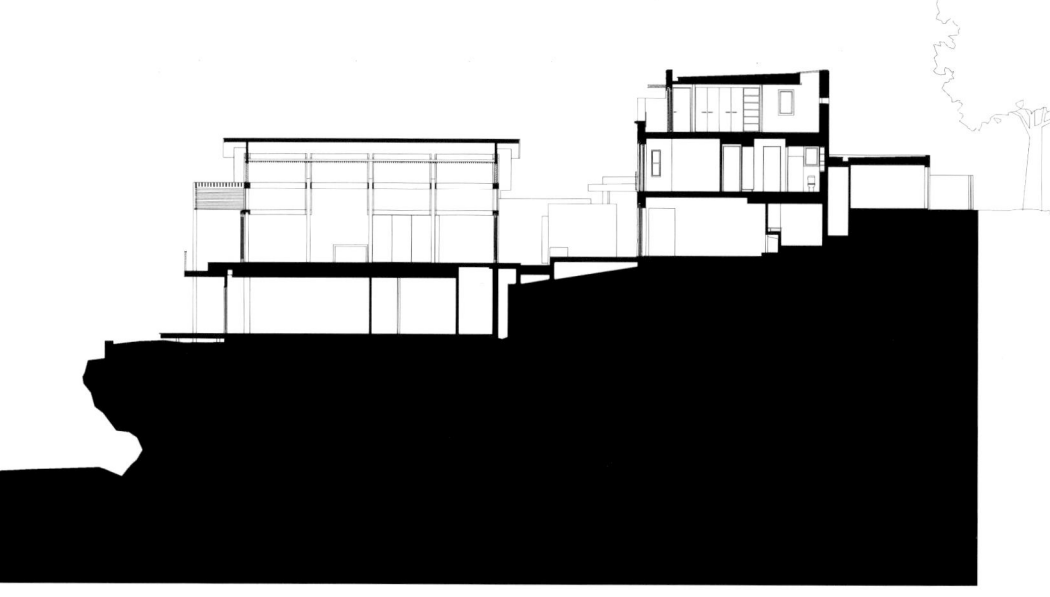

Longitudinal section

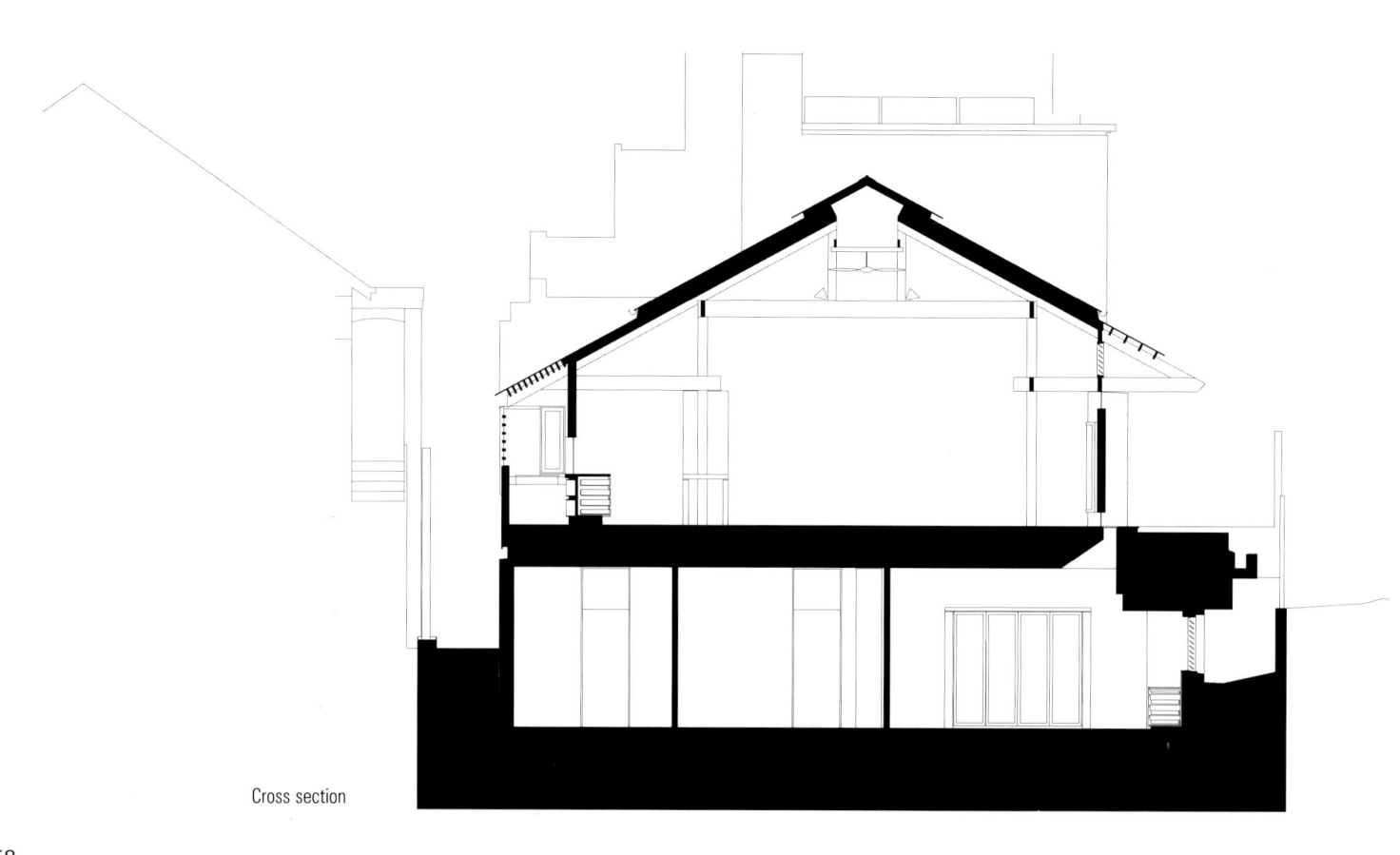

Cross section

58

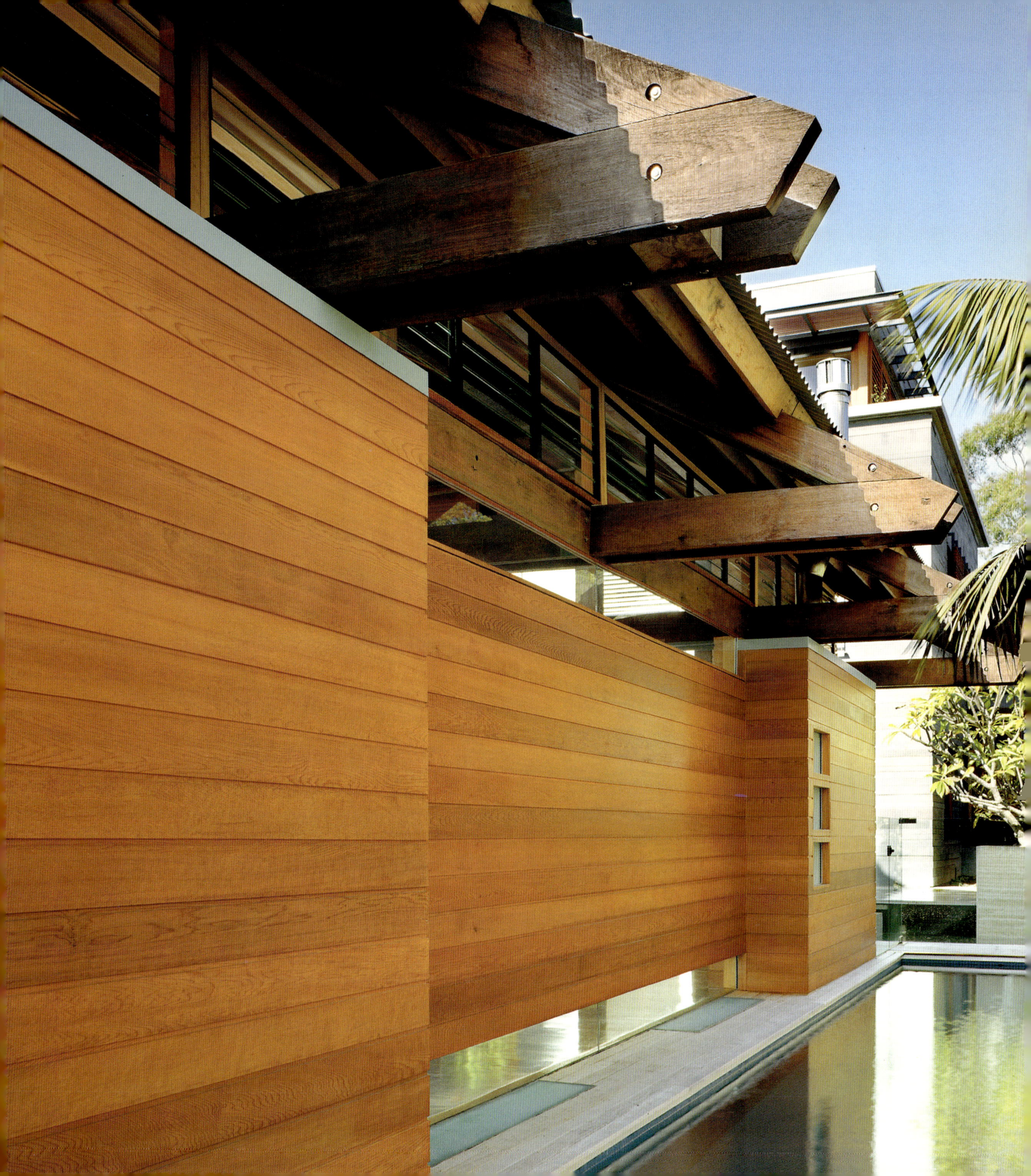

Wortmann & Bañares Arquitectos
House in La Cerdanya

Photographs: Lluís Casals

La Cerdanya, Spain

The layout of this one-story house is a simple 148ftx33ft (45mx10m) rectangle. The home comprises a single space fragmented here and there into various rooms: living/dining room and kitchen, bedrooms, suite, bathrooms (one on the other side of the garage, with independent entrance) and a guestroom with its own bathroom. A sense of fluidity within a single continuous space has been achieved through a peculiar distribution, in which the dividing walls never give way to the façade. Rather than being enclosed within four walls, the bedrooms instead feature large sliding partitions that roll open and, in the process, disappear. All of the functional spaces are interconnected.

Taking into account the central role that the landscape would play, a path was developed that encircles the house along the interior face of the façade. Functional elements supported by the building's perimeter - built-in closets, shelves, sinks and work surfaces, whose presence helps dilute and justify the opacity of the façade - have been placed along the length of this interior route. The outer skin has been designed in the style of an industrial farming structure, from which an "urban loft" emerges.

A modern tone has been struck in the reinterpretation of the local area's standard materials. The stone façade is here ventilated and features a horizontal layout that is more typical of wood. The traditional sloped roof in slate here rests on an exposed lightweight metal structure.

The mobile floor-to-ceiling shutters along the façade establish a fragile barrier between interior and exterior. Their linearity and transparency naturally bring them closer to the landscape.

Finishes in granite, aluminum and wood are modulated according to the predominant horizontal rhythm, paying meticulous attention to the linear ideal that encompasses the entire home without interruption.

The project can be schematized as a "simple container" that provides a sophisticated functional program, but one which manifests the will to find a new way of experiencing domestic space, where the occupants are in close contact with each other and with nature.

Most of the fixtures and furniture were meticulously chosen by the owners.

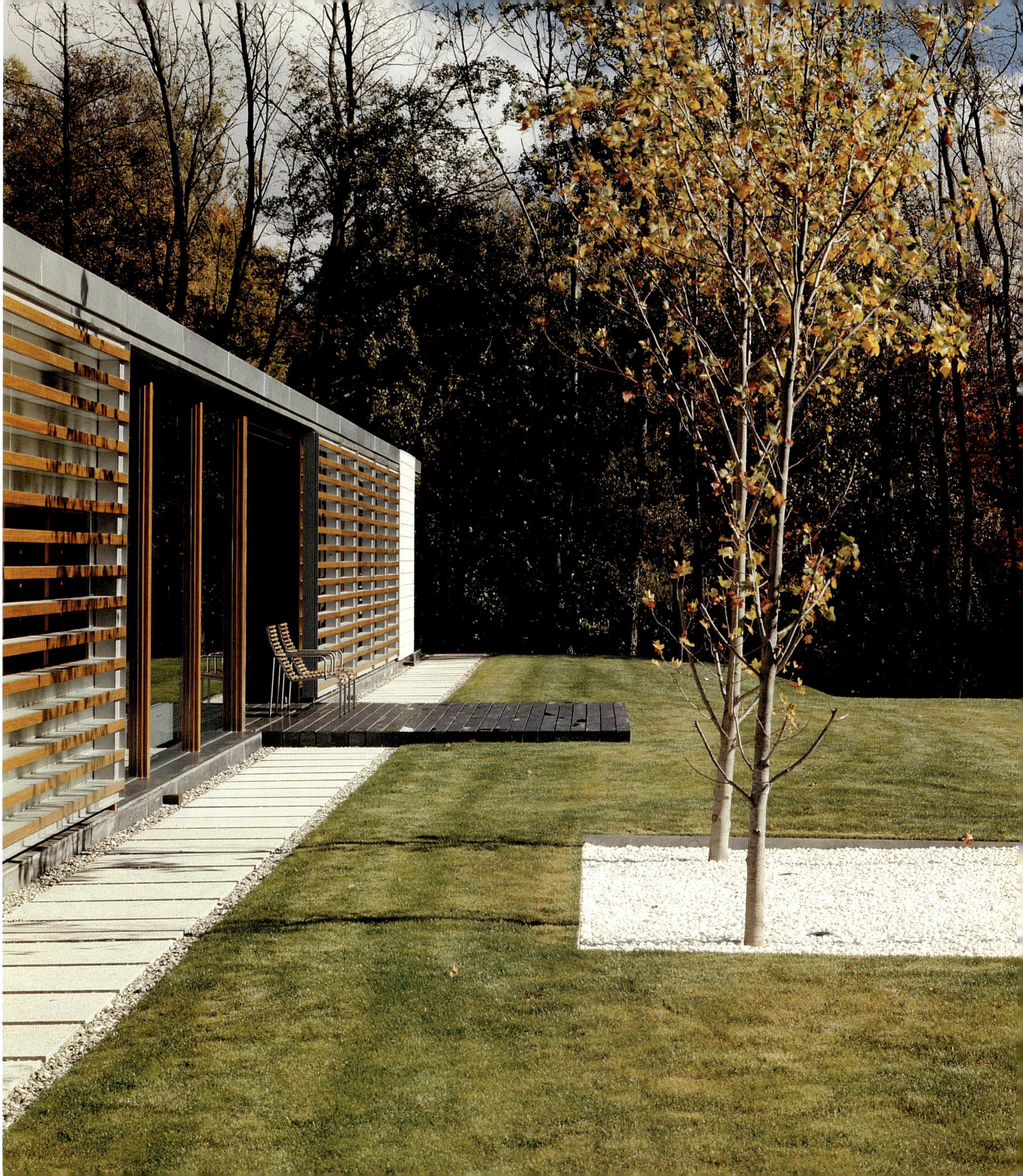

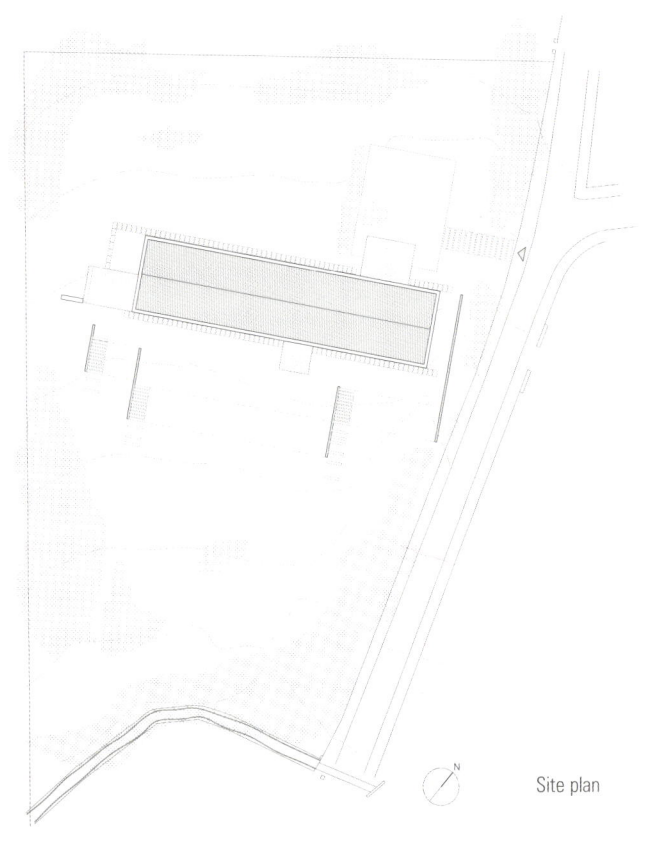

Taking into account the central role that the landscape would play, a path was developed that encircles the house along the interior face of the façade.

Site plan

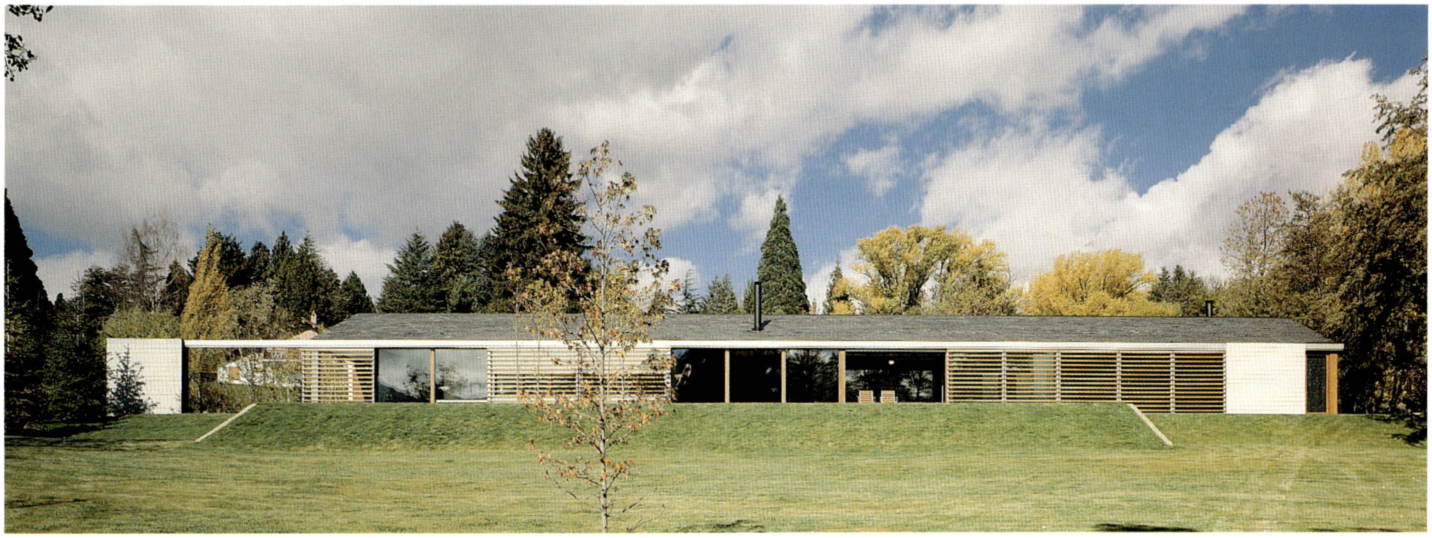
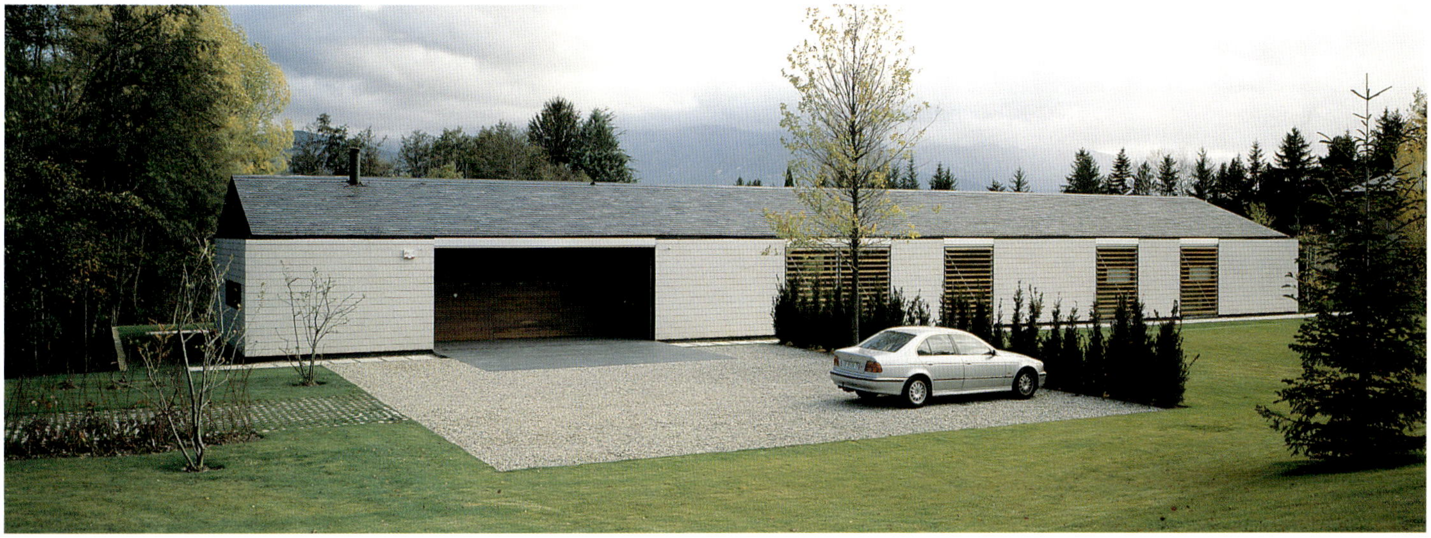
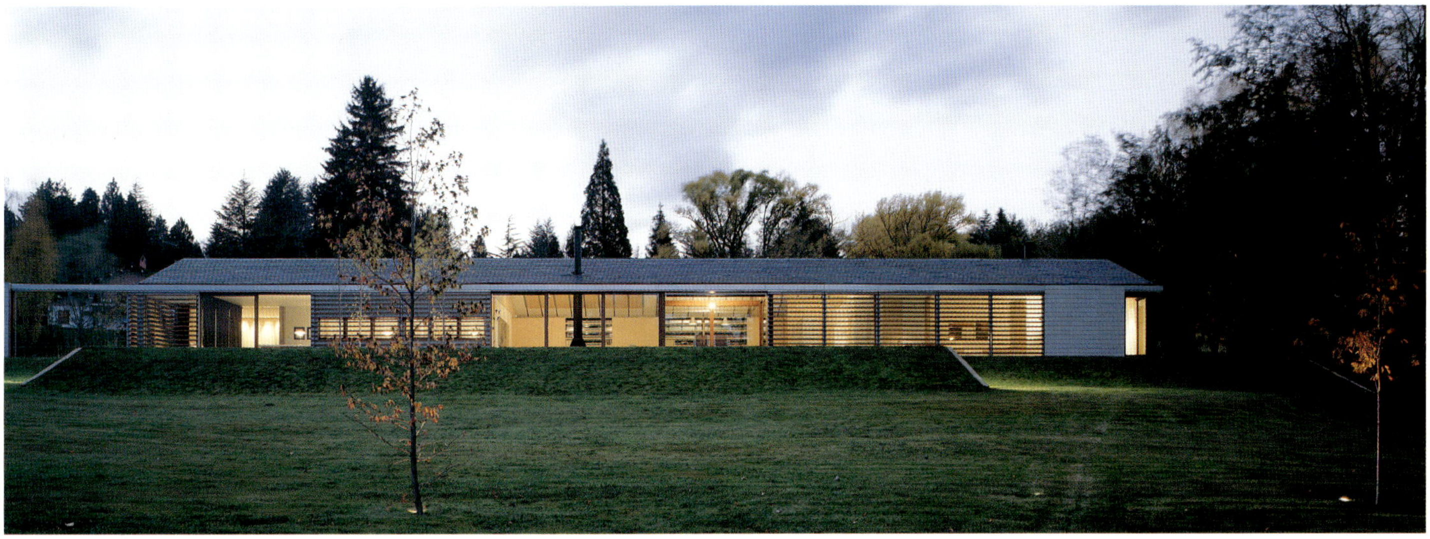

Ground floor plan

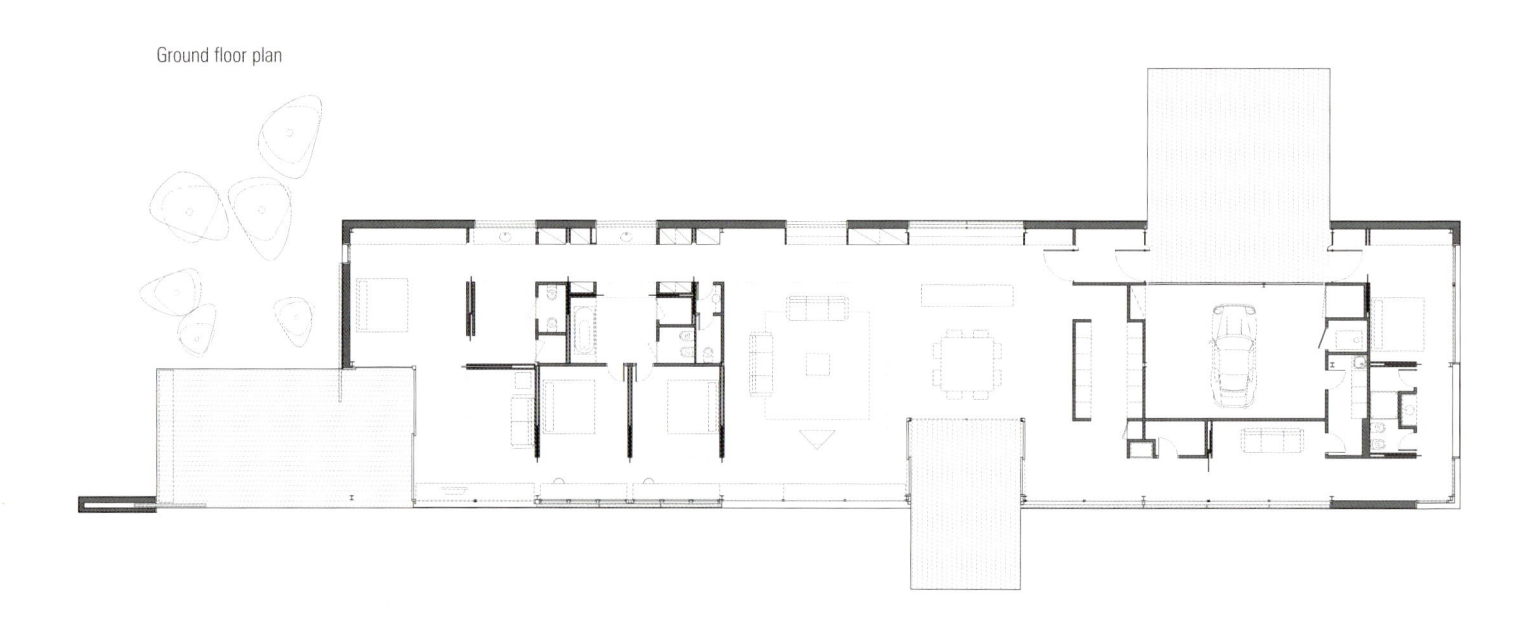

64

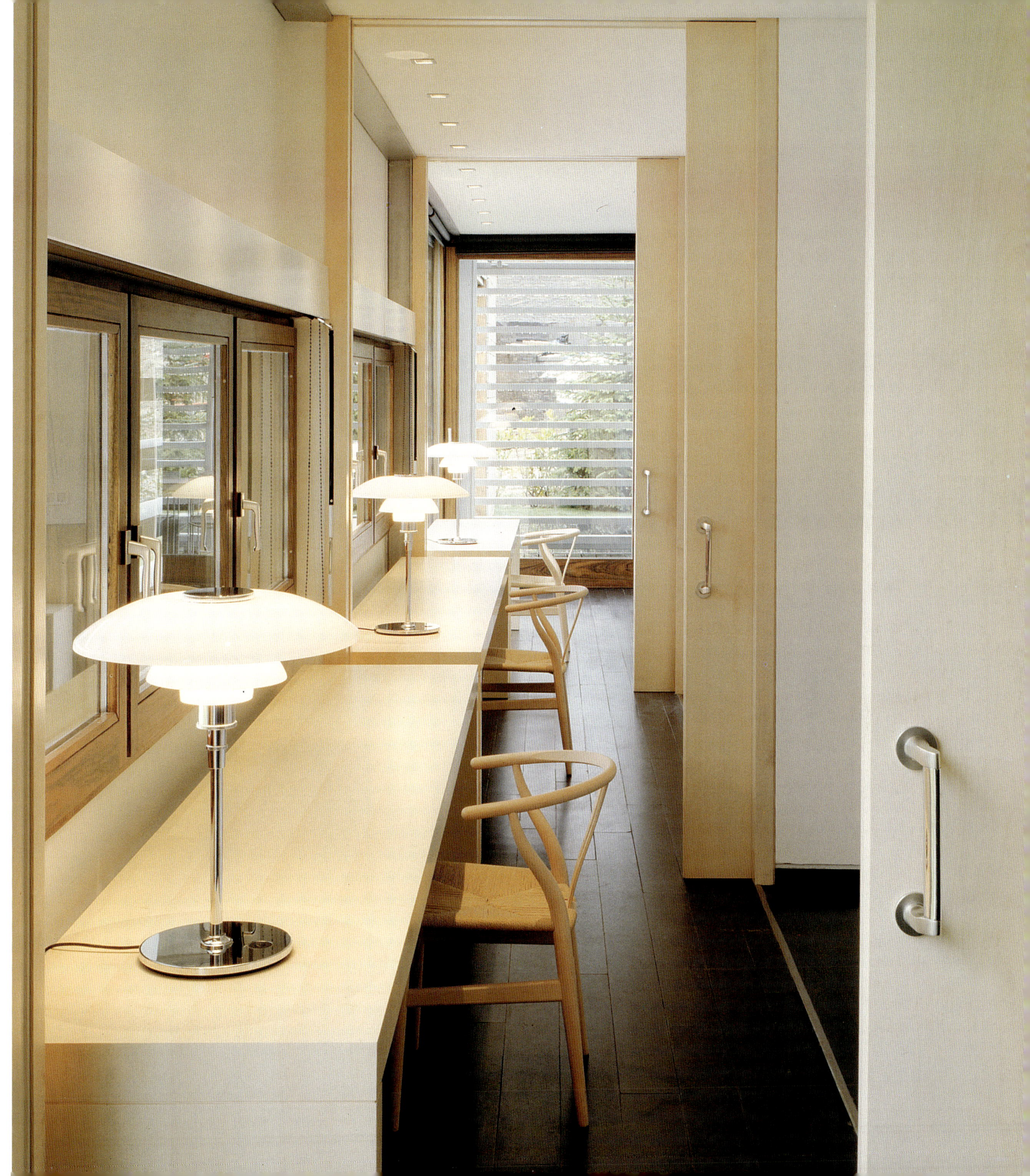

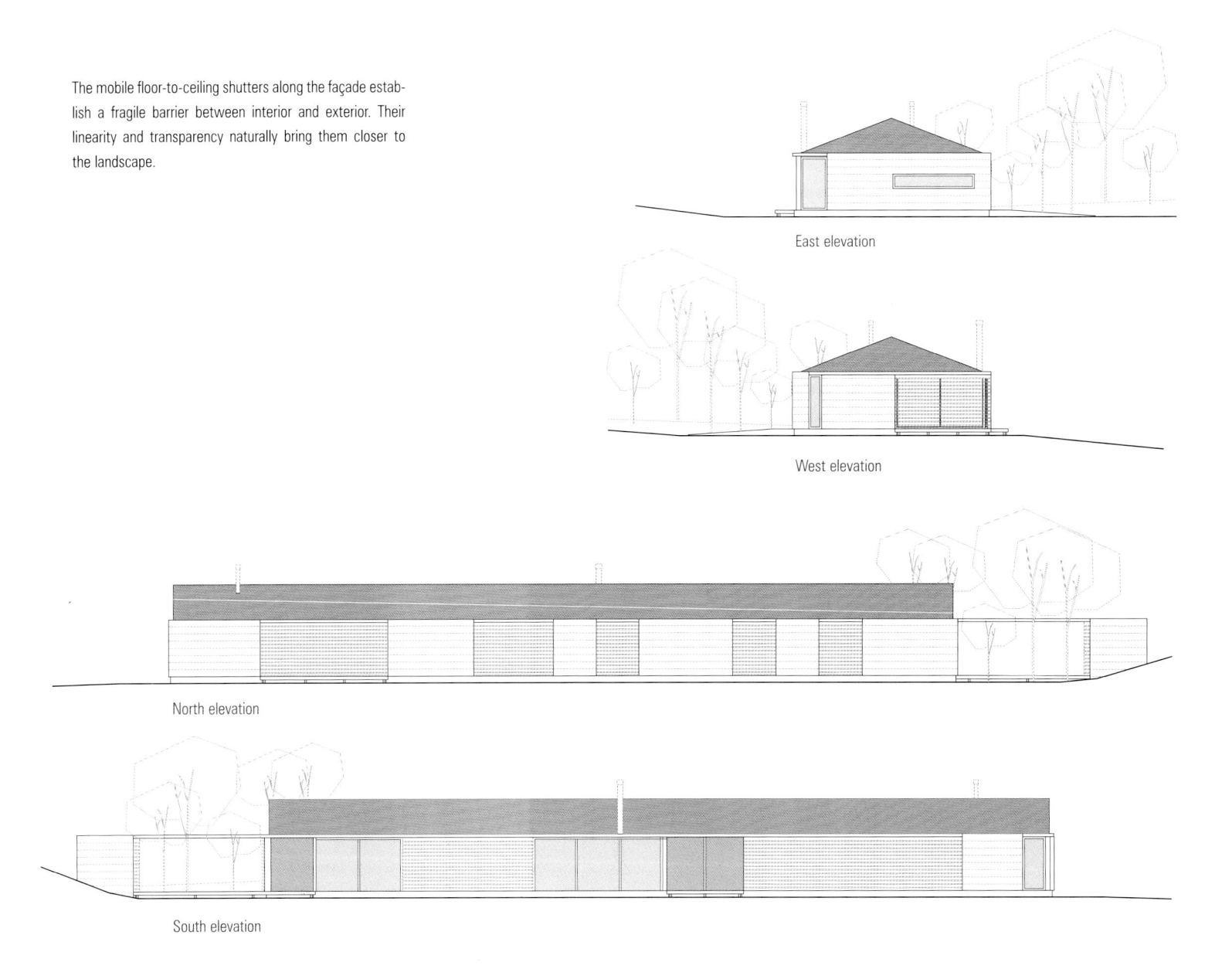

The mobile floor-to-ceiling shutters along the façade establish a fragile barrier between interior and exterior. Their linearity and transparency naturally bring them closer to the landscape.

East elevation

West elevation

North elevation

South elevation

Cross section

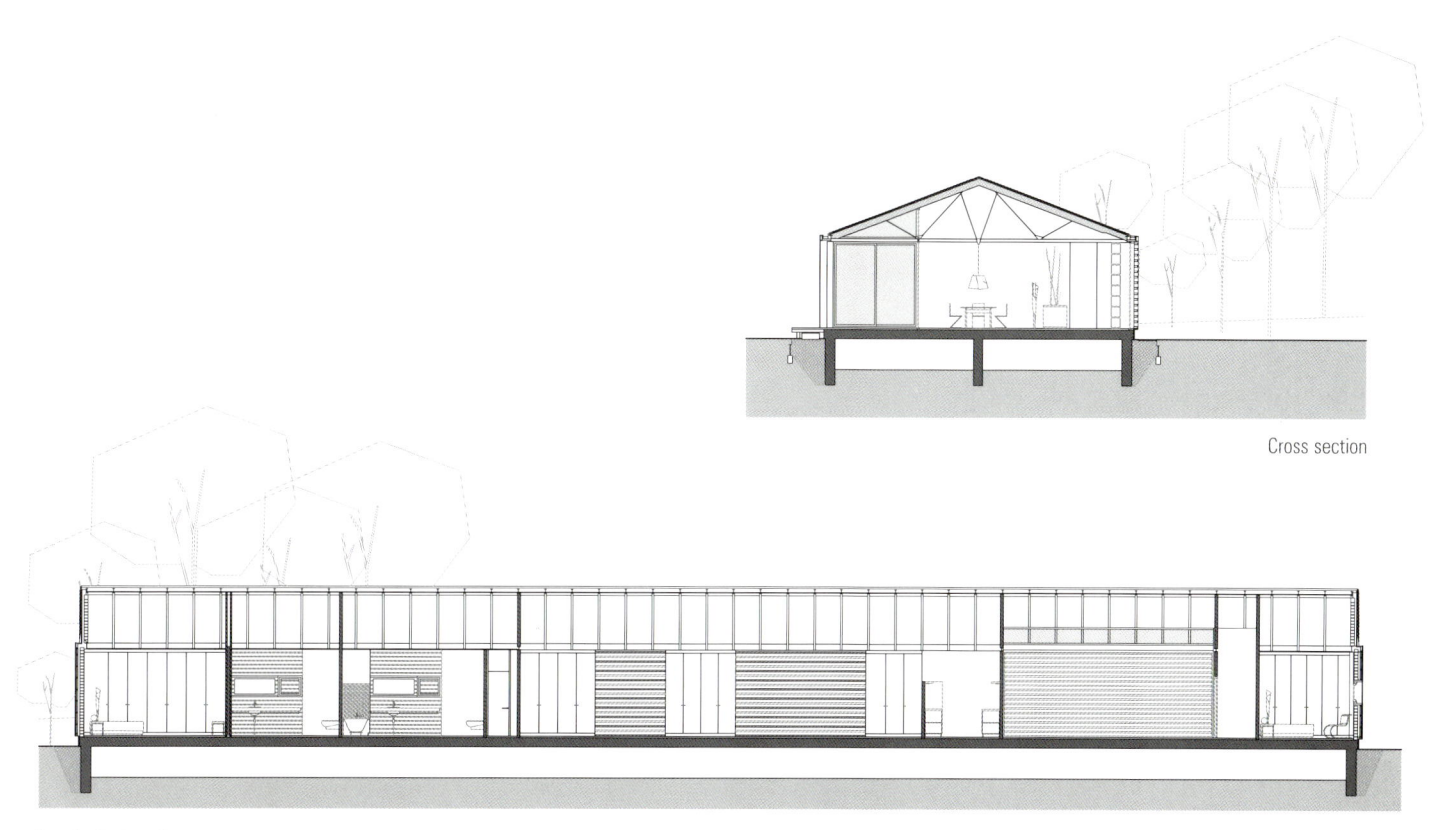

Longitudinal section

67

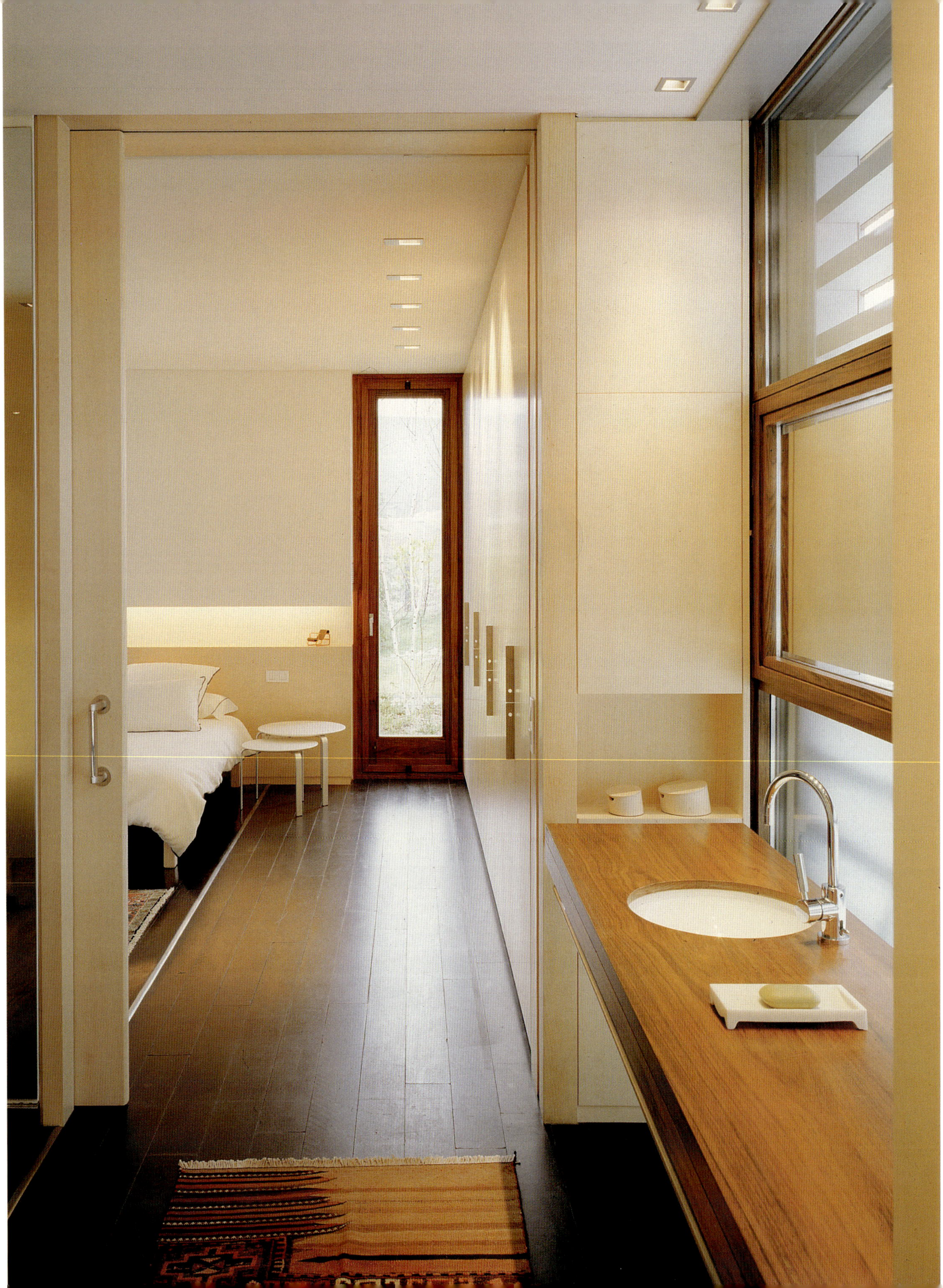

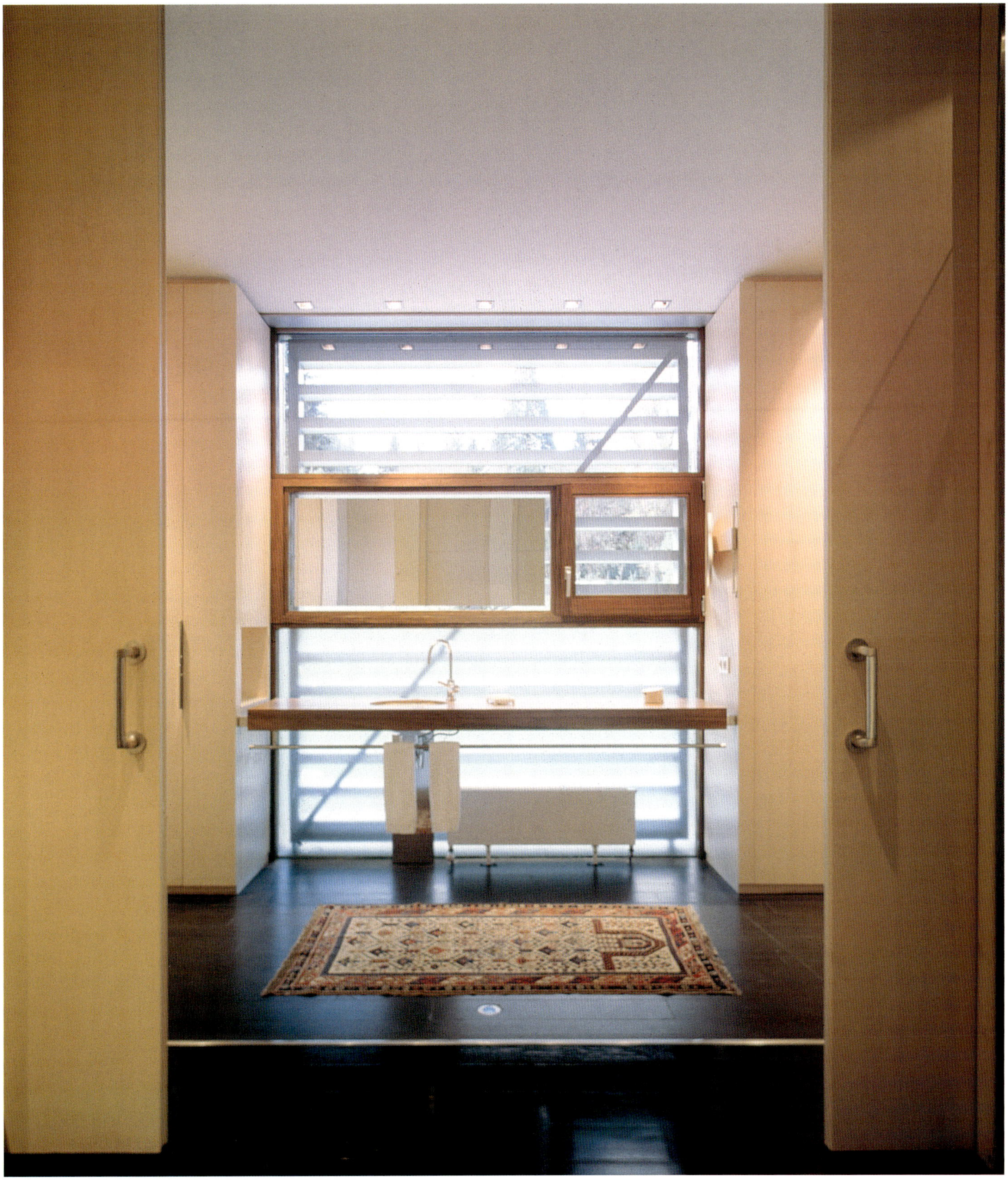

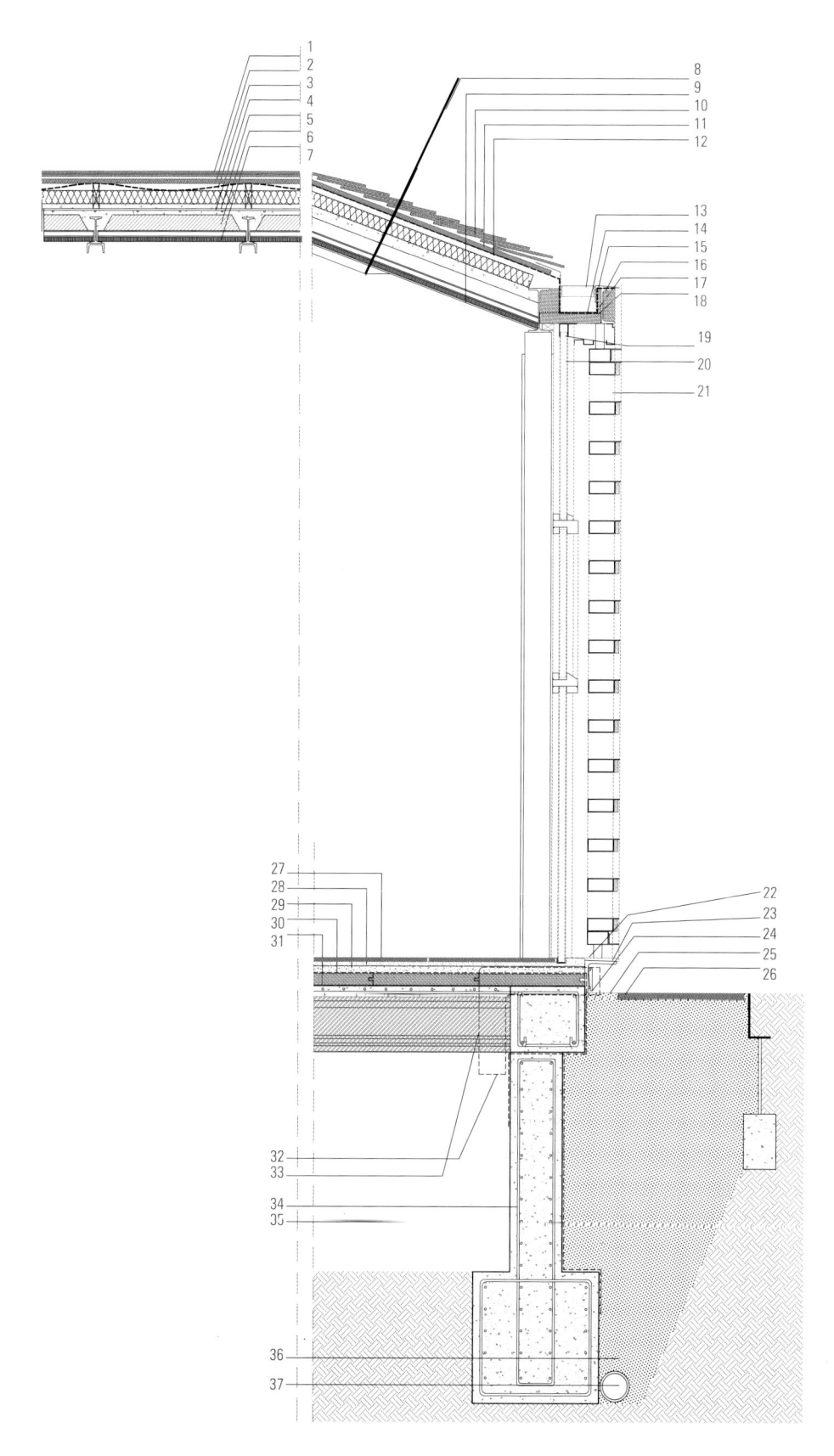

Construction section

1. Slate roof
2. 20 mm board
3. Butyl mesh
4. Welded wire mesh
5. Concrete
6. 70 cm ceramic siding
7. Water-repellant beech plywood cladding
8. 60 mm UPN
9. 120 mm IPN
10. Slate roof
11. 20 mm board
12. Butyl mesh
13. Practicable snow-repellant grille
14. Resin-clad galvanized steel gutter
15. Sheet metal finish
16. 160 mm UPN
17. Insulation
18. T50-6 stanchions every 90 cm, with foam between
19. 50 mm U profilein matte steel
20. 5+5/12/5/12/6 Stadip glass
21. Automatic sliding shutter with aluminum structure and wood cladding
22. Bedding
23. L-150-5
24. Sheet metal in matte steel
25. "Pea gravel"
26. 90x60x3 cm granite slab
27. 20 mm slate paving
28. 20 mm bond coat
29. 30 mm plate
30. Butyl mesh
31. HD polystyrene foam
32. Sanitary ventilation slab
33. Slab of prestressed joists
34. Foundation
35. Butyl plate
36. Gravel
37. Drainage tube

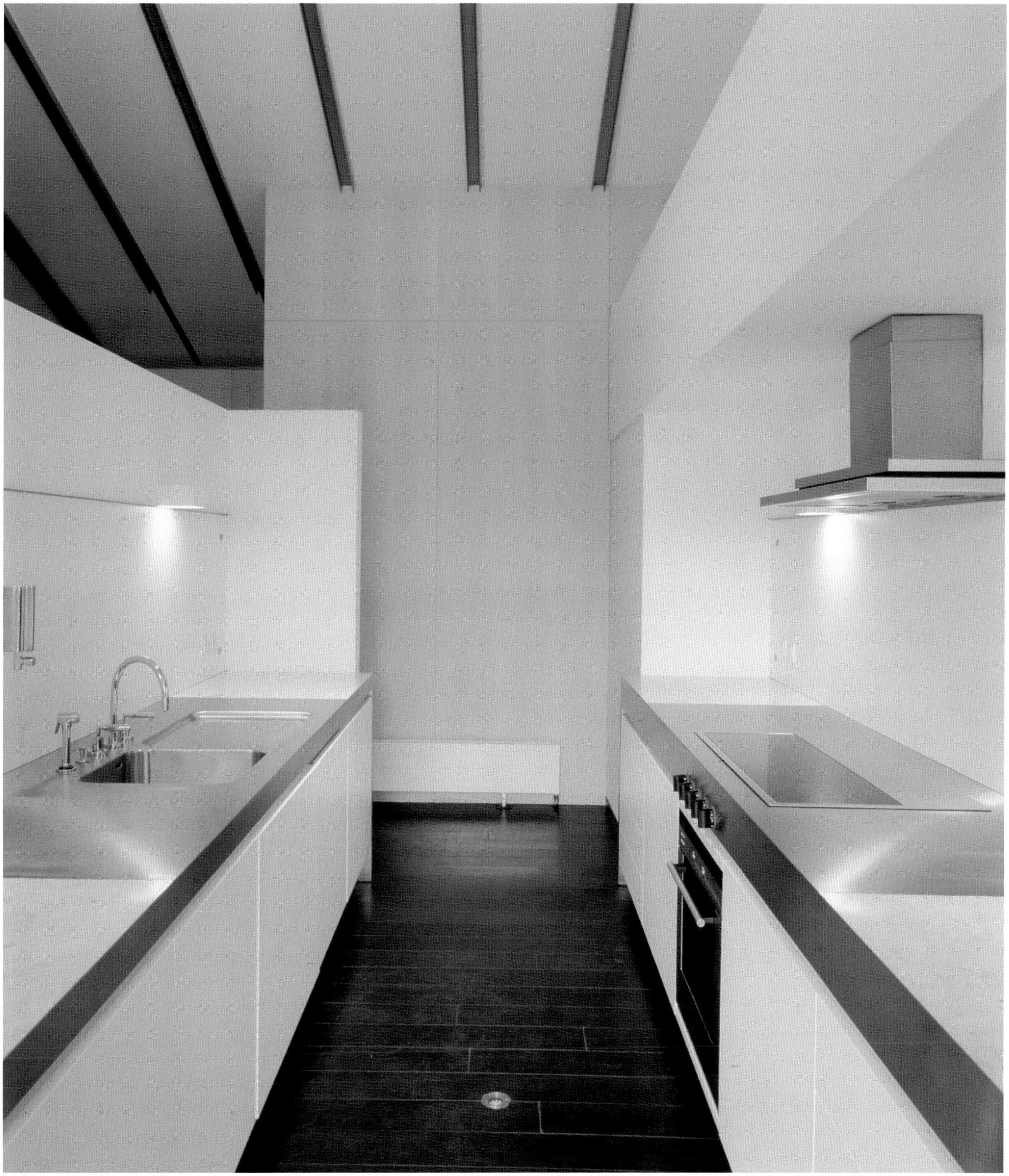

JAHN Associates
Pearl Beach House

Photographs: John Gollings

Pearl Beach, Australia

A holiday house is primarily about retreat and relaxation. This low-cost beach house with a total floor area of some 1894 sq ft (176 sq m) was designed for a professional couple who work in Sydney and have grown children. It was their aim to enjoy the atmosphere of Pearl Beach and its low-key social life through regular weekend visits. They were seeking a lightweight, almost transient building - one that would be airy and casual as well as weather well over time.

In Australia, it is common that many 'beach houses' are physically separated from the beach by spaces belonging to the public domain - such as a street, parking area, pathway or reserve. This poses the question of how to address the competing issues of privacy and views, indoor and outdoor living, and public/private relationships as experienced both during the day and night.

Given that the main living areas face the beach across the street and enjoy morning and afternoon sun, an outdoor eating/relaxation space or 'pavilion' addressing the view and sea breezes was incorporated into the design, instead of a terrace, balcony or verandah. This room, together with the linear volume of the house set against the southern boundary, helps to shield the north-facing rear garden from direct view.

The more traditionally enclosed living areas are contained in an adjoining volume of two stories - with the master bedroom enjoying an elevated view of the ocean, kitchen and living room spaces below. A separate 'pavilion' of guest bedrooms, complete with en suite bathrooms is separated from the main building by a metal-clad shower/laundry block tied together by an external 'boardwalk'. Moving about the building has a distinctly outdoor feel.

The range of materials is simple and classic: timber boarding is used extensively throughout the house, the floors are either clad in blackbutt flooring or tallow wood decking, all window frames are aluminum and rooms can be closed off via sliding doors with twinwall polycarbonate infill.

This is a simple, yet craftsman-built building made possible by an excellent working relationship between architect, builder and client. While the spaces are modest and the fit out direct, it creates a stage for play and pleasure through the subtly controlled environment.

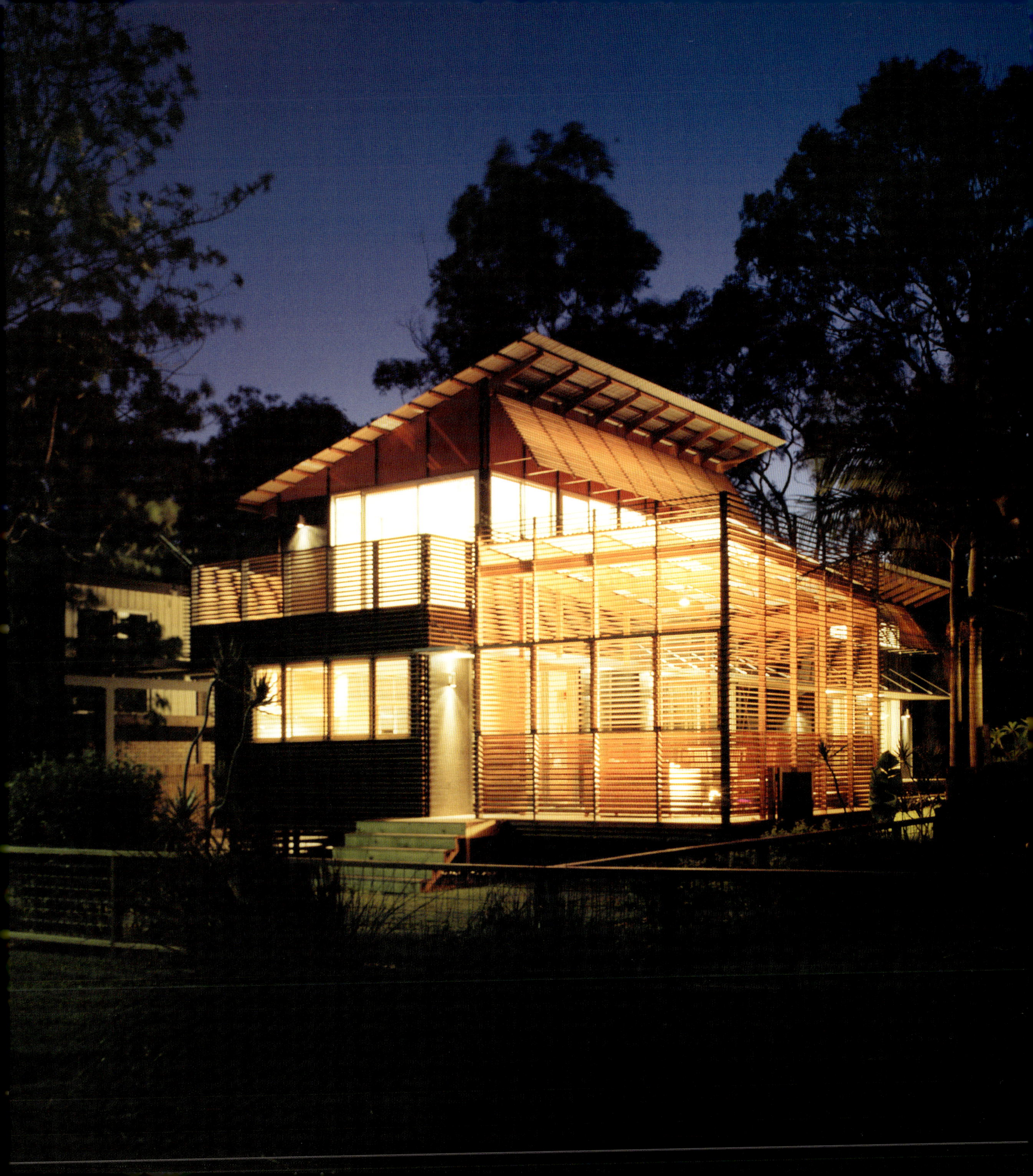

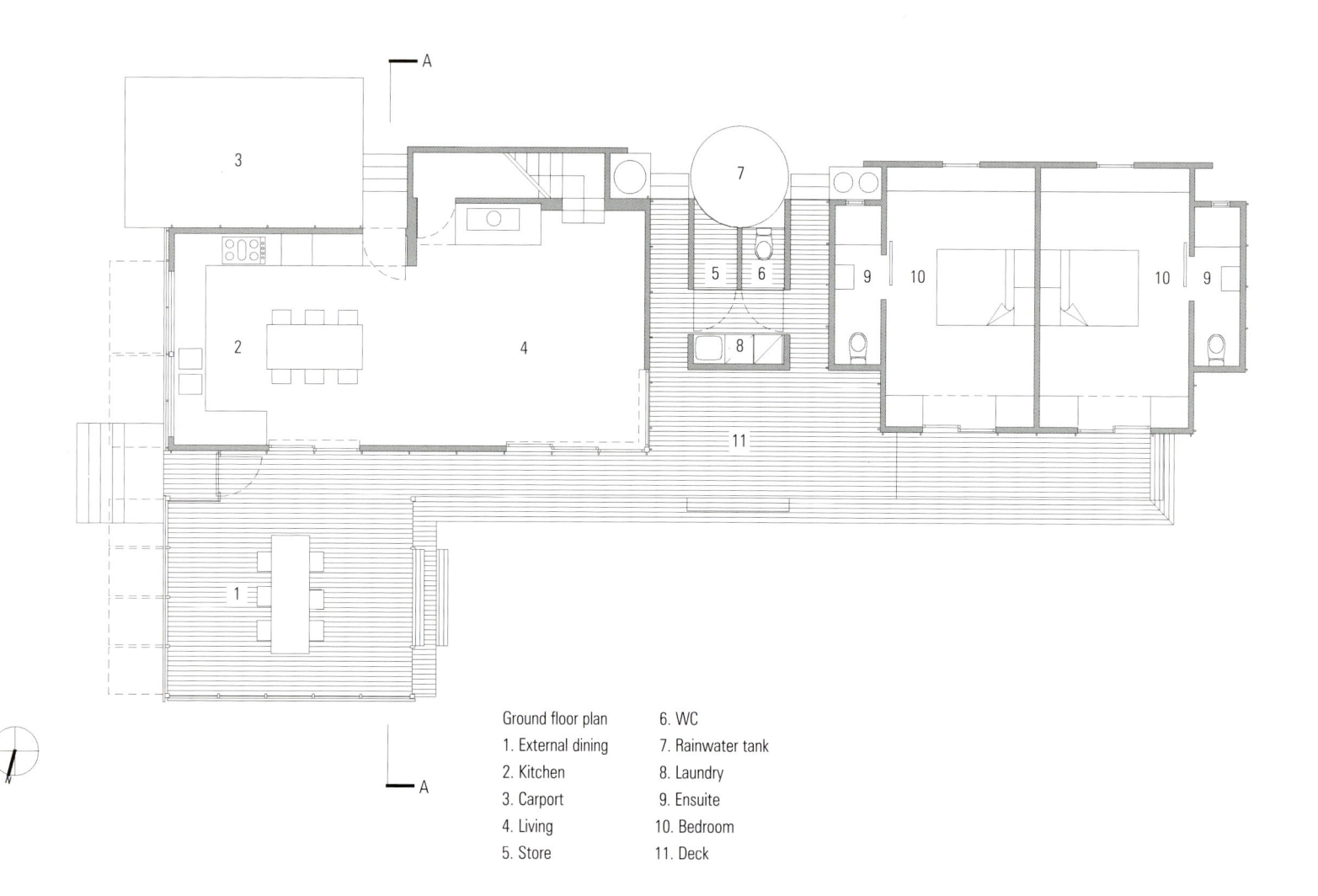

Ground floor plan
1. External dining
2. Kitchen
3. Carport
4. Living
5. Store
6. WC
7. Rainwater tank
8. Laundry
9. Ensuite
10. Bedroom
11. Deck

75

First floor plan
9. Ensuite
10. Bedroom
11. Deck

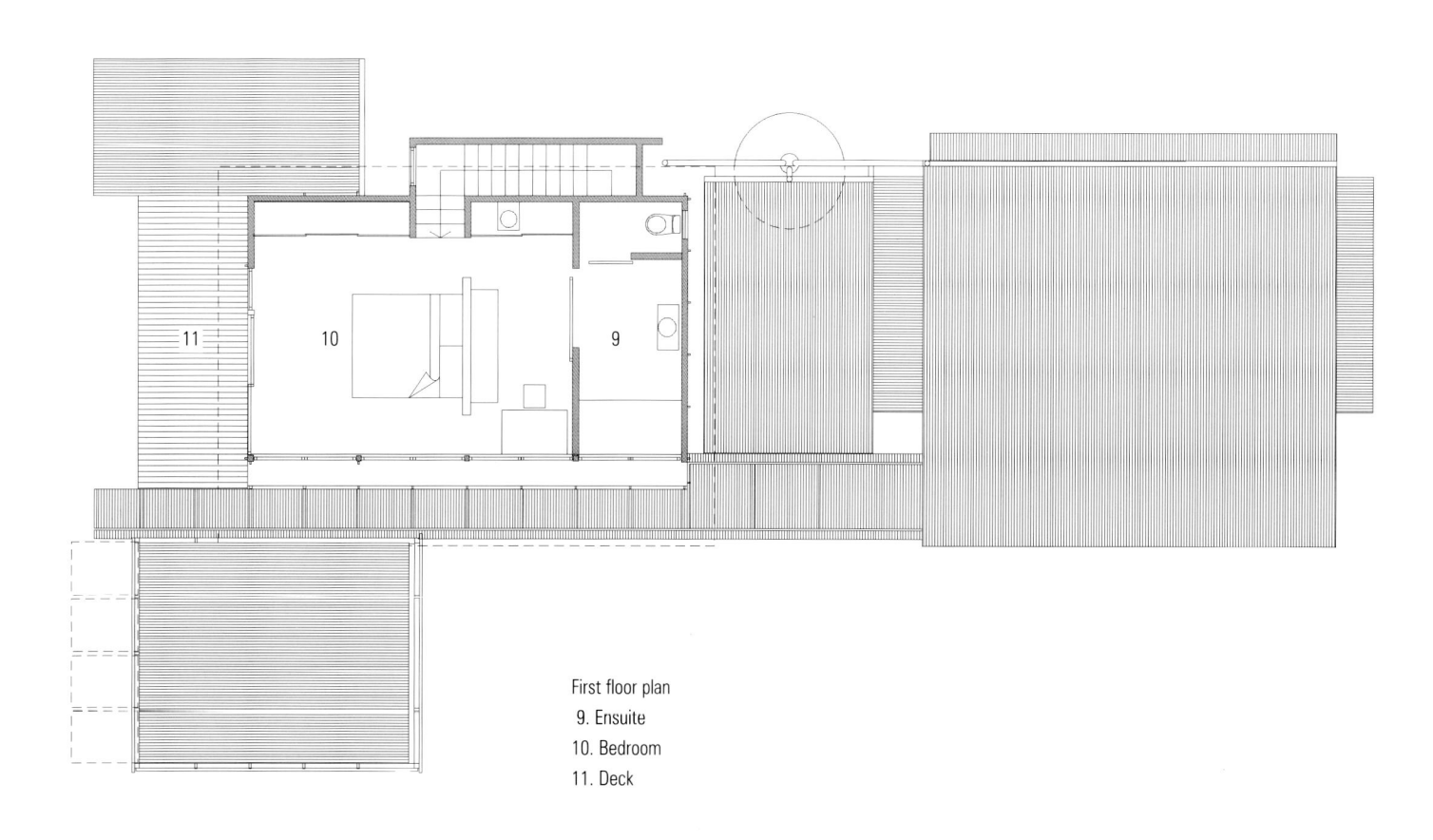

Given that the main living areas face the beach across the street and enjoy morning and afternoon sun, an outdoor eating/relaxation space or 'pavilion' addressing the view and sea breezes was incorporated into the design, instead of a terrace, balcony or verandah.

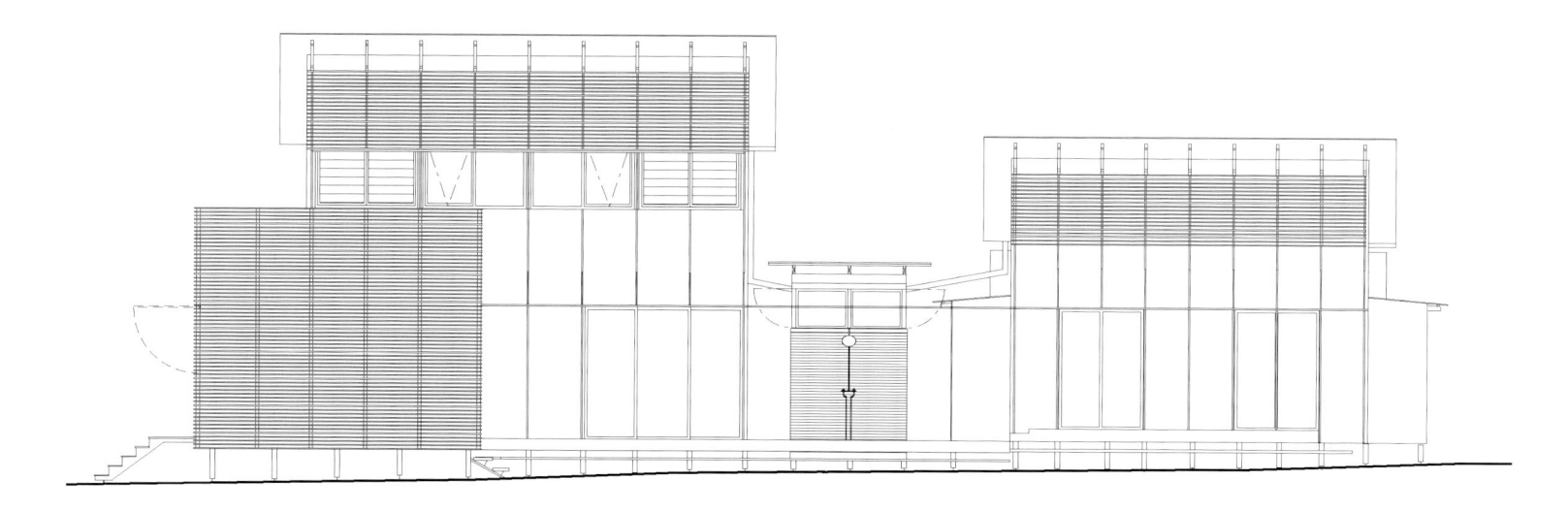

North elevation

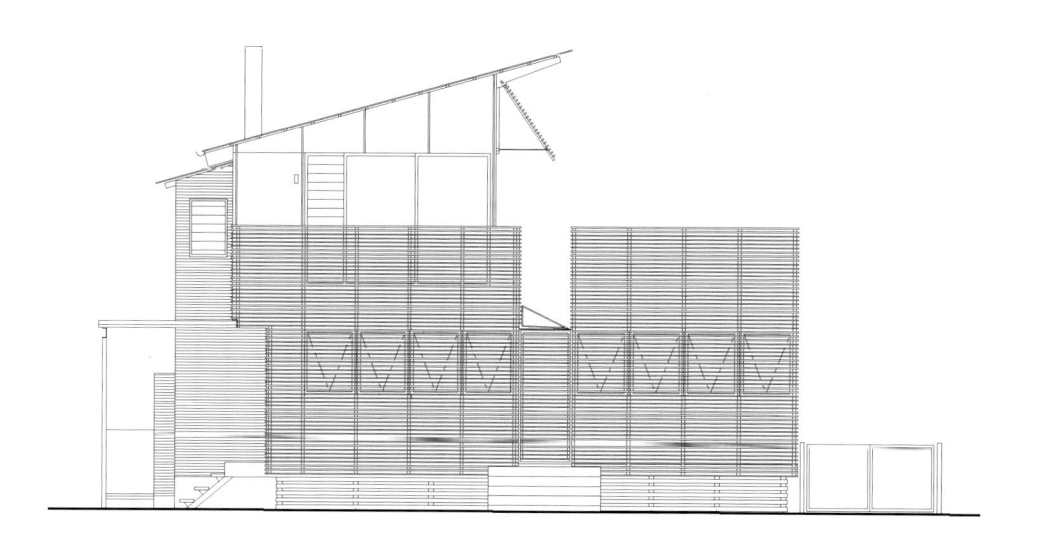

East elevation

The gallery, together with the linear volume of the house set against the southern boundary, helps to shield the north-facing rear garden from direct view.

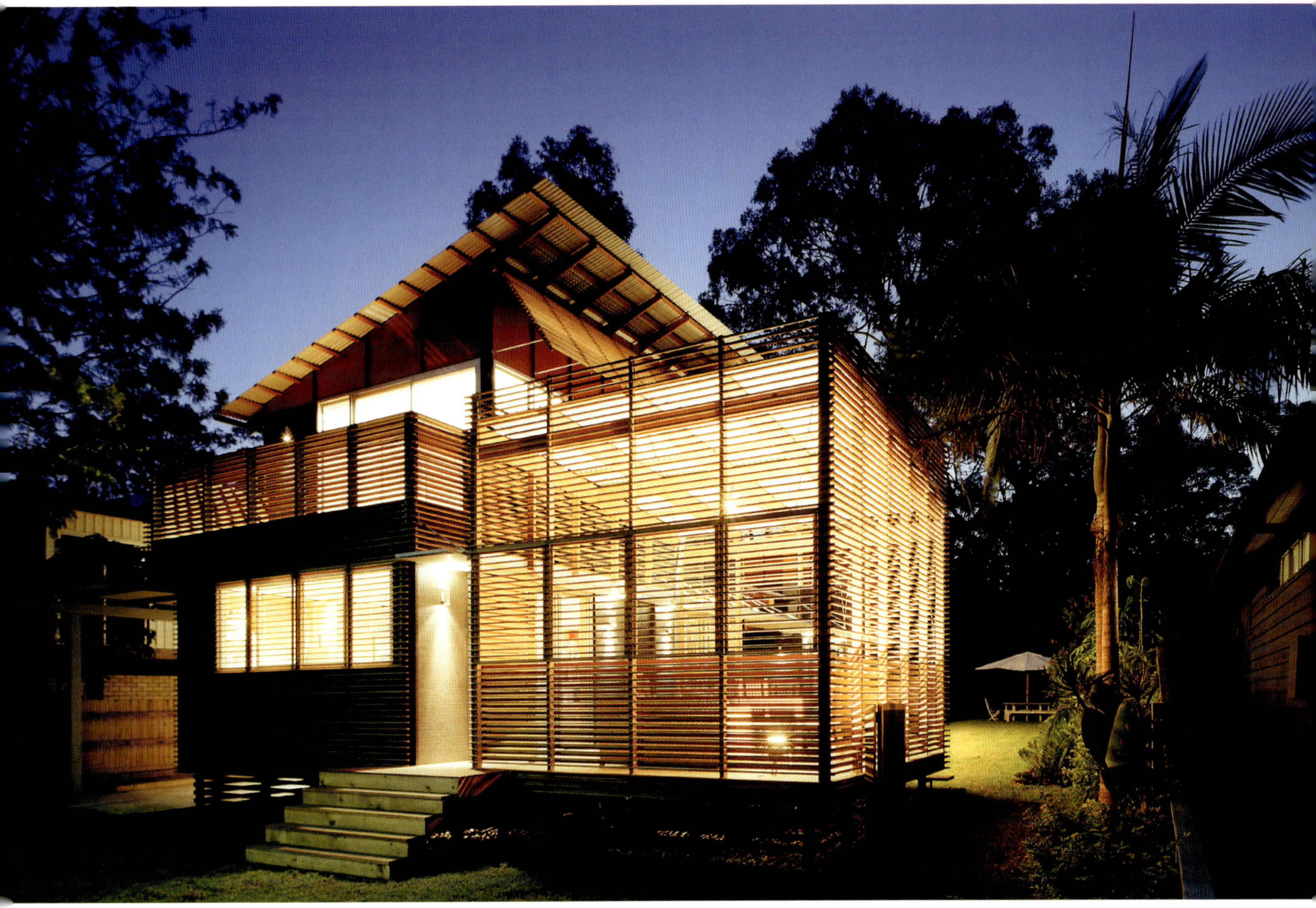

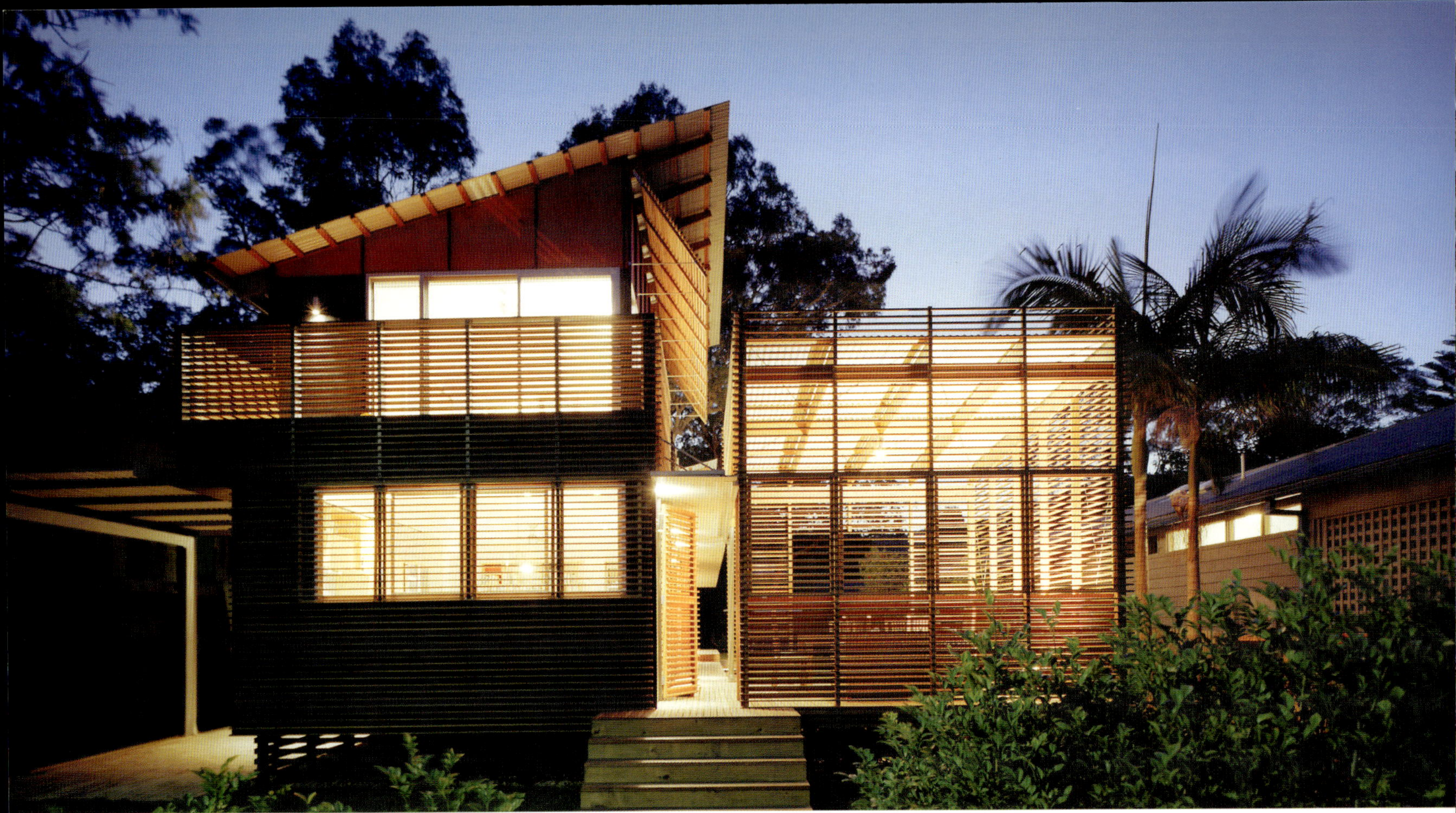
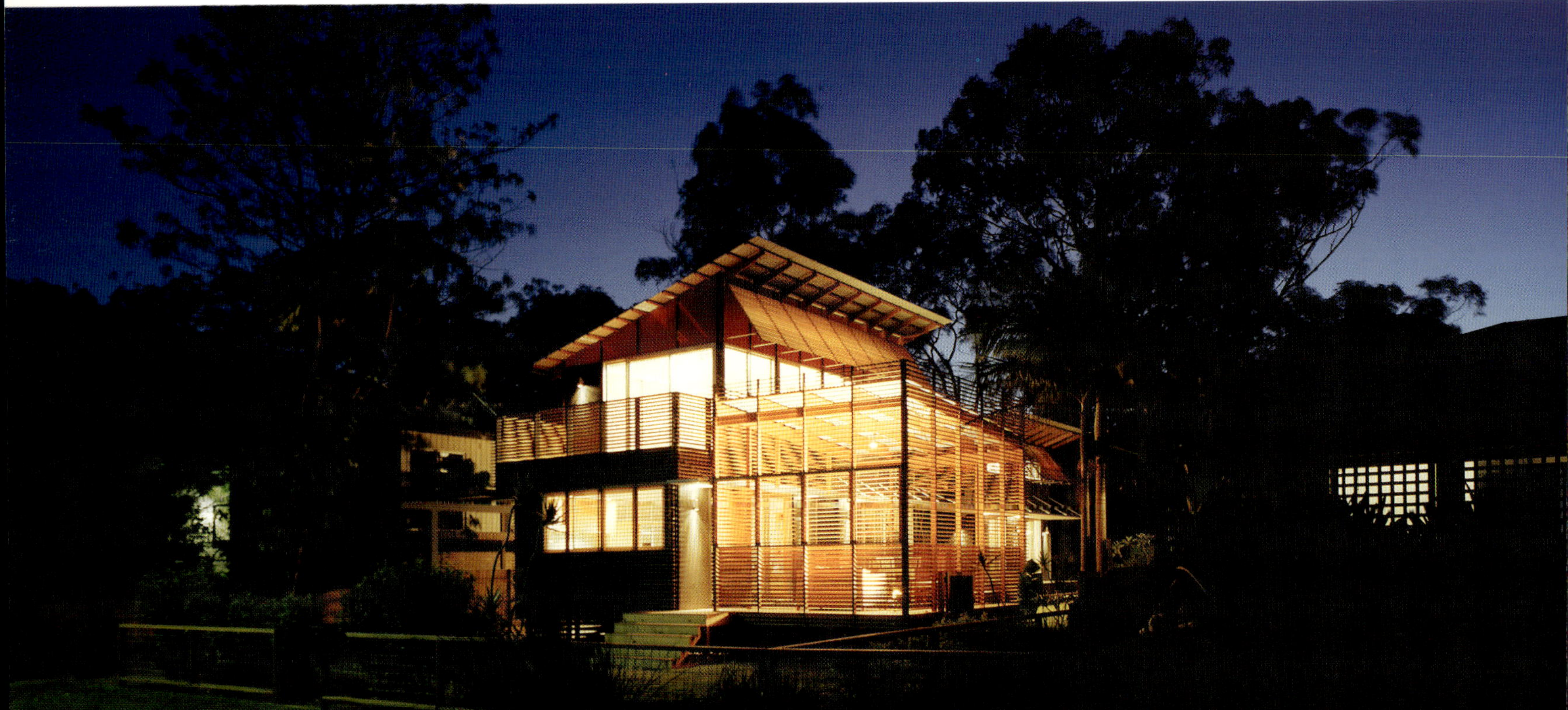

Section AA

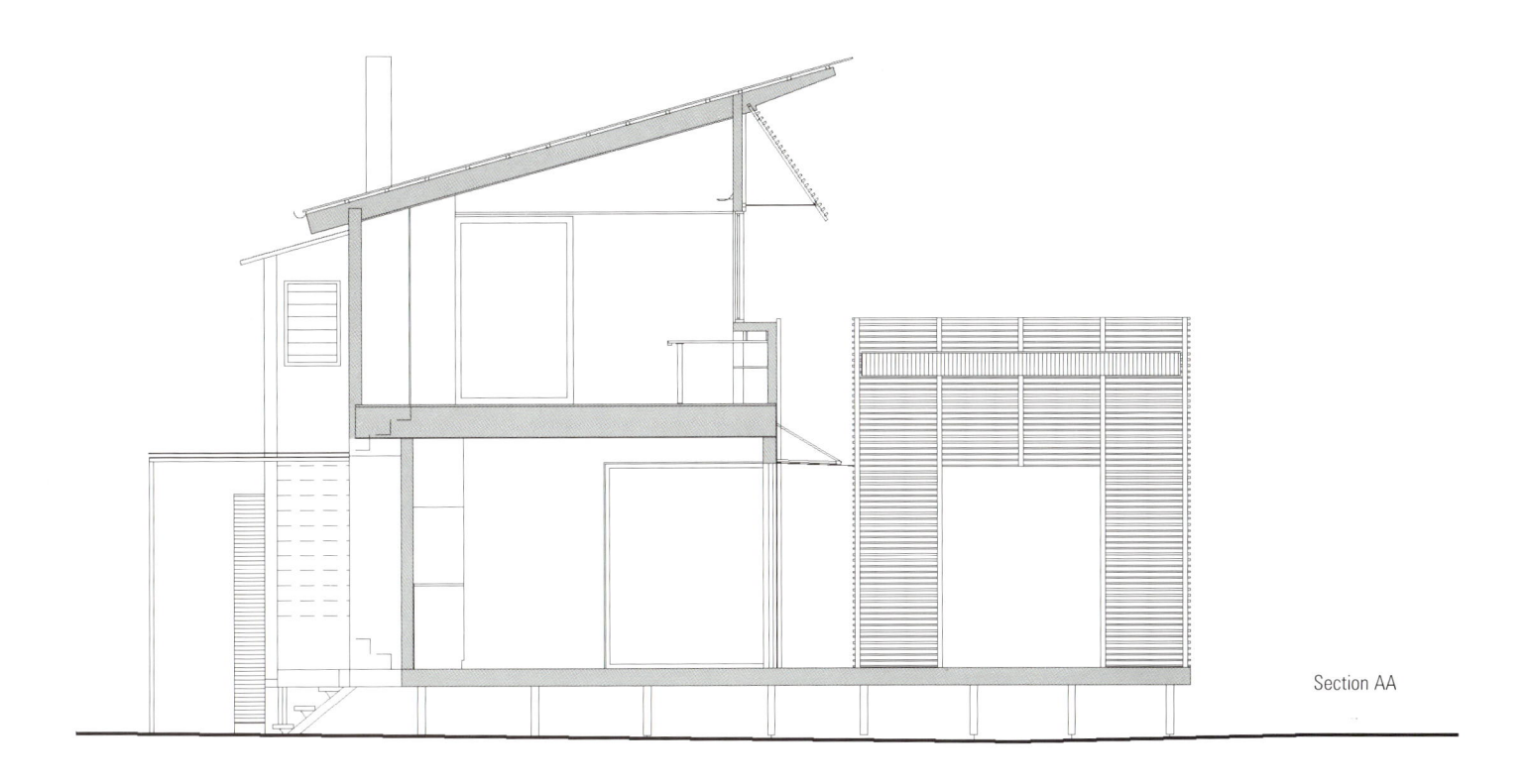

81

Wingårdh Arkitektkontor AB
Villa Astrid

Photographs: James Silverman

Brottkärr, Göteborg, Sweden

The dramatic landscape of the Swedish west coast becomes overly domesticated when housing construction takes over. Boulders are terraced to make gardens, wild ravines are transformed into roads and plots of land. The rare places that still have a concentrated atmosphere are those that are left over, being either too difficult to build on or impossible to tame.

Villa Astrid has just such a location. The house has not made the setting any less dramatic, instead interpreting the character of the location. The twist away from the road, the steep cliff and the view out towards the sea have been given form using architecture's most fundamental aspects - openness and enclosure. The closed elements, walls and roof, constitute a durable armor of patinated copper plate, while the open elements - the glass sections - appear like carved holes in this solid structure. This sculptural approach could well have stopped at rigid formalism if it weren't for the house's affectionate relationship with nature. Its design has not sprung from principles or abstract theories, but from a summary of the requirements of the site and the provisions for the area for a roof gradient of 14 to 30 degrees and a roof base height of 9.84 feet (3 meters).

The house is closely bound to its site. The rocks on which it stands pose naked inside the house and form a wall in the deep courtyard that brings light to the ground floor living room. The upper-floor rooms, designed for work and leisure, focus on the view, giving the house a counter twist, like a person whose hips and shoulders turn slightly in different directions.

This house has been designed for a middle-aged couple, with one child, who entertain at home a great deal. The contrast between the open character of the entrance floor and the privacy on the ground floor reflects these functions, while the easily hidden dining room, which is also part of the entrance floor, offers a pleasant surprise.

The simplicity of this structure makes it very robust. The concrete joists rest on walls built of lightweight concrete. The tie beam system is insulated with foam glass, sealed with asphalt against the concrete. This provides full insulation under the copper skin. The structure of the house makes it completely waterproof without any incorporated organic materials. Copper ions from the façade can be neutralized by crushed limestone along the plinth.

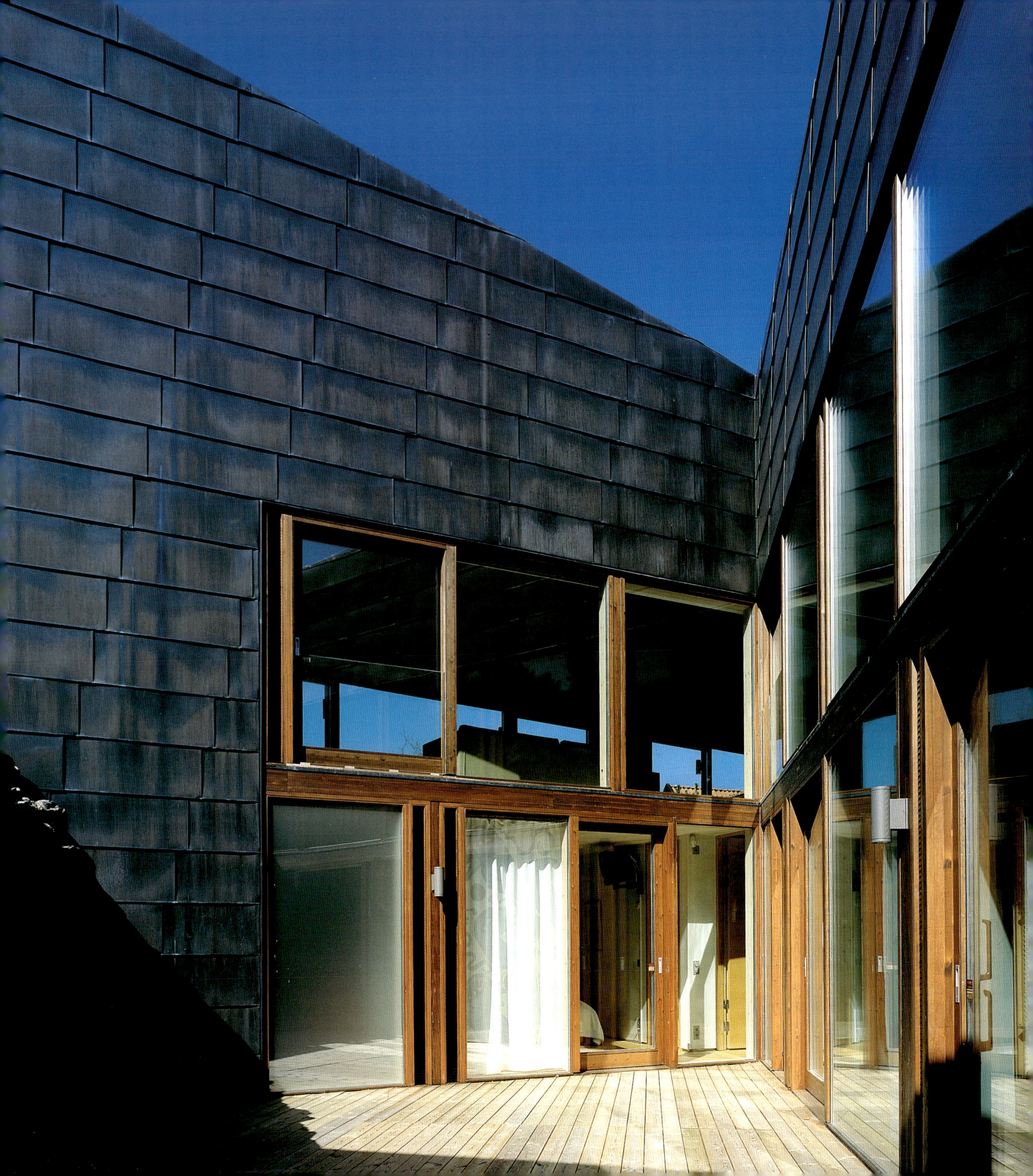

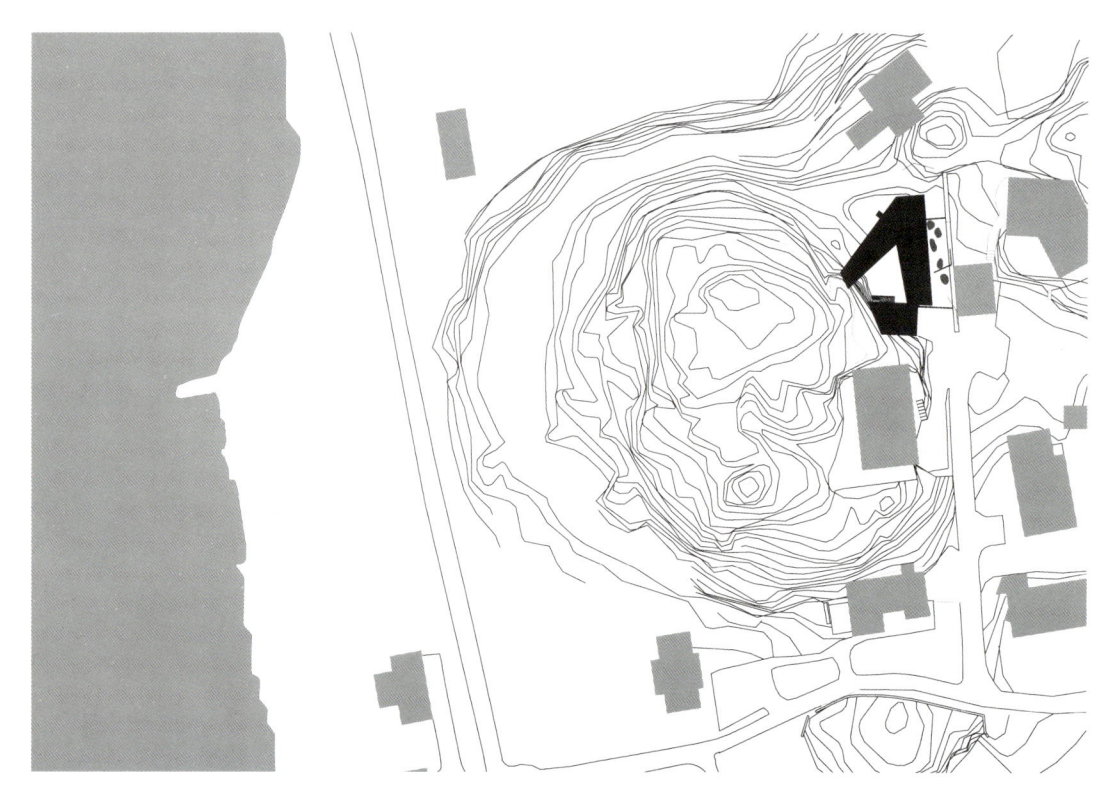

The house is closely bound to its site. The rocks on which it stands pose naked inside the house and form a wall in the deep courtyard that brings light to the ground floor living room.

Site plan

85

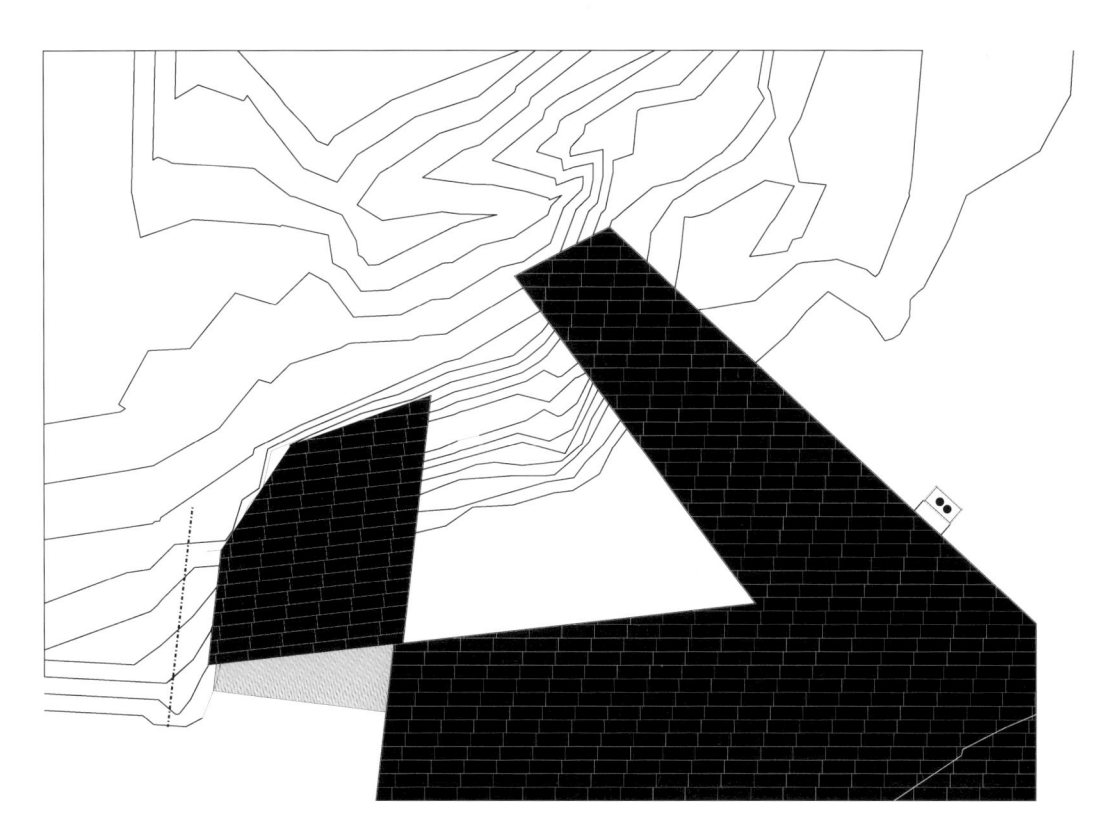

Roof floor plan

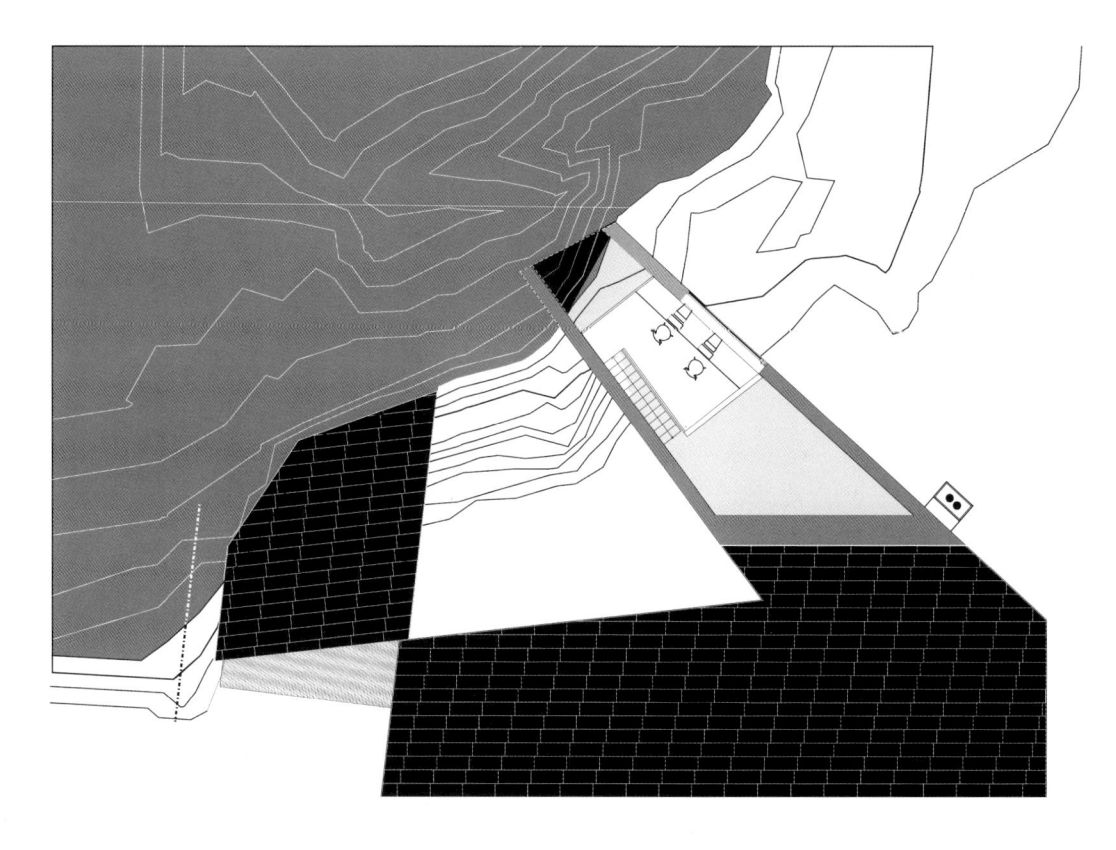

Third floor plan

86

Second floor plan

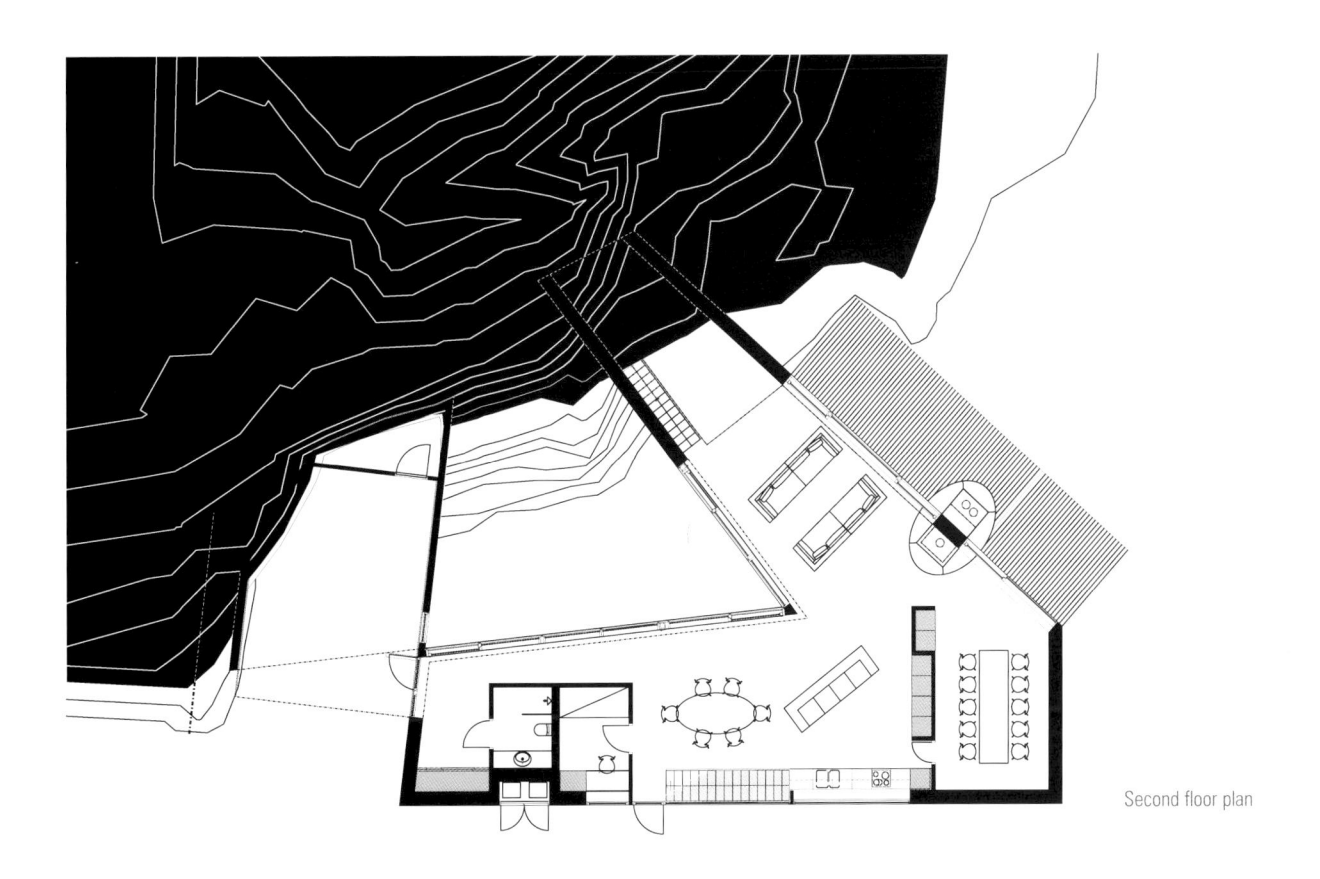

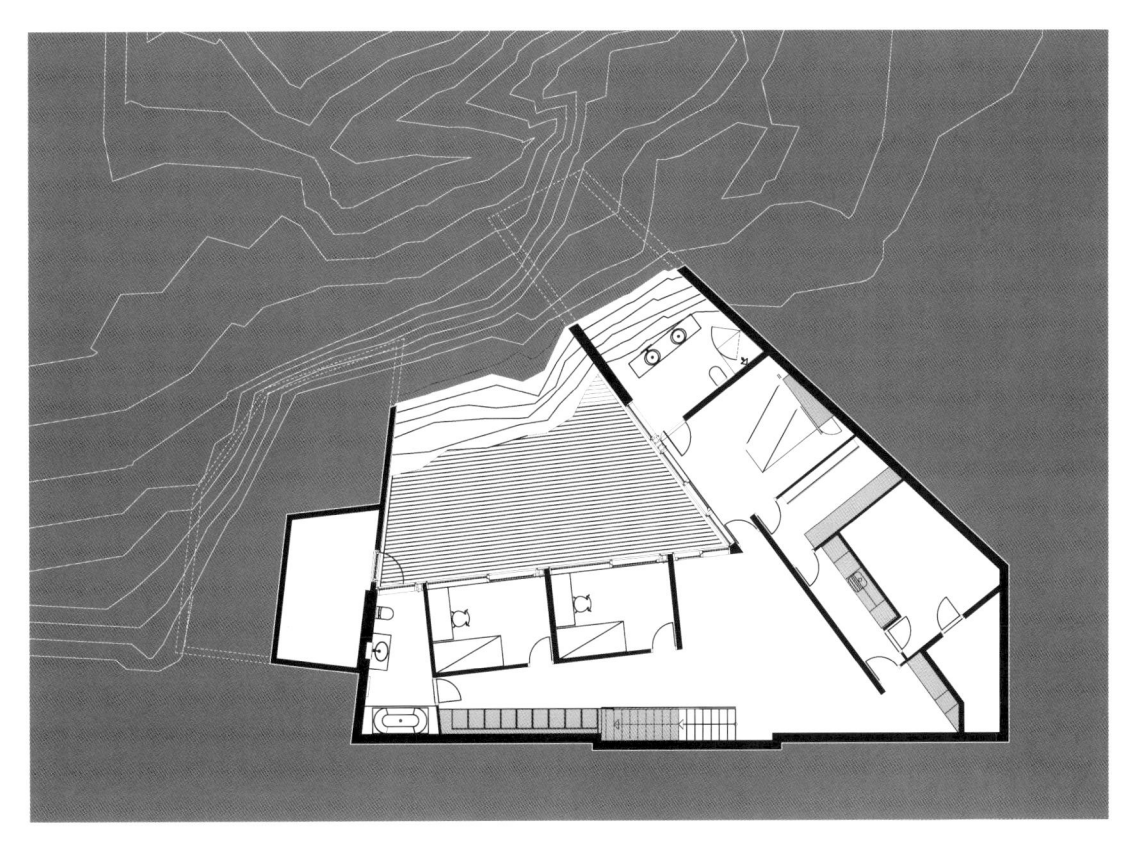

First floor plan

87

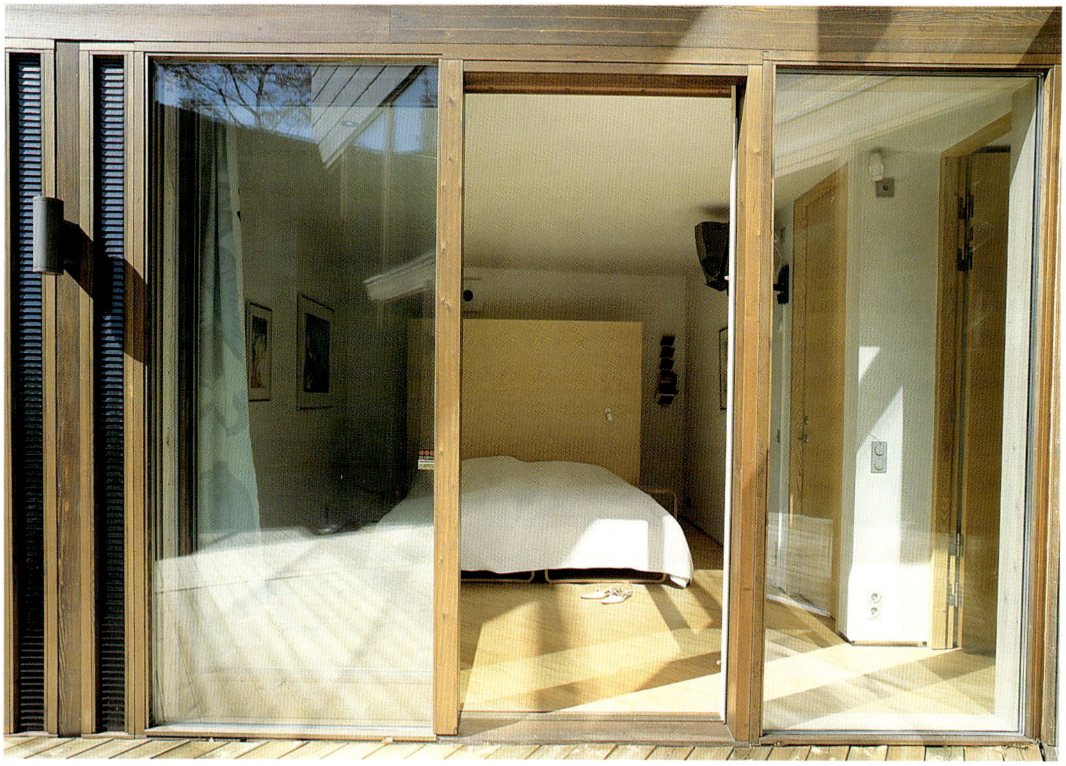

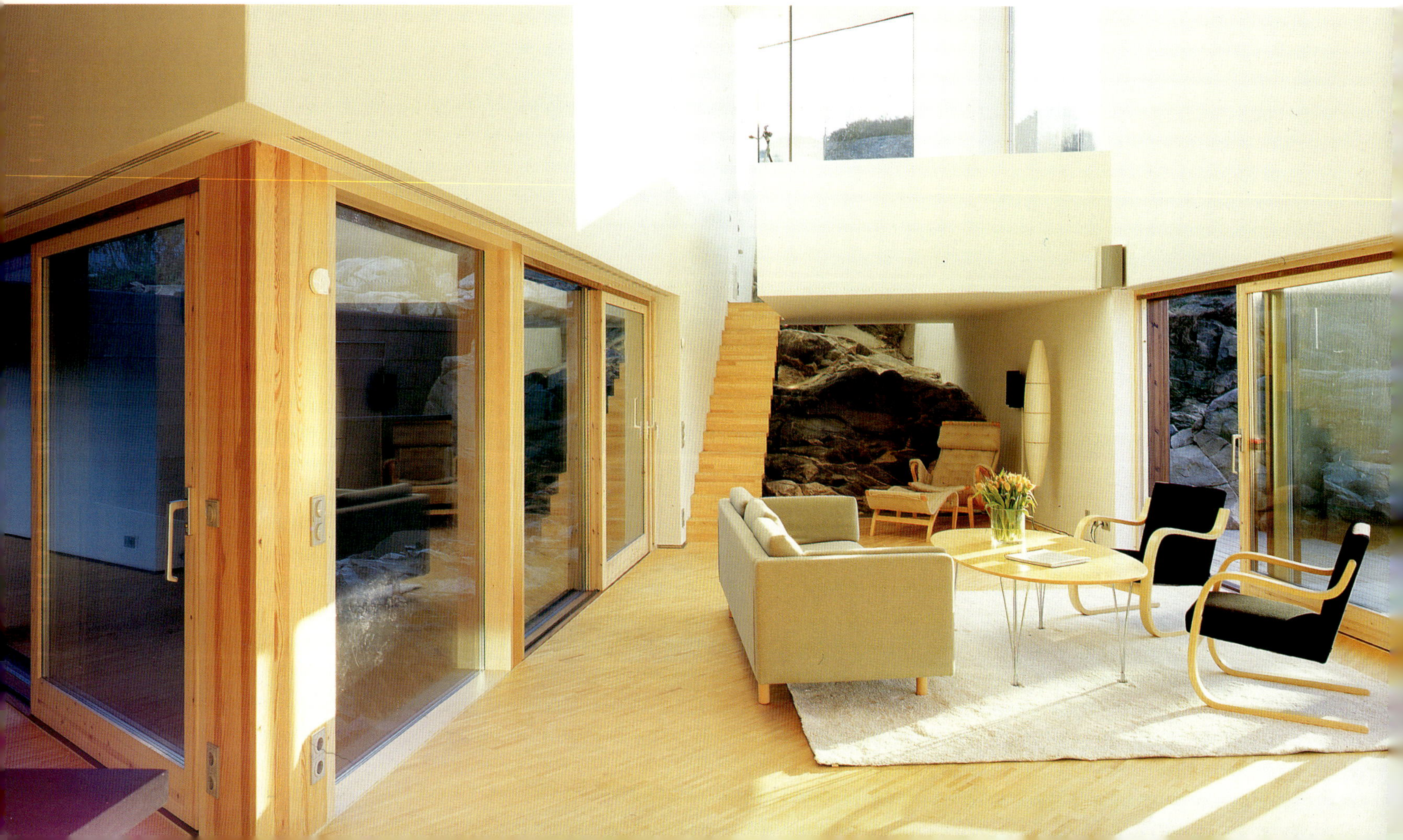

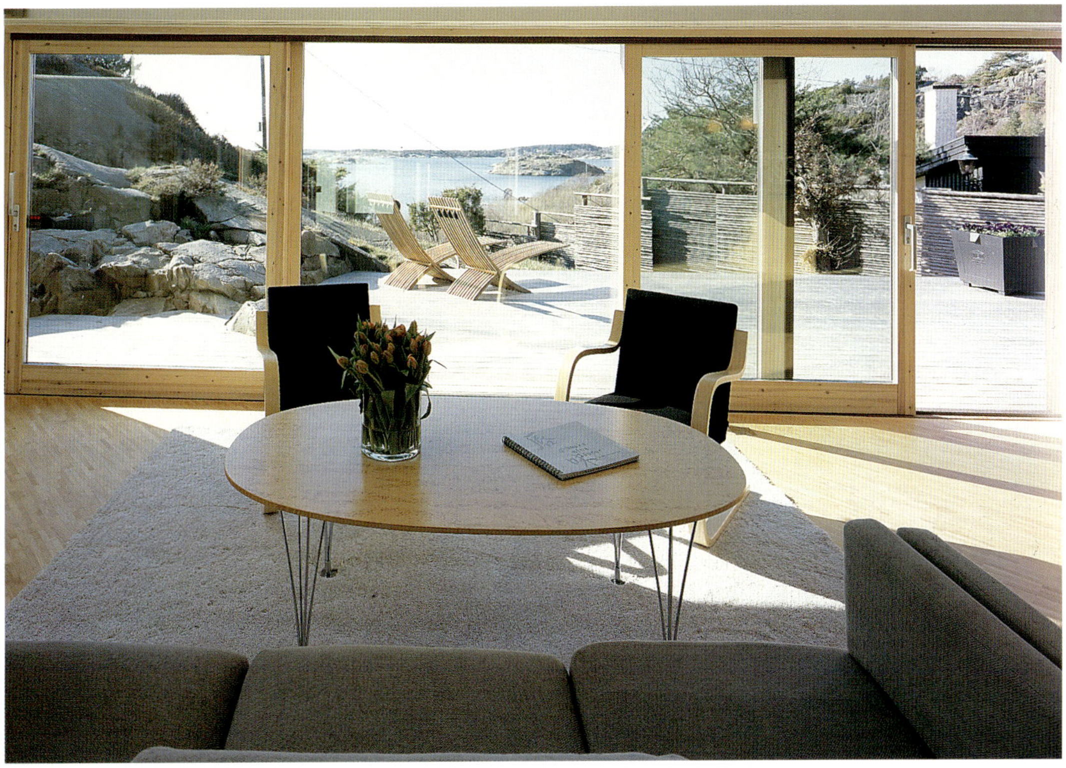

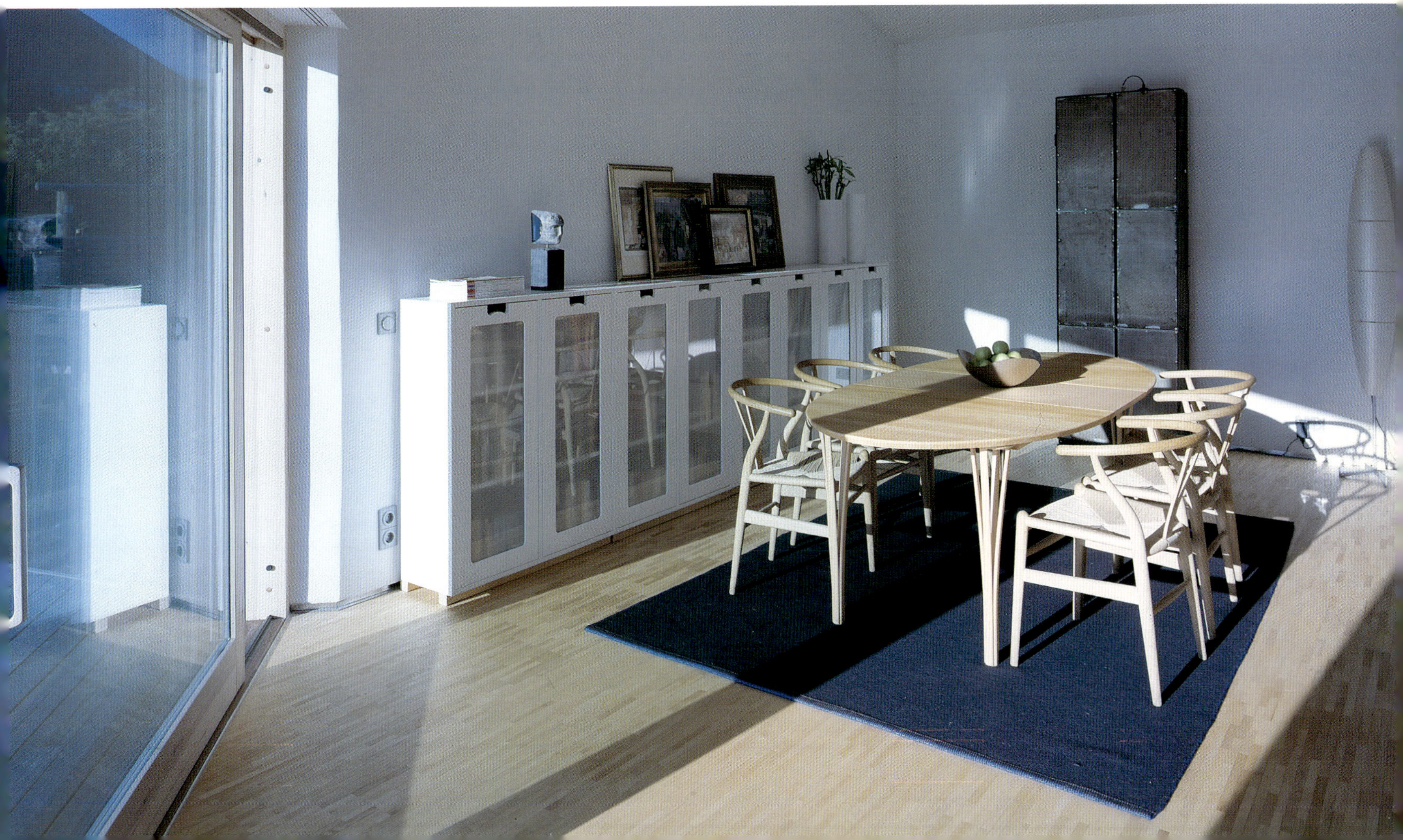

90

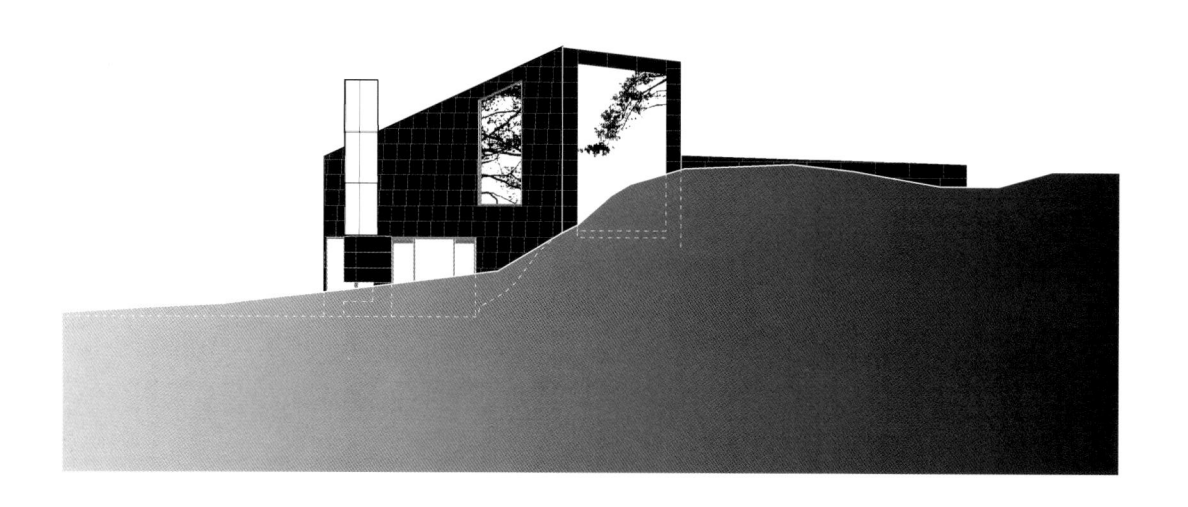

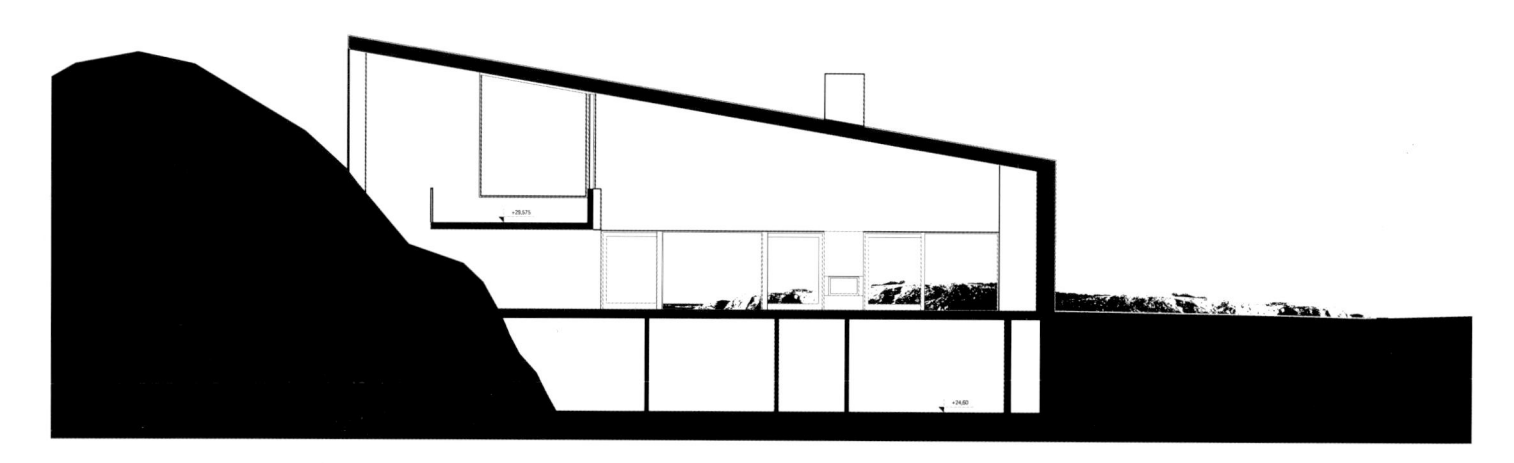

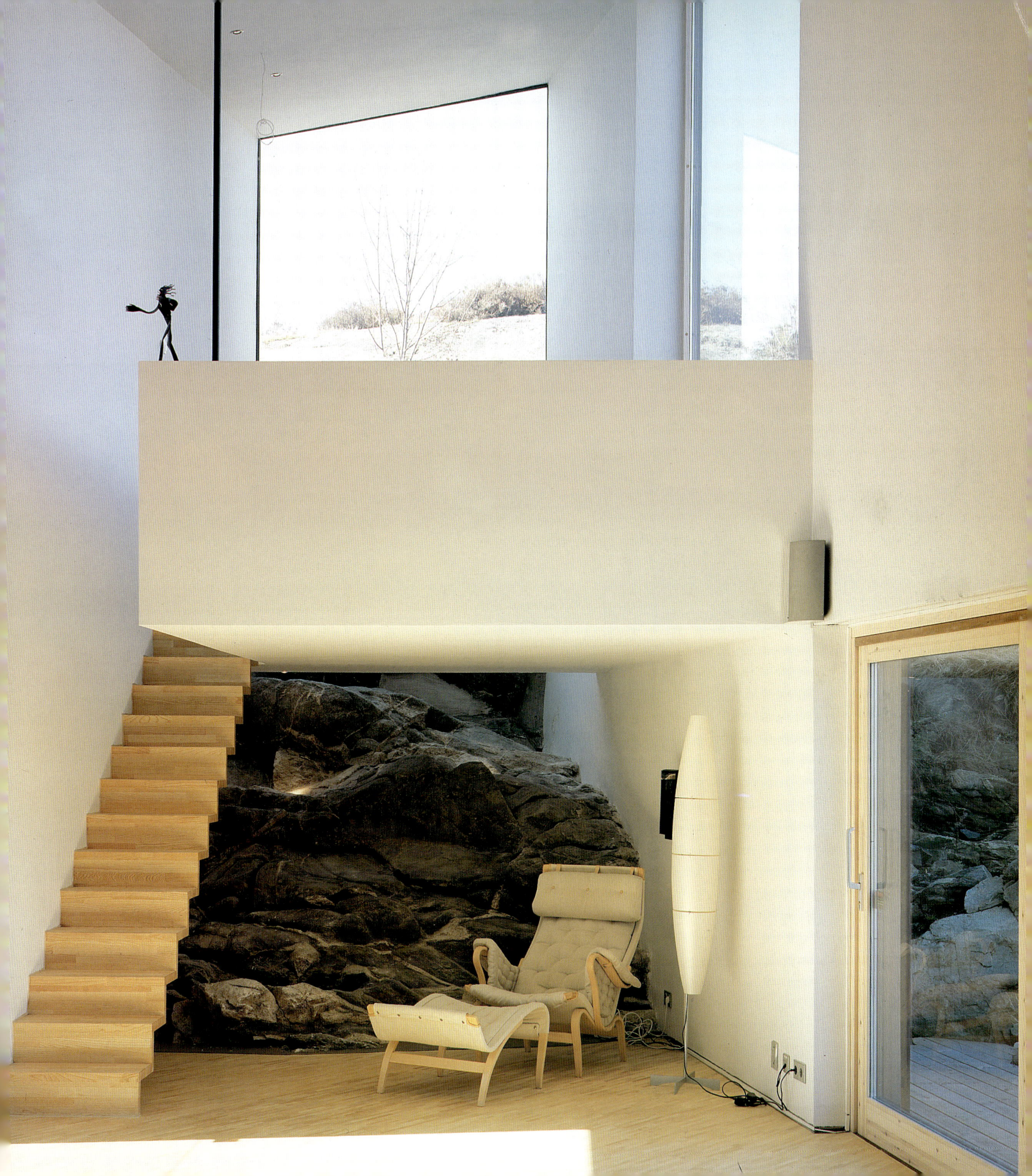

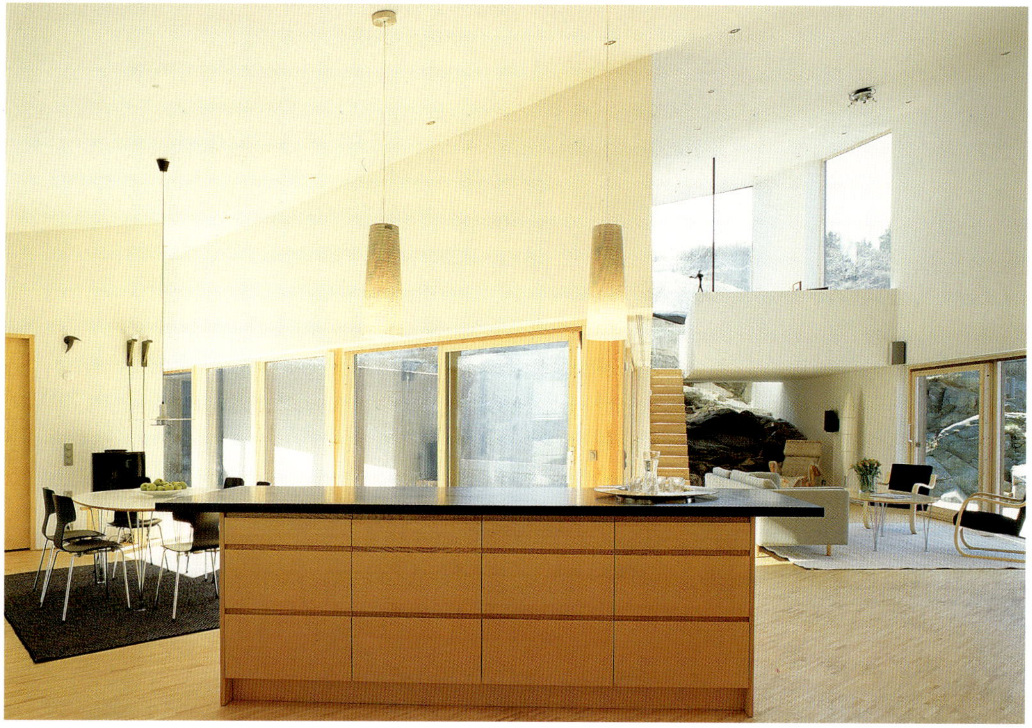

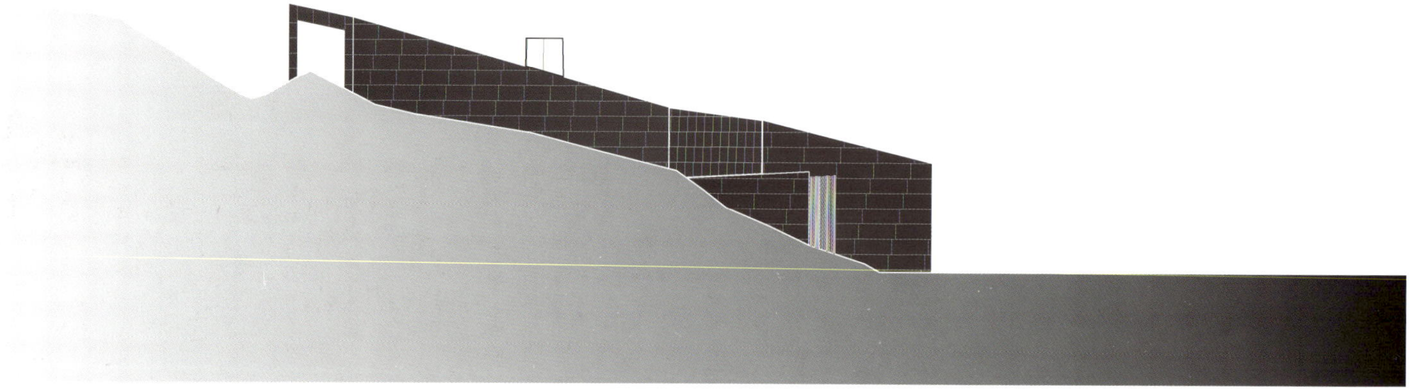

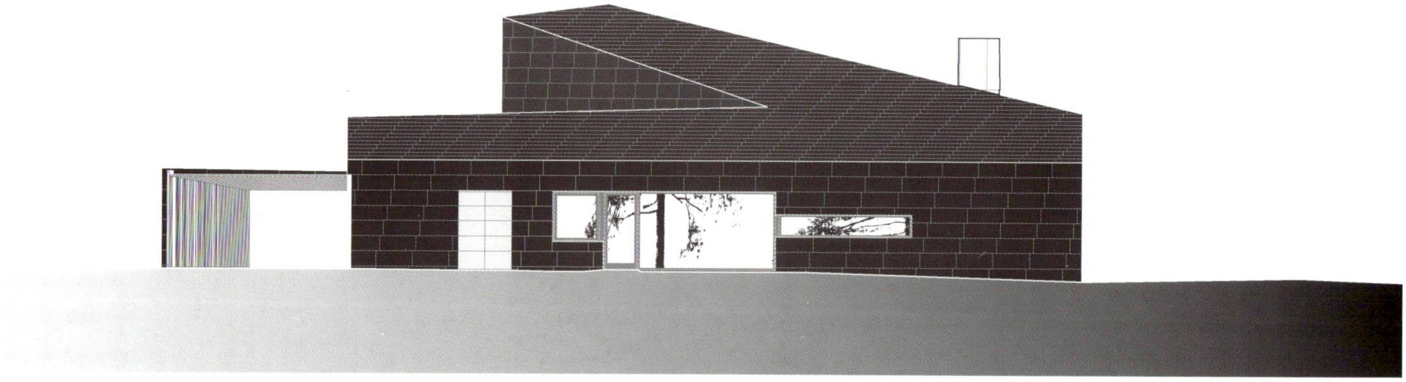

93

The structure of the house makes it completely waterproof without any incorporated organic materials. Copper ions from the façade can be neutralized by crushed limestone along the plinth.

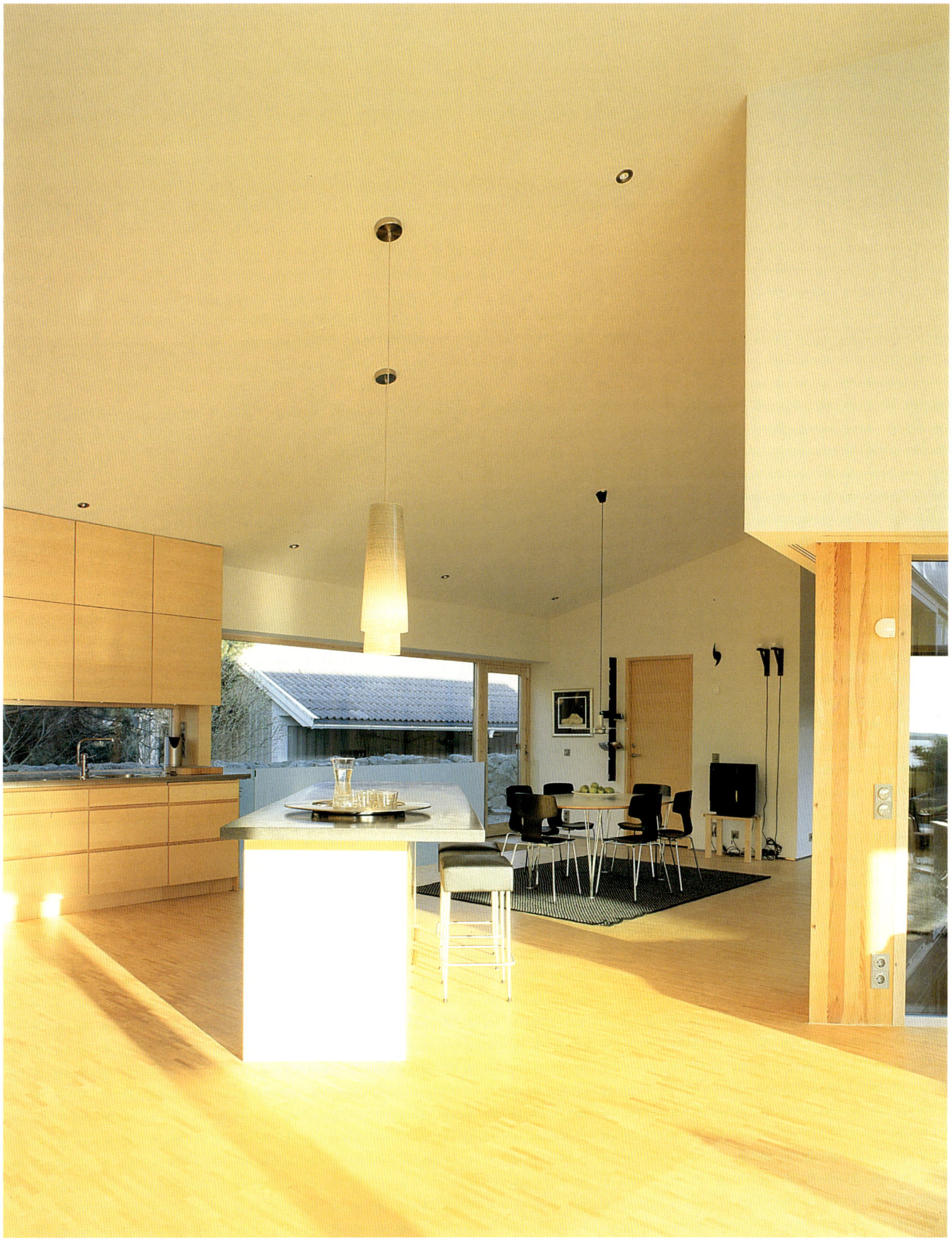

E. Cobb Architects
Lakeshore in the Cascade Mountain Range

Photographs: Steve Keating

Seattle, USA

The site was selected for its unique character, year around recreation and proximity to Seattle. The topography is extremely steep. Sloping down continuously from the road to the water, the site drops 54 feet (16.5 meters) over 126 feet (38.4 meters) in distance.

Most of the adjacent shoreline is crowded with tall fir and cedar trees, with the exception of a few developed lots that have cleared virtually all trees. This project uses trees as a spatial asset, not a view obstruction. Instead of clear cutting trees, the house positions occupiable spaces high in the tree branches, allowing a line of trees to be a thin, selectively pruned veil between the house and lake.

The house is configured as three parts: a box on top, a narrow two-story slab at the bottom, and a lightweight cantilevered shelf between the two.

The top box is a two-car garage with elevator, mudroom and storage. A concrete deck warps to meet the sloping driveway. An exterior stair leads down to the entry, which is the space between the box and shelf. The two story base was planned to maximize sleeping spaces. The bar is thin, stretching the spaces to maximize lake exposure and minimize the excavation for the foundation heel cut. The bedroom bar contains four bedrooms (two connected by a climbing wall), a kids' bunk cabin, two bathrooms, two built-in day beds and a built-in hall bunk.

The third floor is rotated and extended off the sleeping bar to position and orient the living area for views. This move also creates an exterior roof deck above a portion of the sleeping bar. The "shelf" is entirely open, with a galley kitchen defining a living space on one side, and dining on the other. The dining table anchors this floor with meals, games and projects. The living space furniture is built-in, allowing for maximum capacity and additional sleeping opportunities. The living shelf is virtually all glass facing the lake.

A disappearing "bunk box" was designed in the upper bedroom. Two flush wood doors open to reveal a built-in bunk cabin. In addition to the steel access ladder, each bunk has its own hidden door accessing separate landings of the stair. The kids can go to their individual bunks directly from the stair, and visit each other via stair or ladder. On the stair side of the wall, the two bunk doors are disguised as a wooden panel with chalk trays.

The stair treads are supported by a 22' tall chalkboard. This makes the stair itself is an ongoing art project as well as communication surface.

The design team was challenged for solutions and inventions that went far beyond conventional architecture, design and construction practice. The solutions needed to resolve multiple conditions and needs, offer the unexpected, and appear simple - even "low-tech".

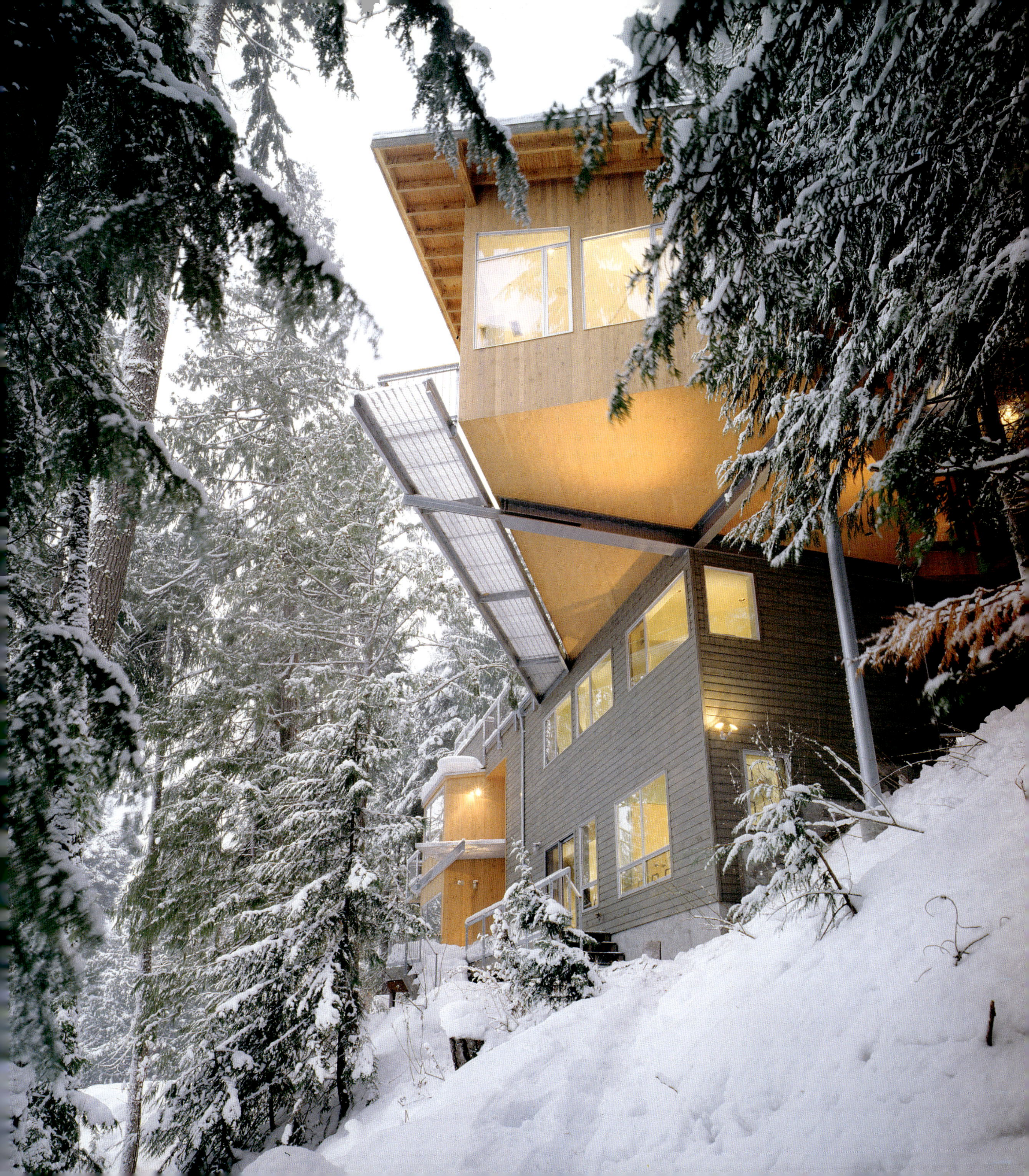

The house works to take advantage of its environment in all seasons, from summer windsurfing to winter cross-country sledding. While outdoor activities are of primary importance, the house itself offers a fun, interesting and comfortable space to live in.

Site plan

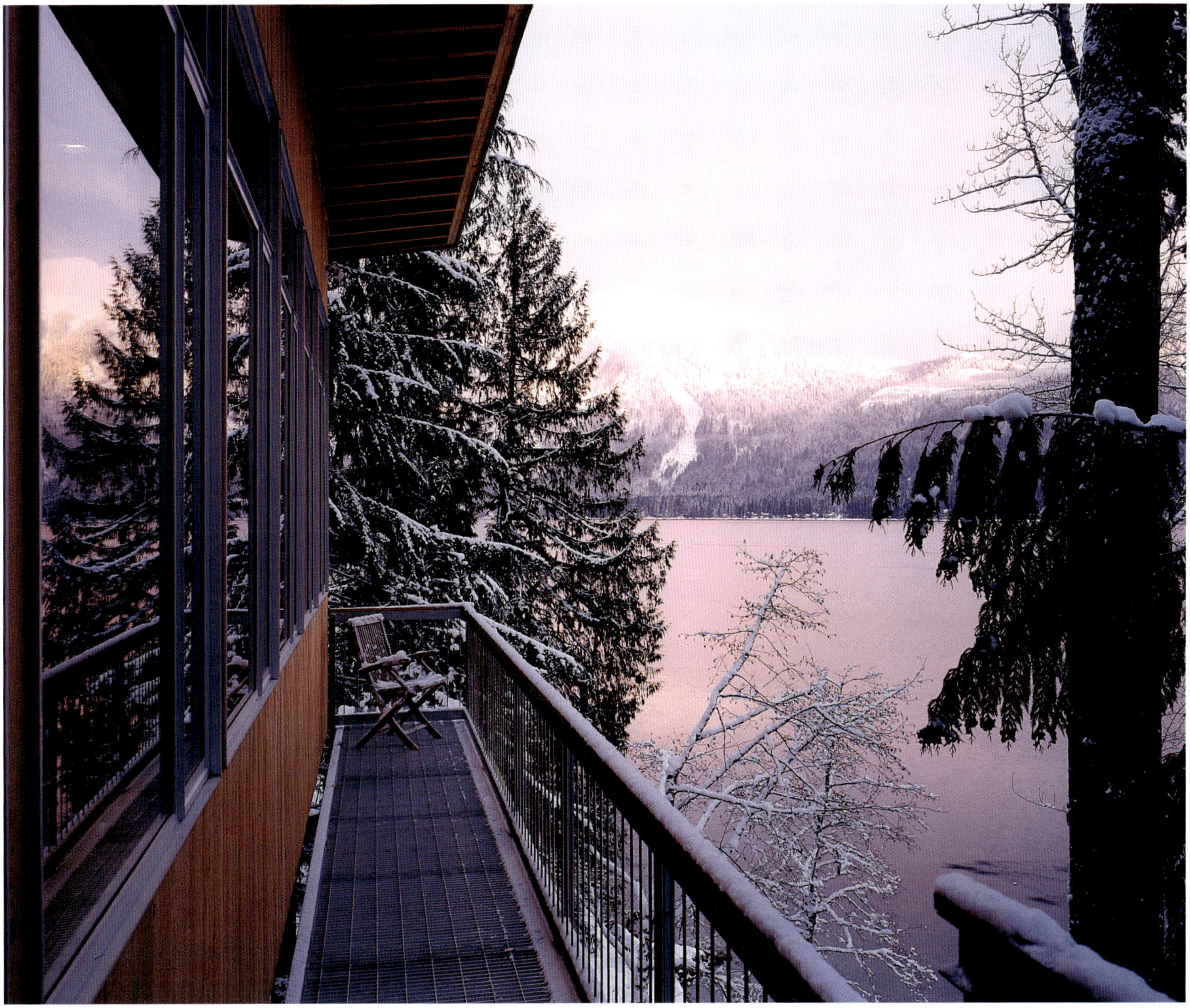

Garage floor plan

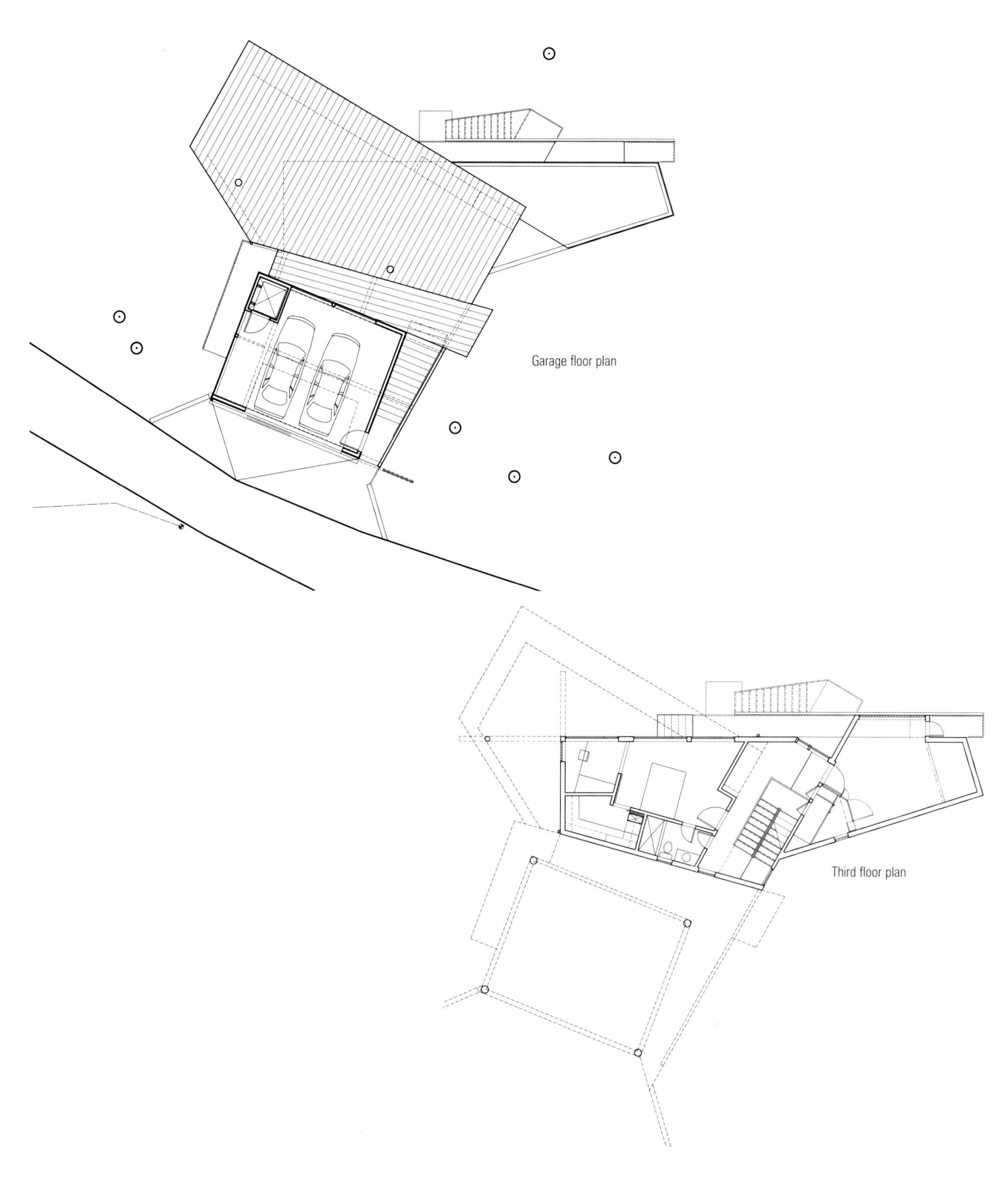

Third floor plan

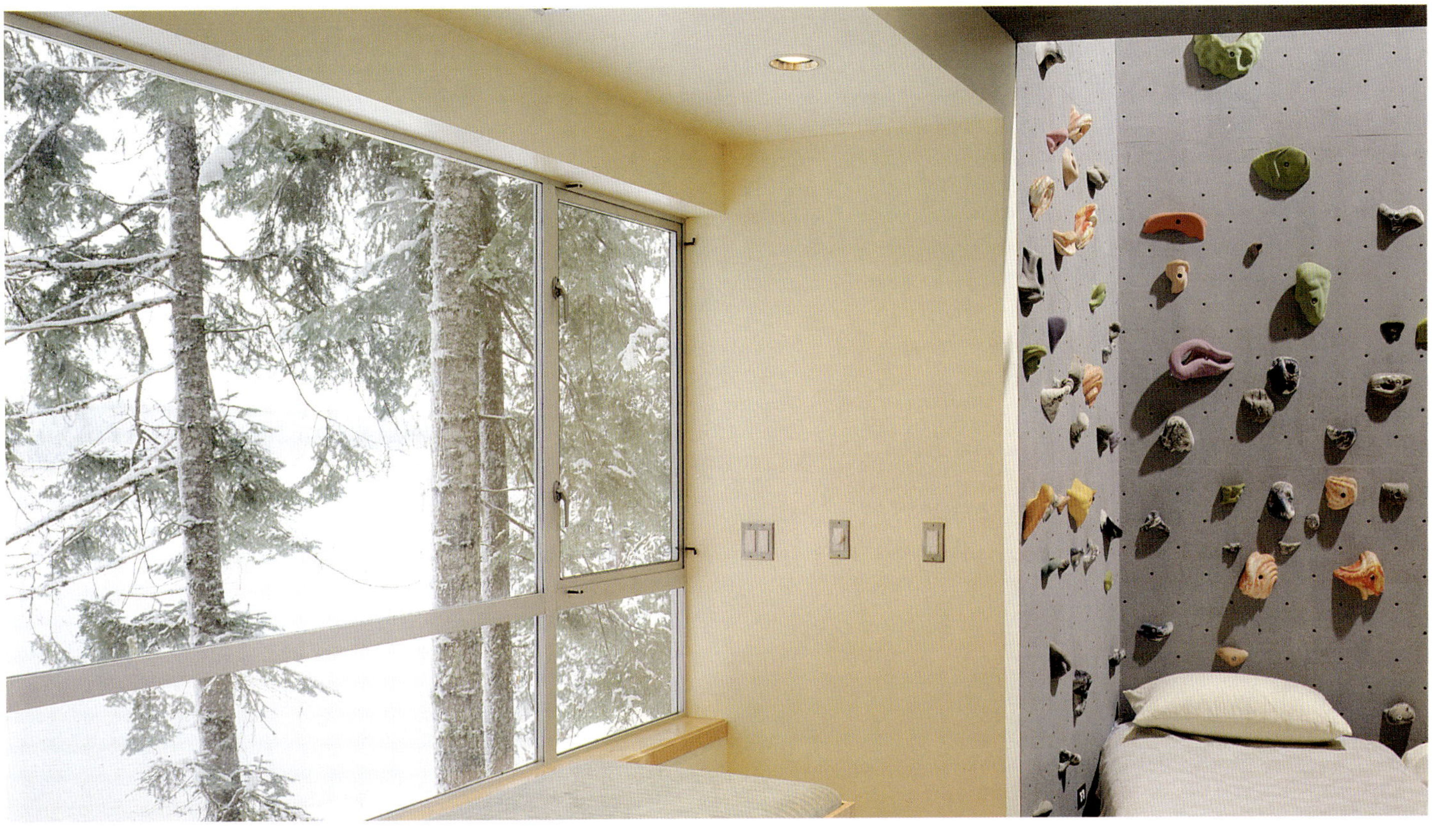

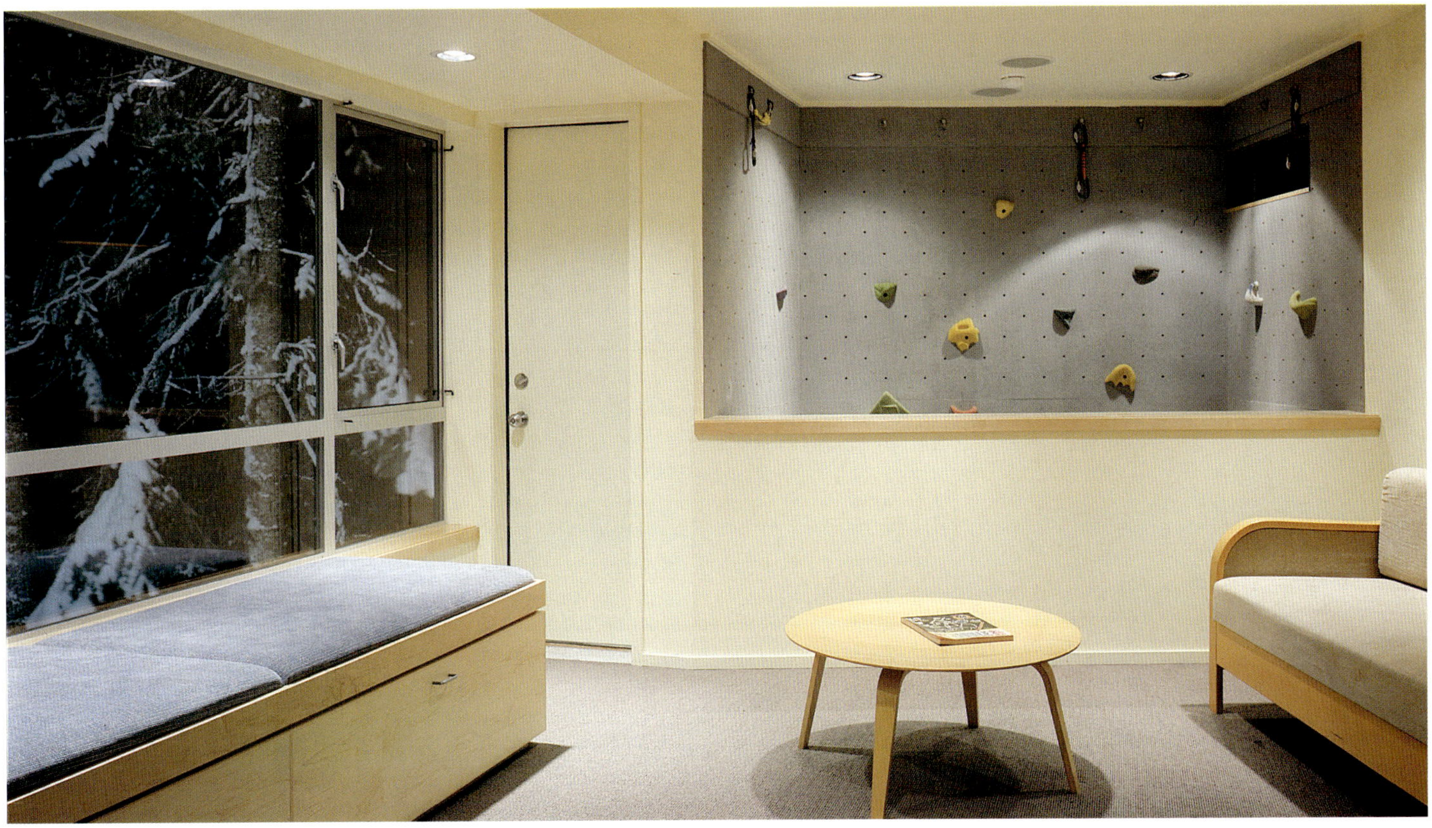

Second floor plan

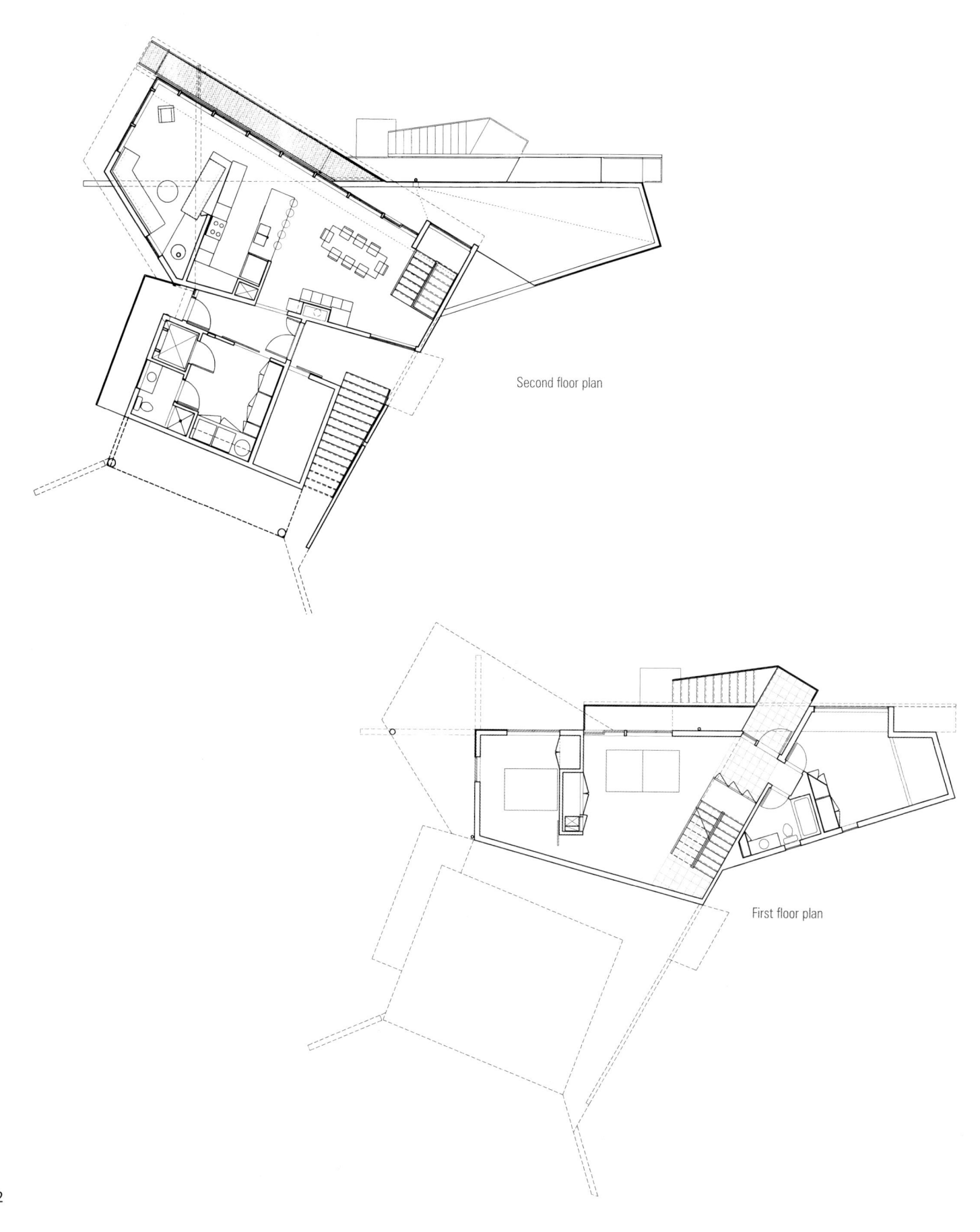

First floor plan

103

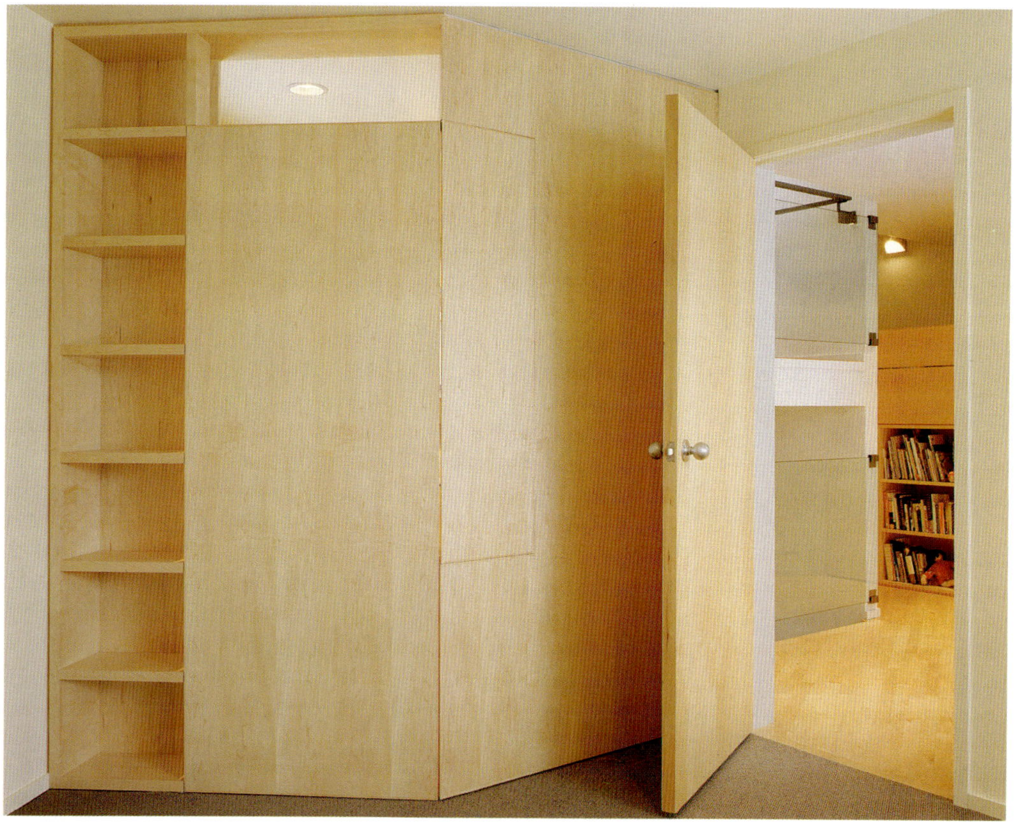

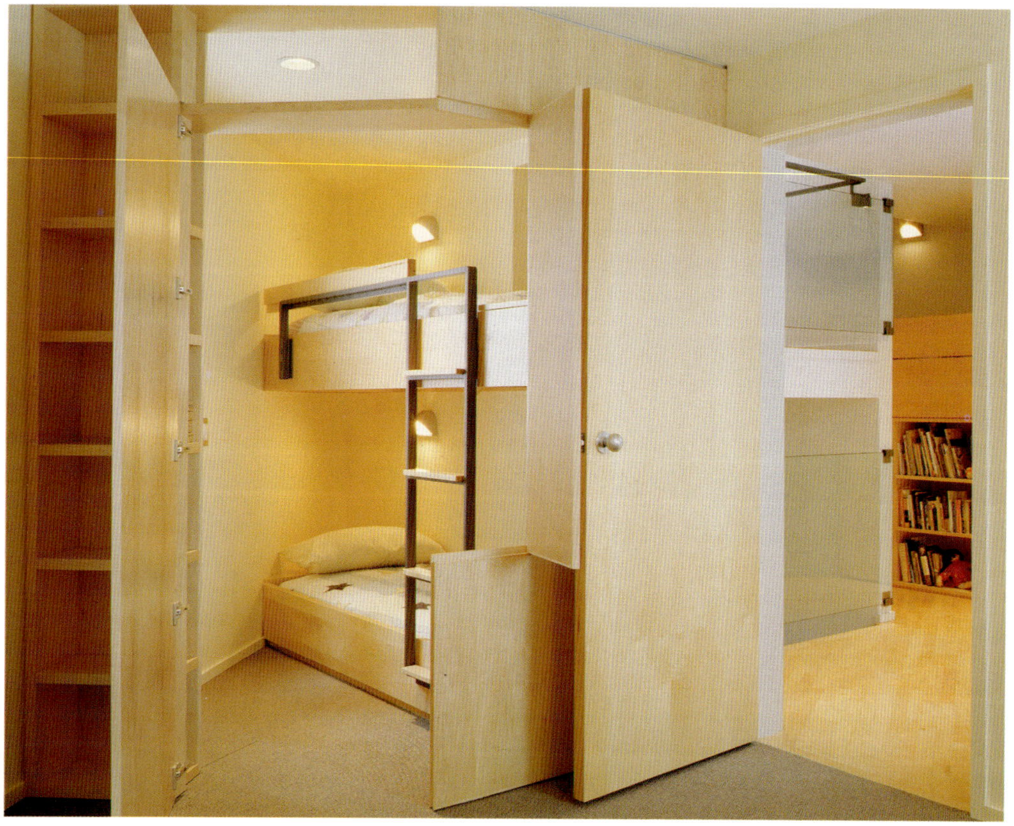

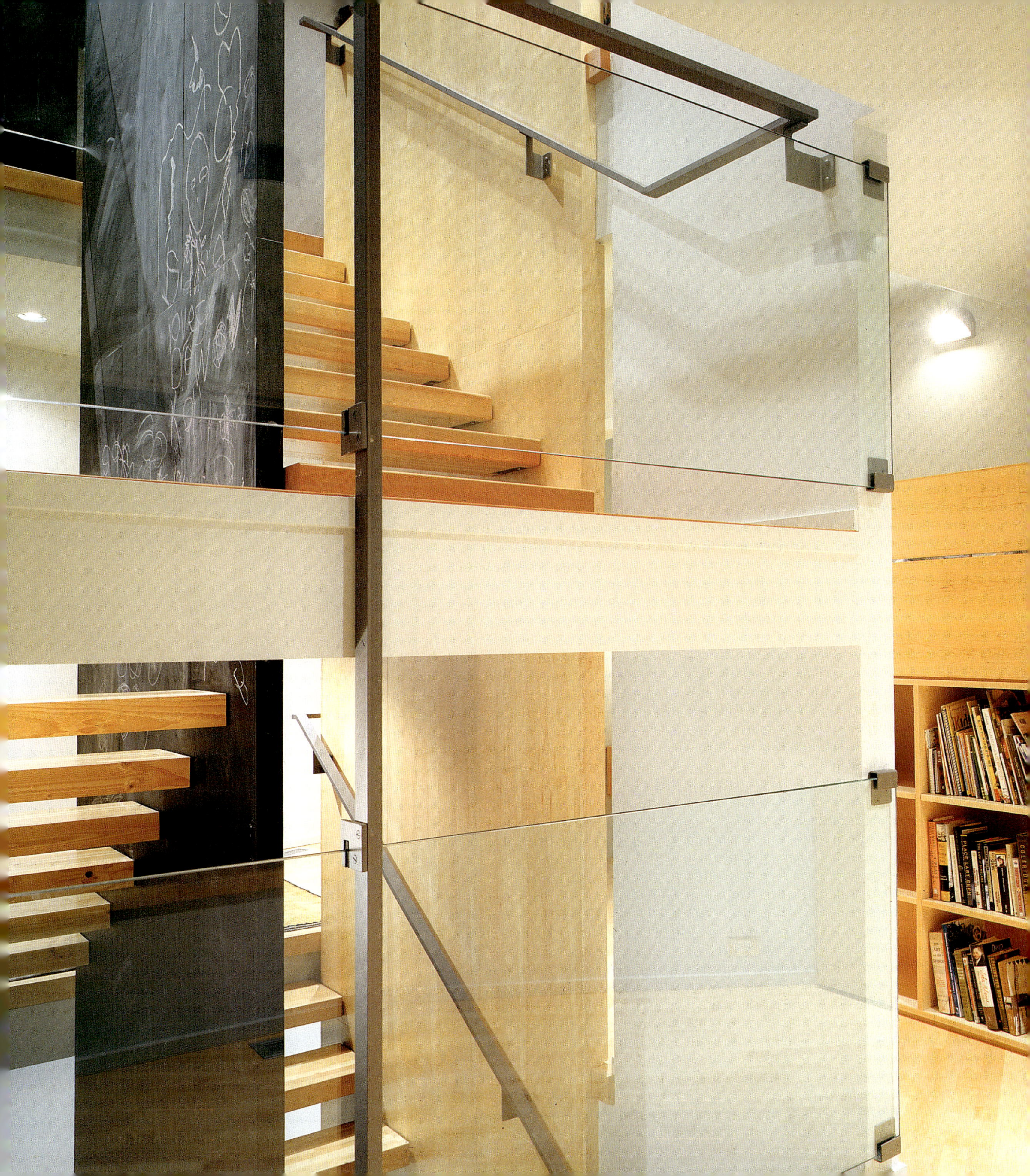

South elevation

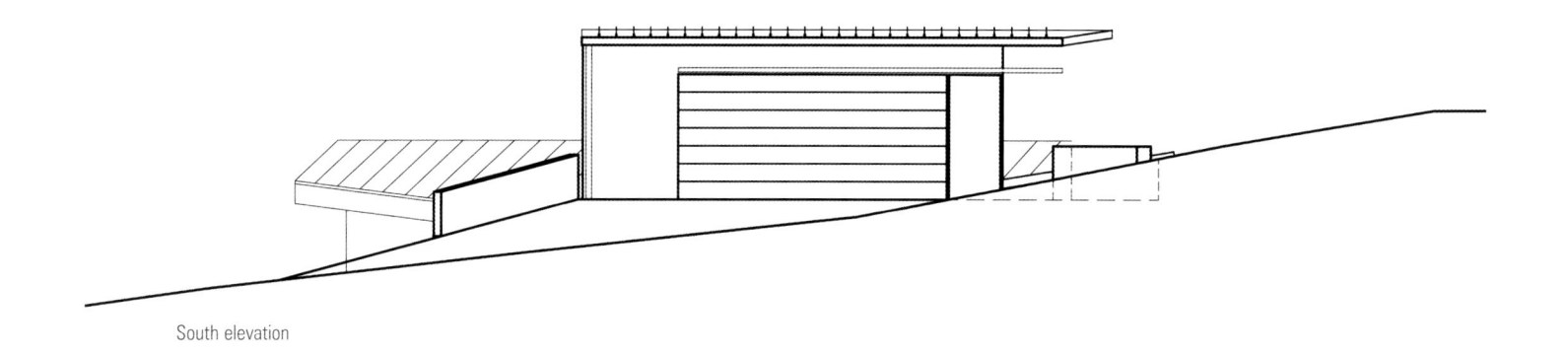

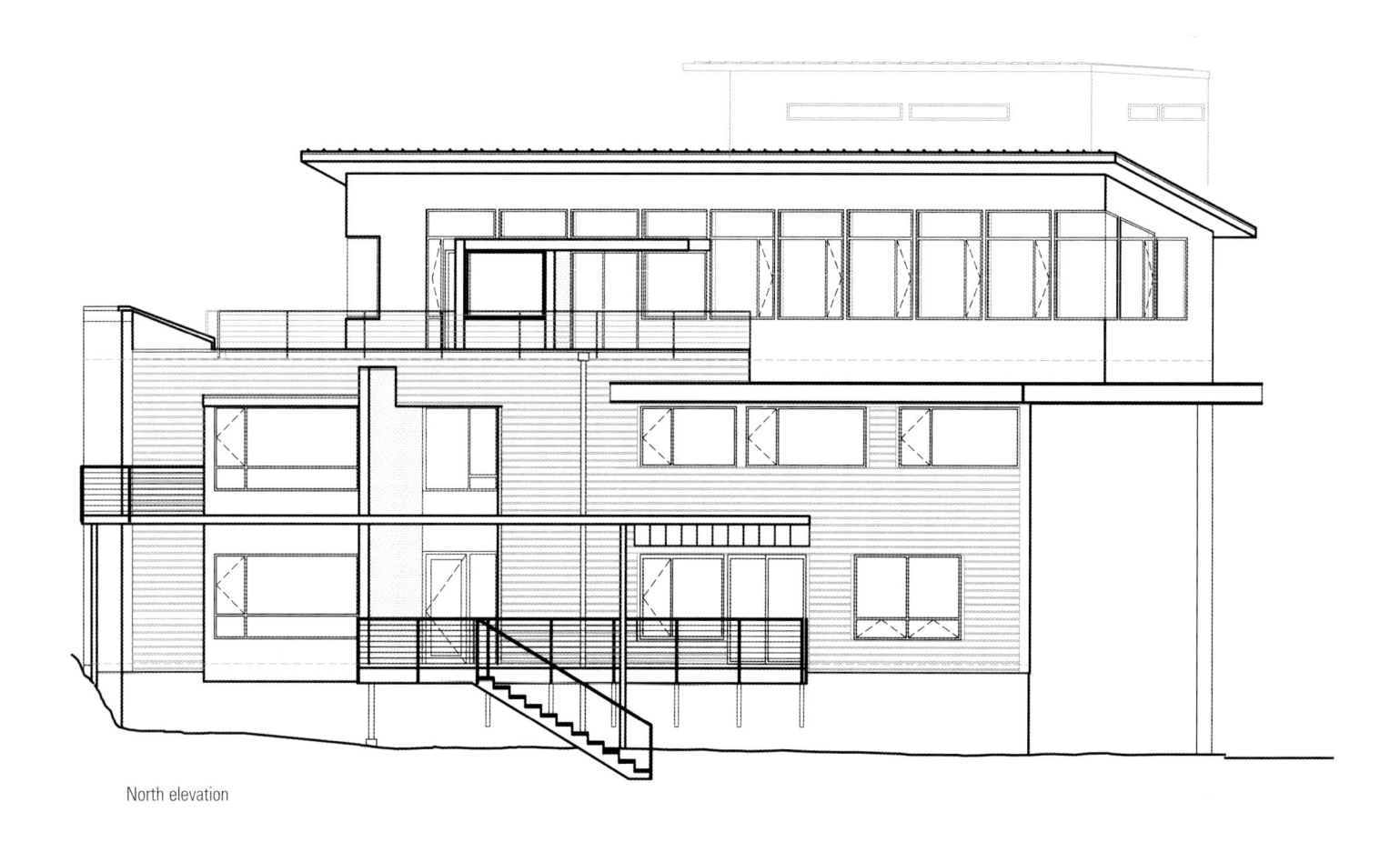

North elevation

106

West elevation

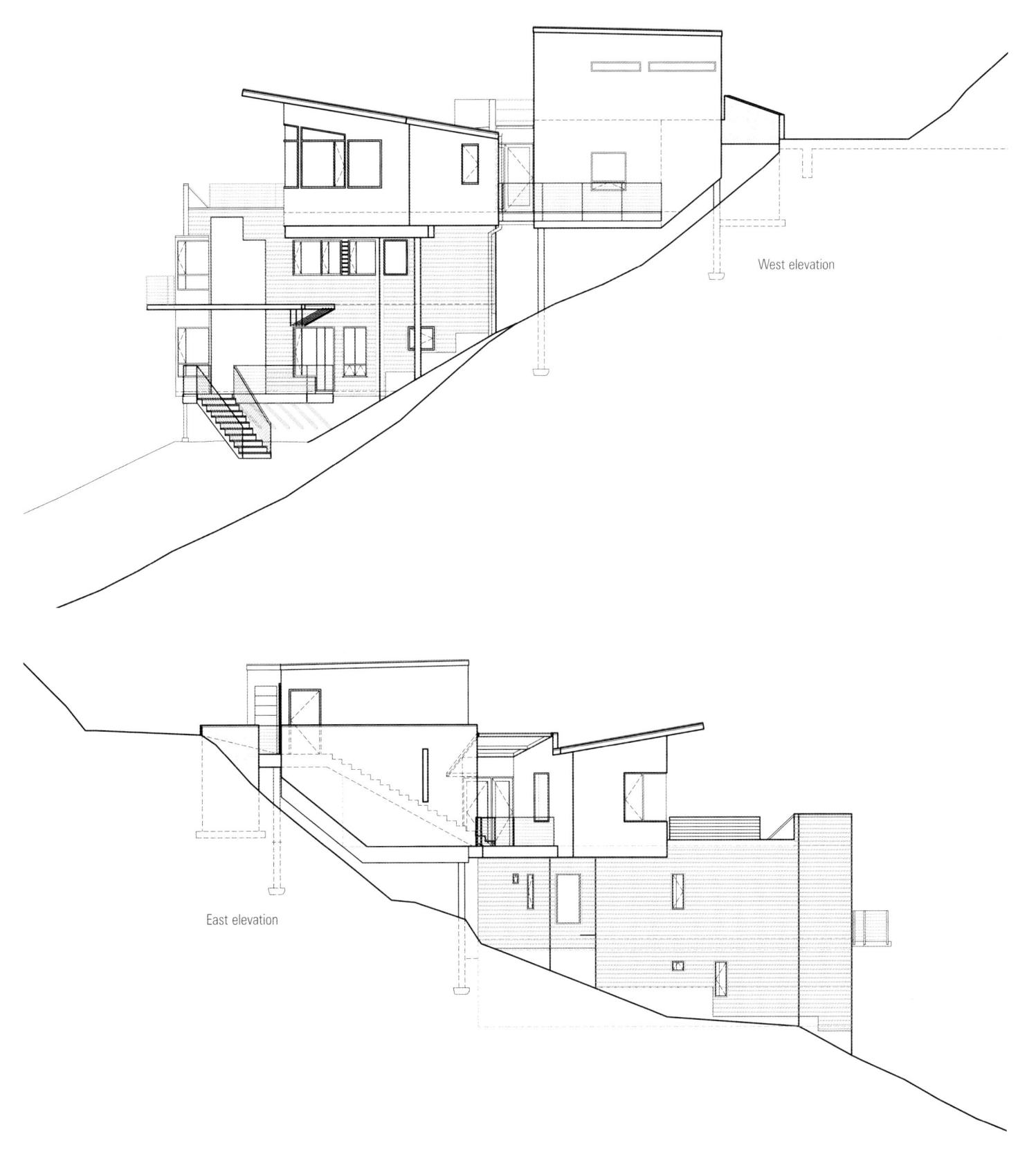

East elevation

Longitudinal section

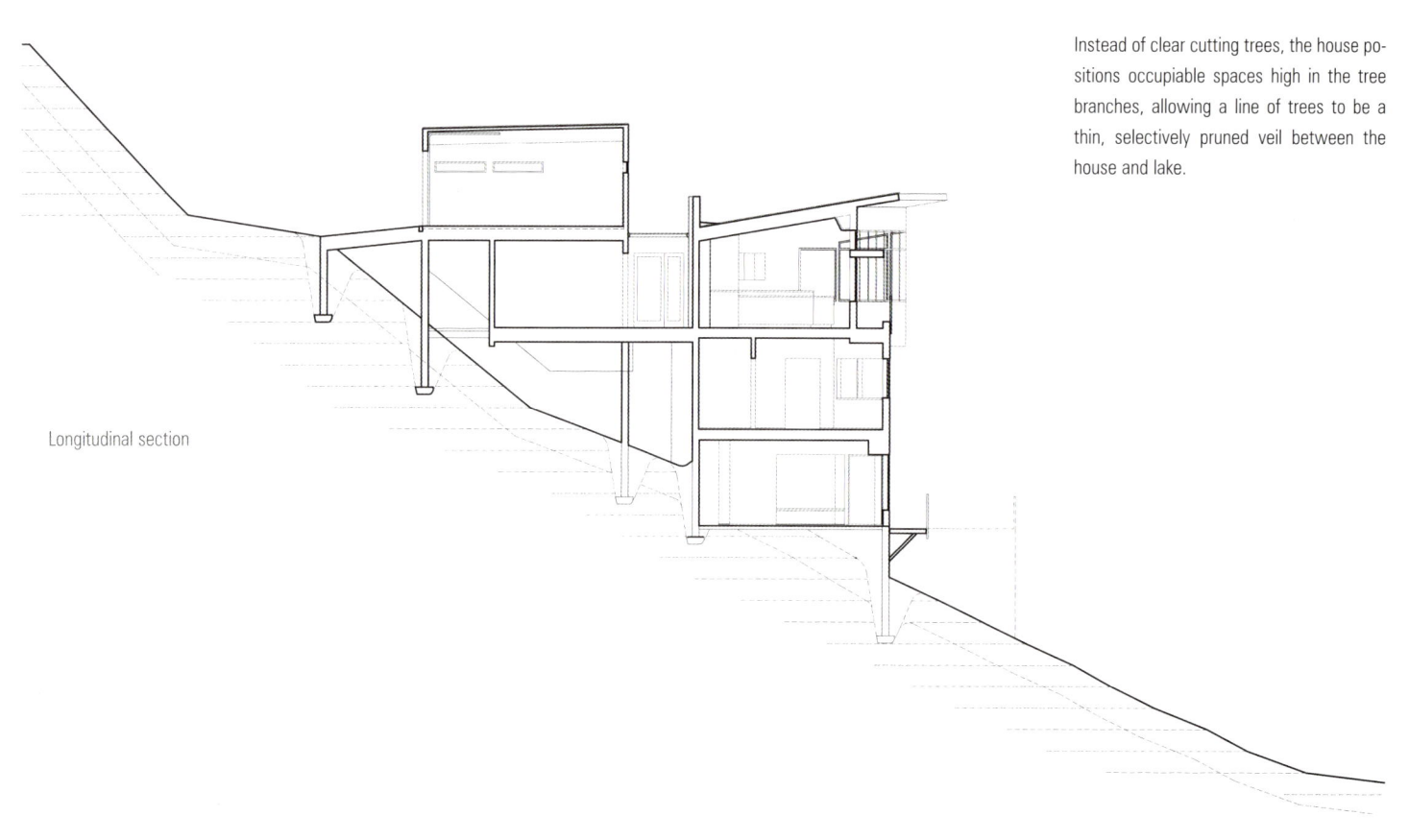

Instead of clear cutting trees, the house positions occupiable spaces high in the tree branches, allowing a line of trees to be a thin, selectively pruned veil between the house and lake.

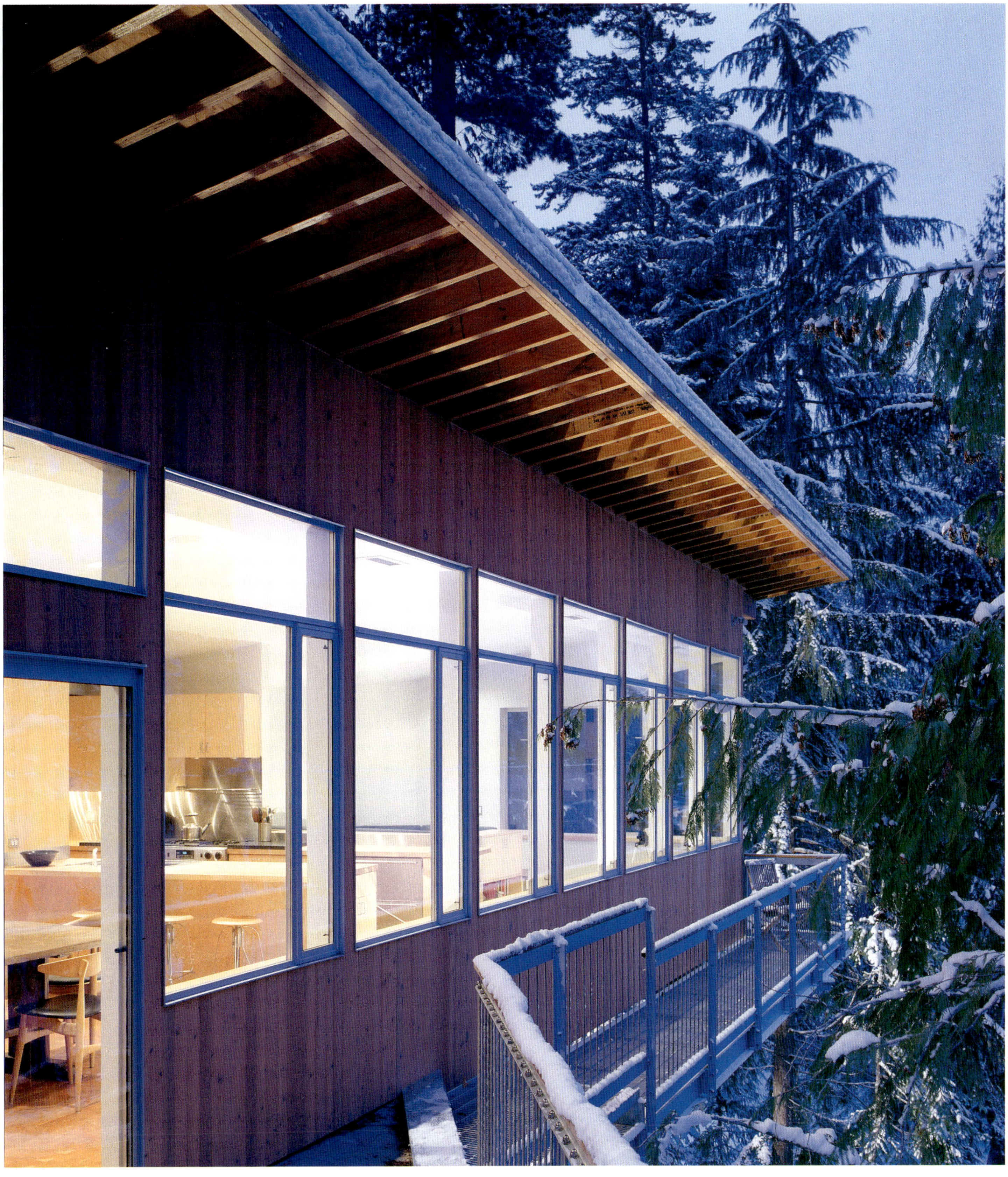

Bellemo & Cat
Cocoon House

Photographs: Mark Munro

Wye River, Southern Victoria, Australia

The house is called "Cocoon" not because it looks like a cocoon, (it actually looks more like a Zeppelin and was built using a mixture of timber boat building techniques and aircraft technology) but because it functions as a cocoon, "both as a nascent Architectural firm and as a family", for the architects who designed it for their own recreational use.

The site itself is on a very steep plot of land with spectacular views as well as excessive exposure to harsh weather conditions. Thus, the design scheme had to simultaneously shield the home from inclement weather while at the same time opening the interior to the view. The end result is a pod-like structure that allows for adequate insulation on all sides of the building except those facing the most desirable views.

Seeming to float amidst the trees, this steel-clad, boat-like cocoon holds in its belly a large glass-faced plywood rectangle facing the westerly ridge of the hills and the ocean. Large sliding doors open this volume out toward the trees, giving the sense of being both inside and out at the same time. The more pragmatic, square-shaped laundry and bathroom areas are located just past this space, while two sleeping cabins are nestled in the "hull", their walls assuming the ovoid shape of the exterior.

Structurally inspired by boat and aircraft building technology, a rectangular structure was built first to house the living and washing areas, later adding a series of plywood ribs to create the shape. Green hardwood battens conforming to the basic shape were then applied, thus creating a monocoque fuselage-style structure. Colorbond shingles form the final exterior skin, serving at once as cladding and structural reinforcement.

The rooms at the ends have no standard post and beam structure, relying instead on the mesh of the timber battens and shingles to form a strong, structural shell.

The building process itself was something of a challenge. Because the plot was so steep and prone to landslides, the builders had to work with climbing ropes and harnesses. Standard scaffolding was out of the question (again, due to the slope) and the round hull of the structure meant that there was no roof to stand on. To overcome this, the ceiling beams and floor joists were left jutting out of the building to be used as secure platforms from which to work.

The exterior cladding of this totally ovoid building required a durable yet lightweight and flexible material. The solution was simple: customizing a standard BHP Colorbond flat sheet into shingles.

Considering its relative low cost and ease of construction (not on this site perhaps, but in a factory) the architects are contemplating prototyping the house as a possible prefab housing model. They are also working on a fabric skin and exposed skeleton.

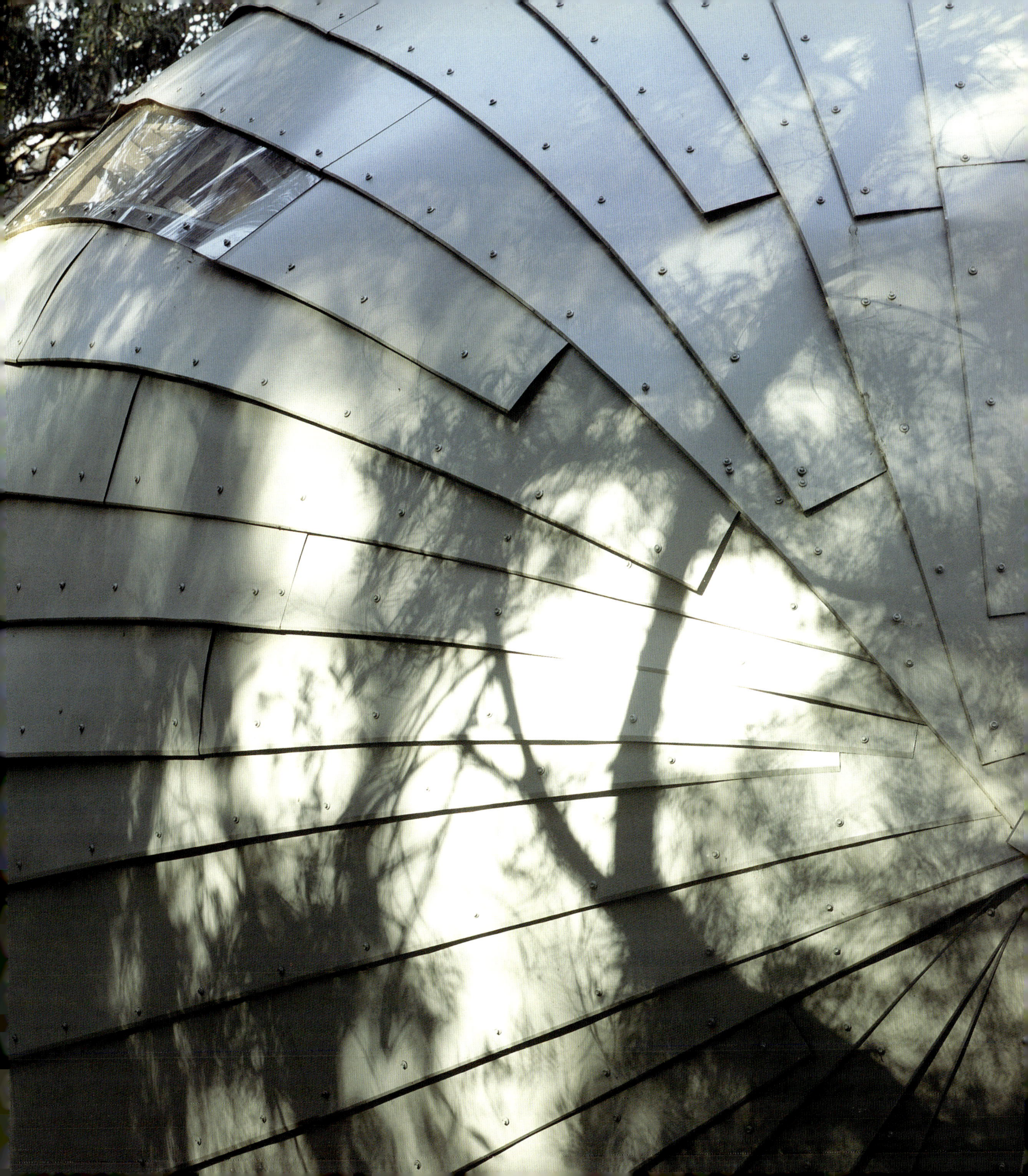

Structurally inspired by boat and aircraft building technology, a rectangular structure was built first to house the living and washing areas, later adding a series of plywood ribs to create the shape.

Longitudinal section

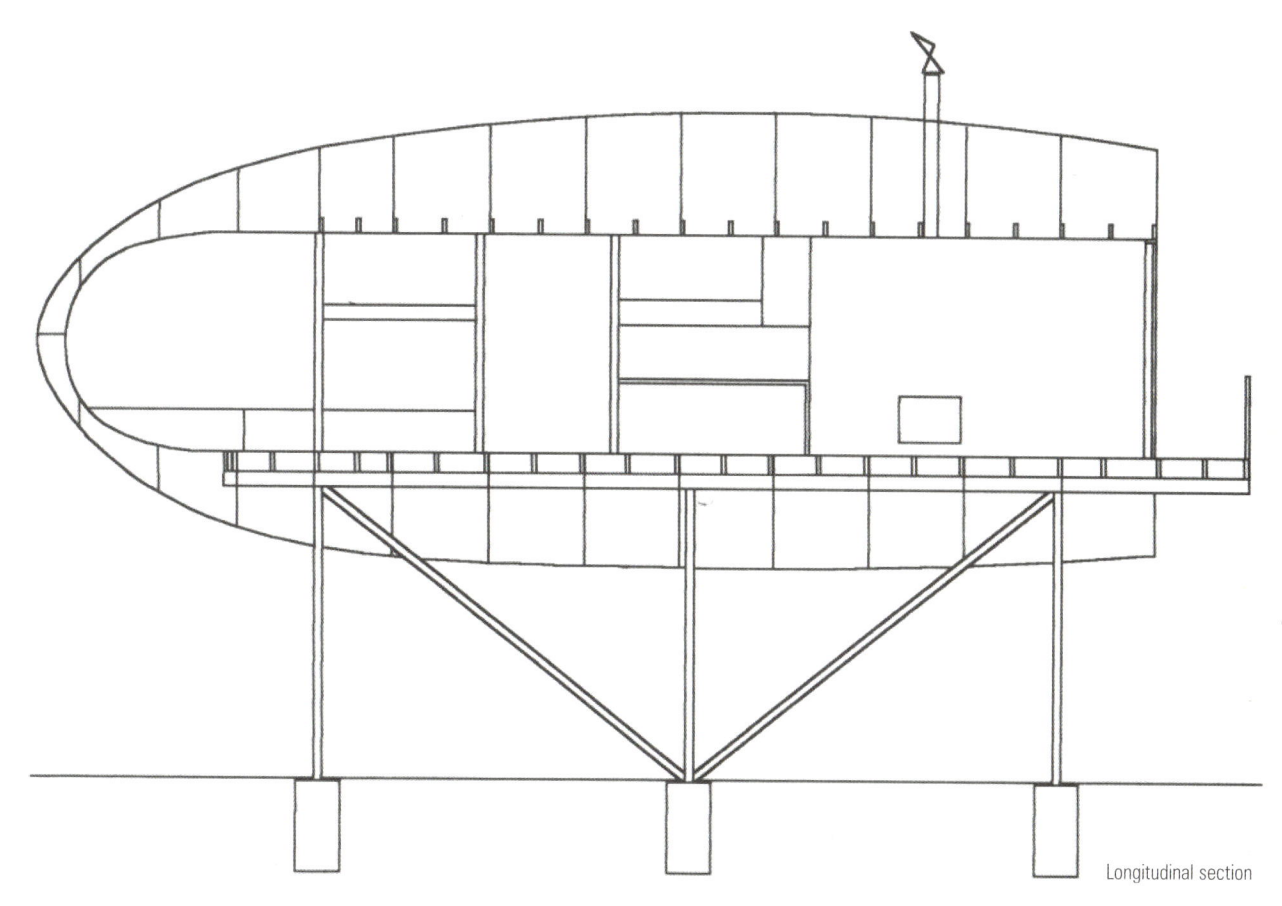

113

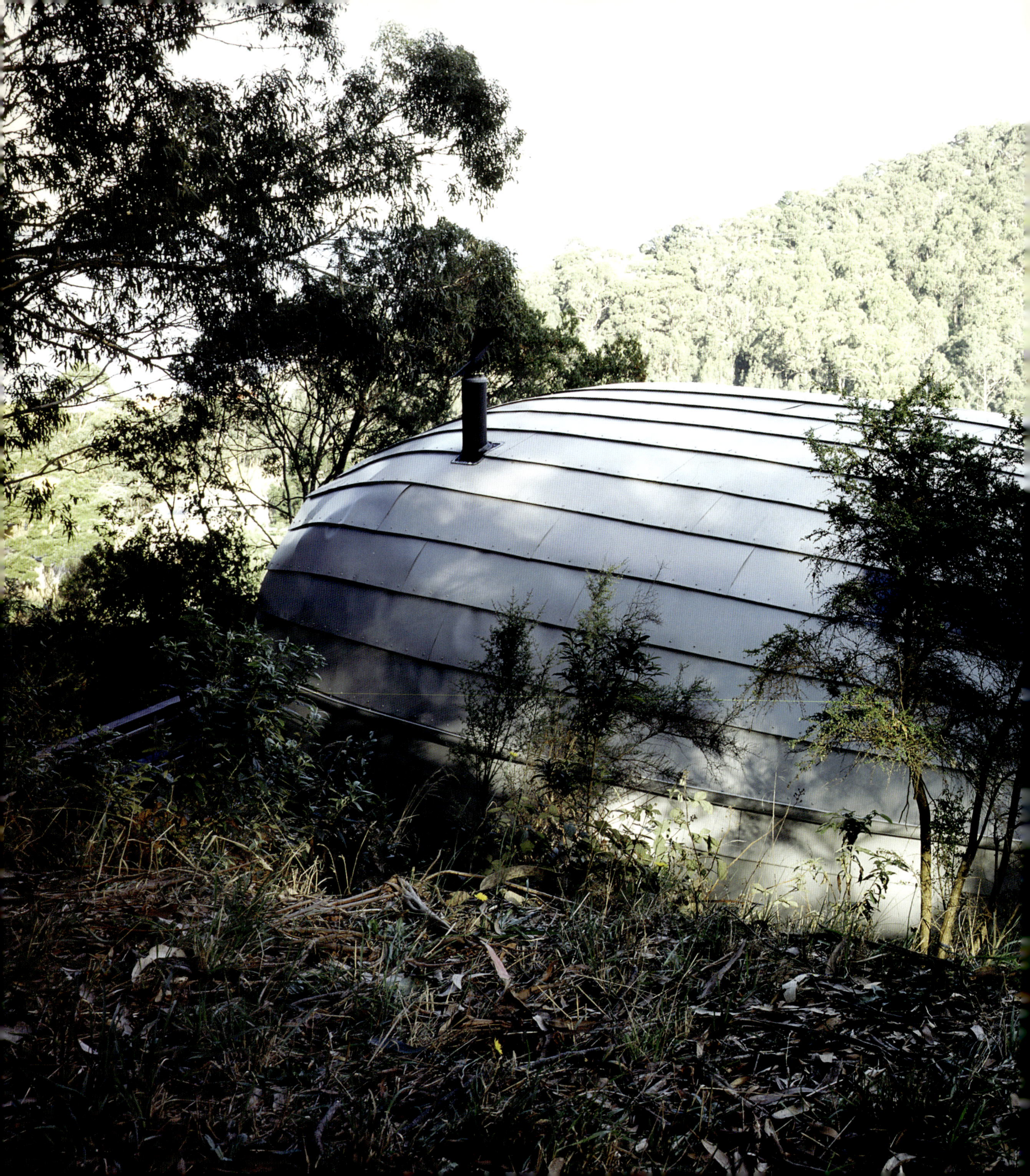

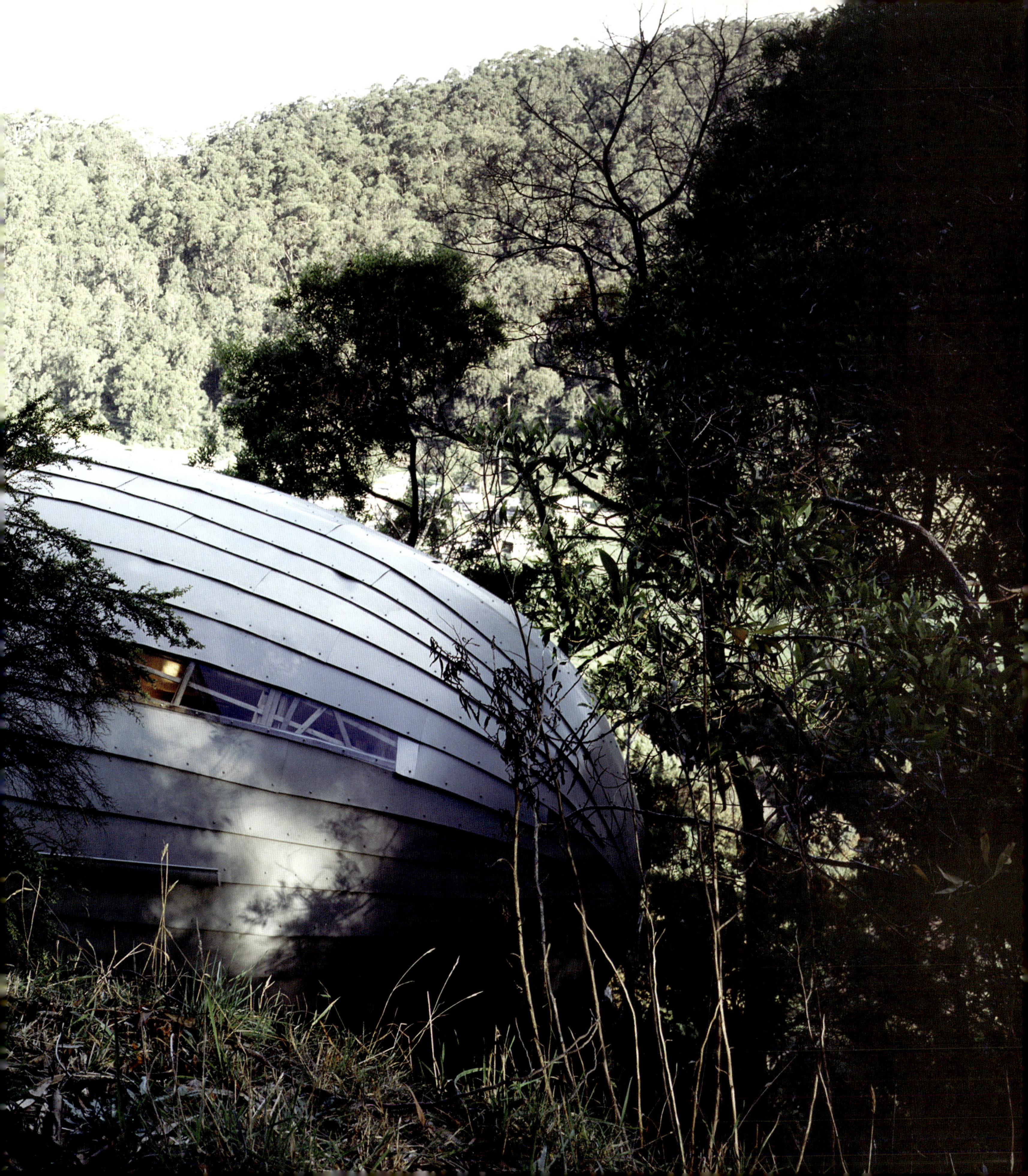

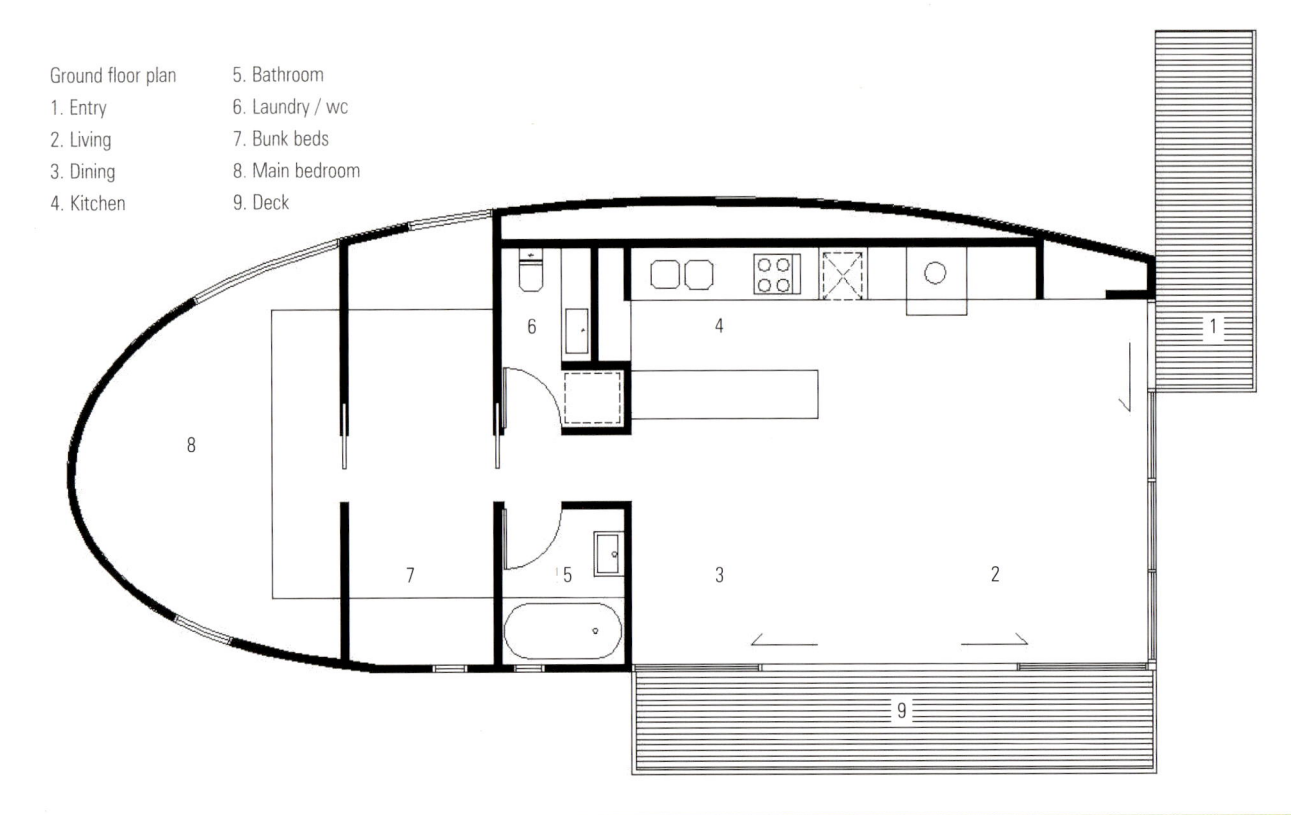

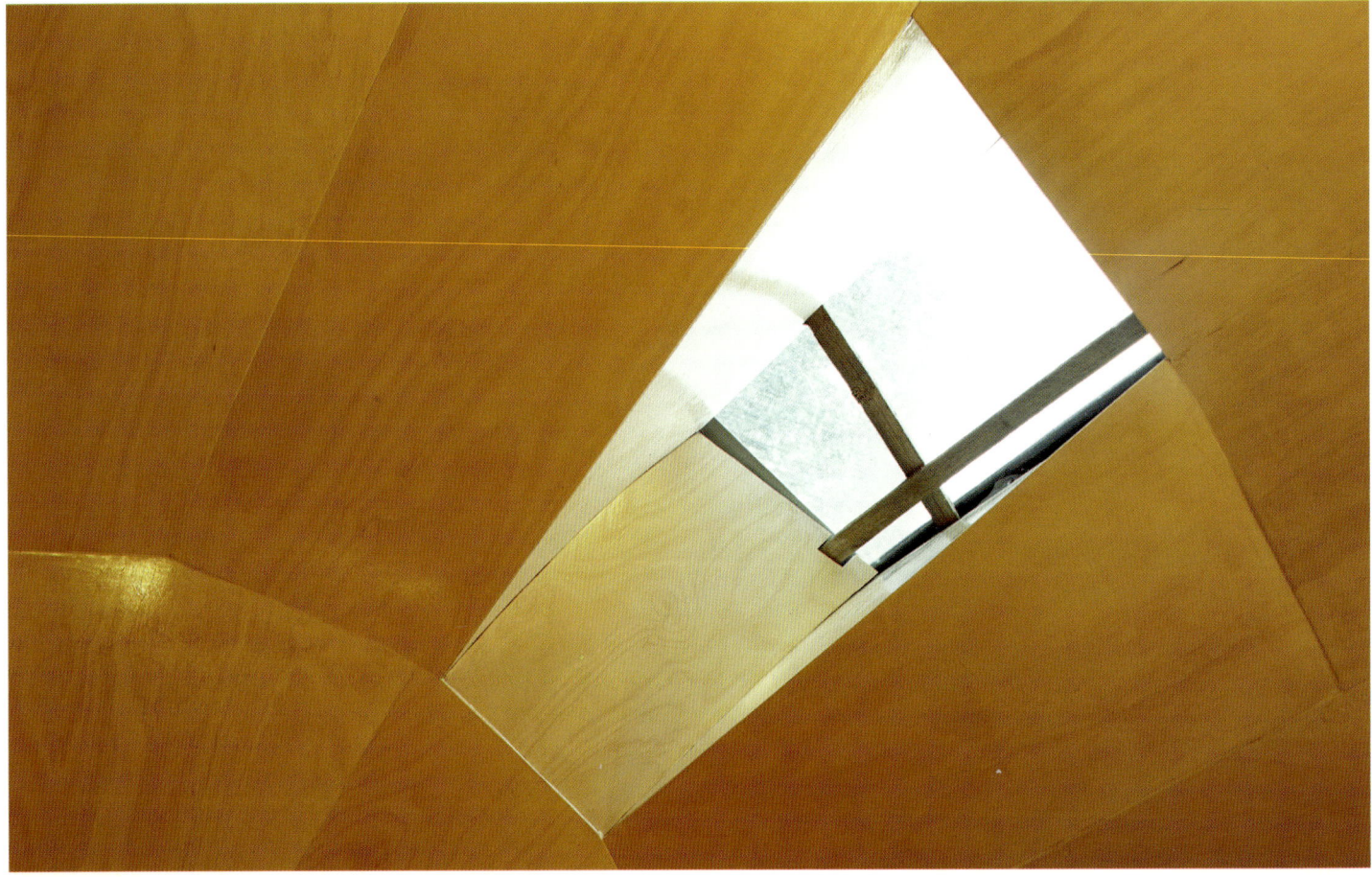

Ground floor plan
1. Entry
2. Living
3. Dining
4. Kitchen
5. Bathroom
6. Laundry / wc
7. Bunk beds
8. Main bedroom
9. Deck

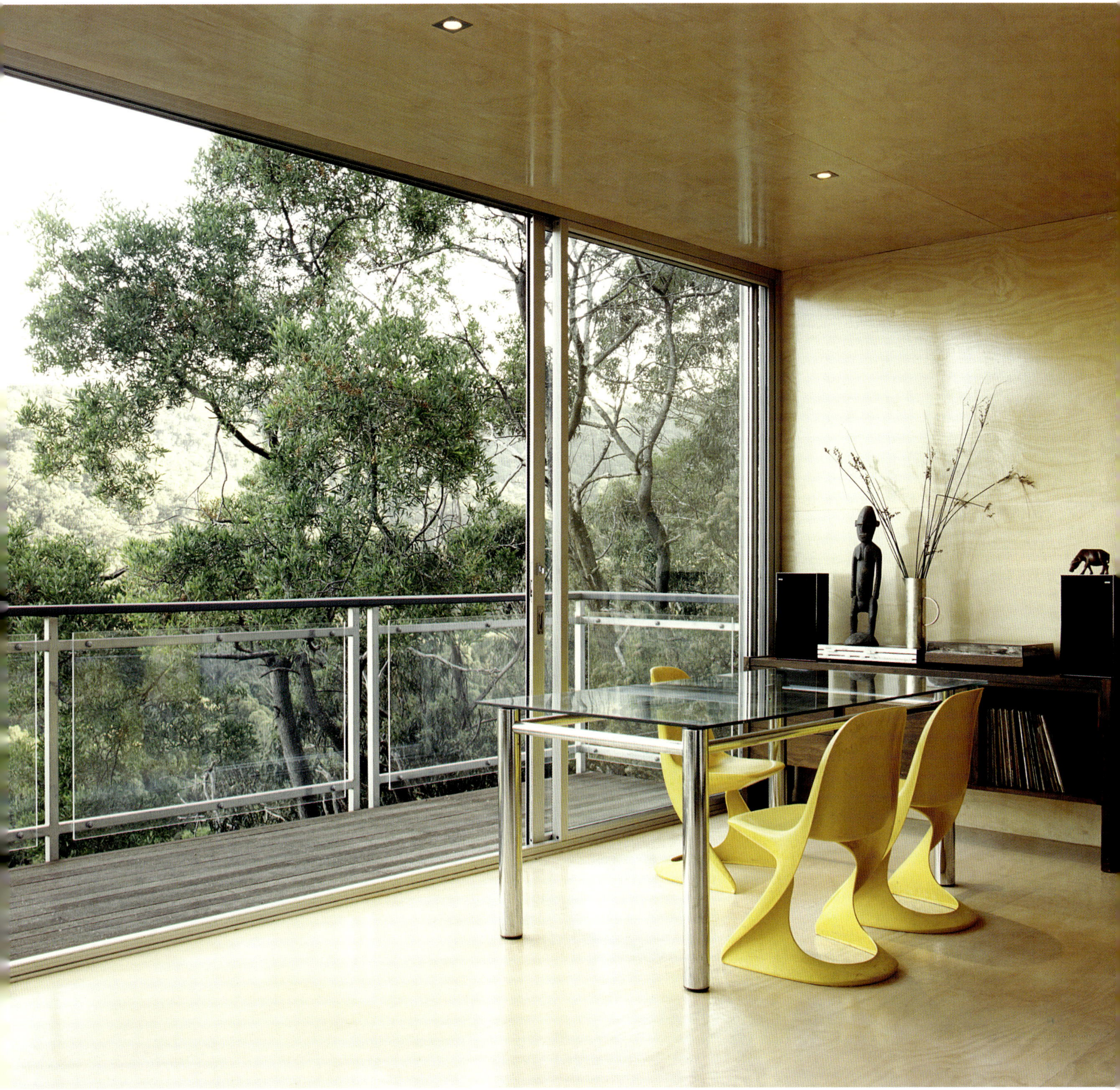

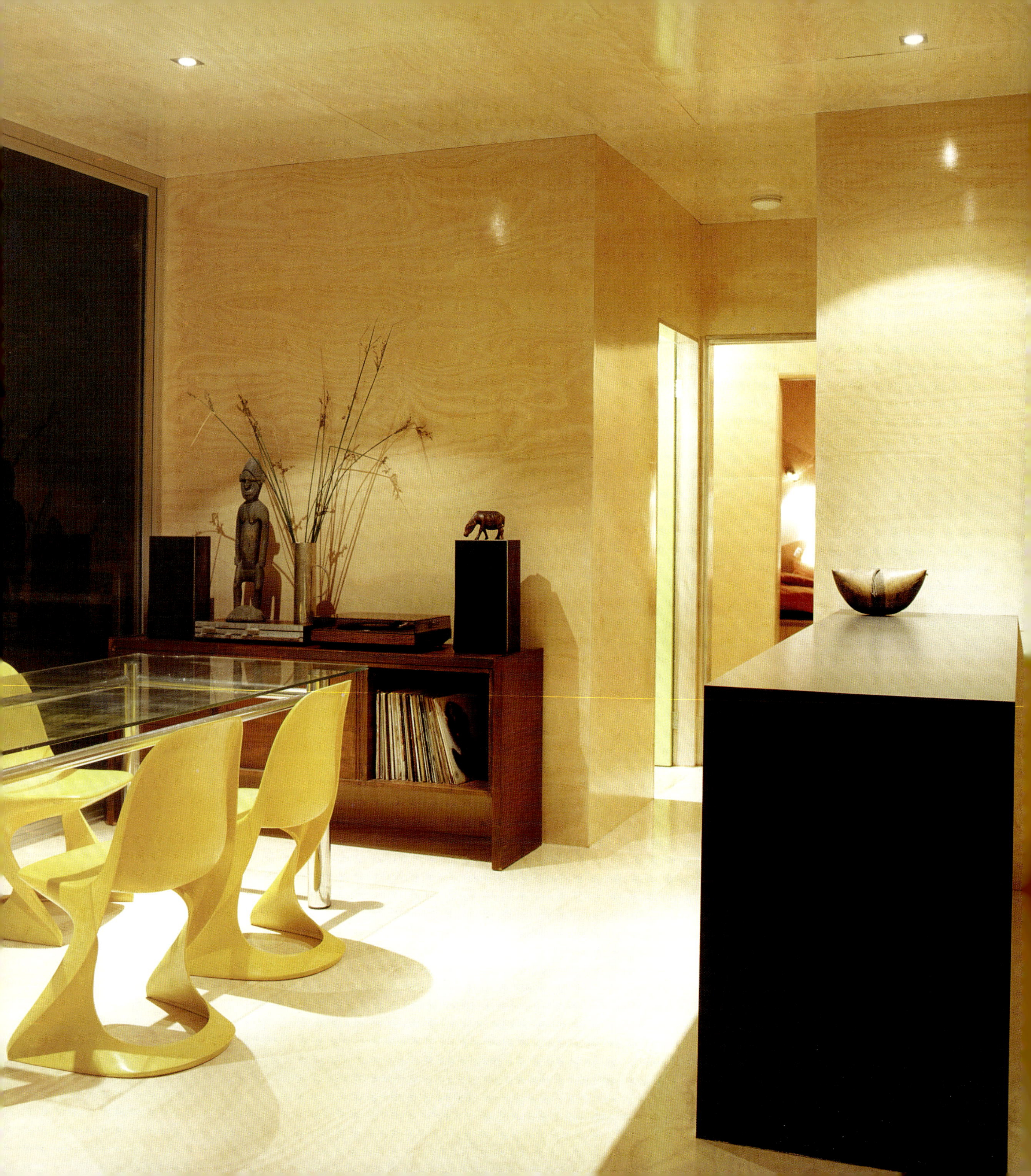

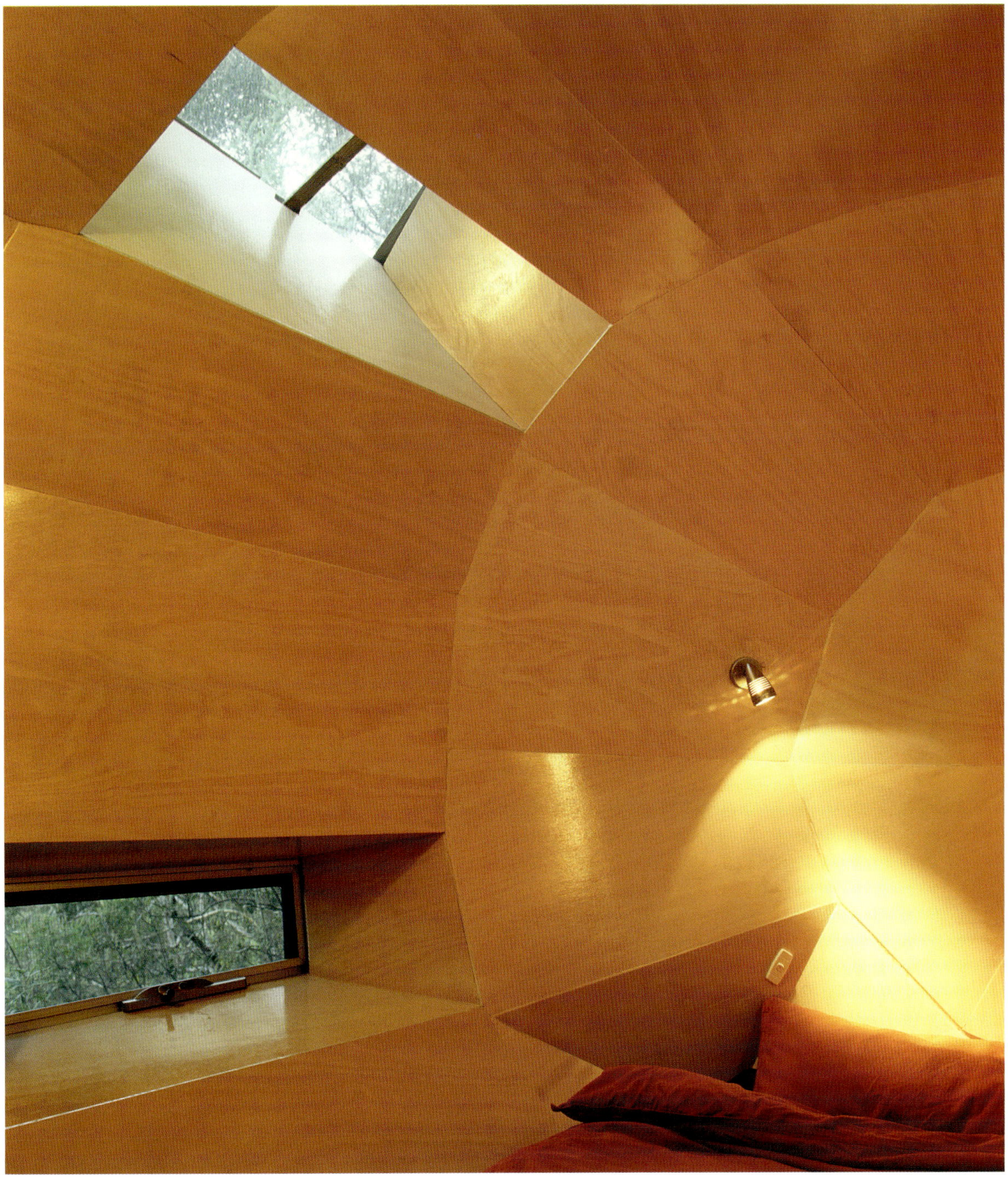

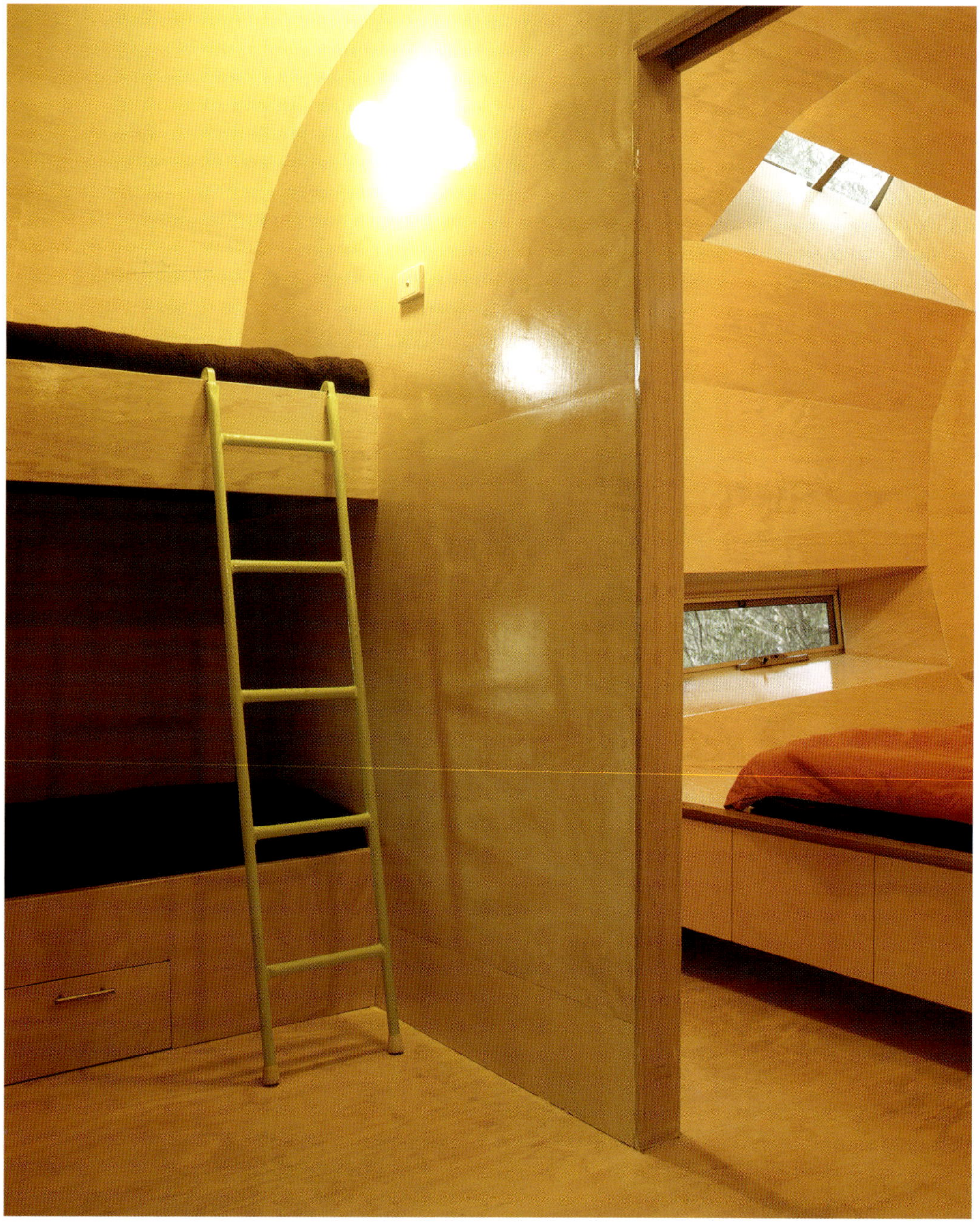

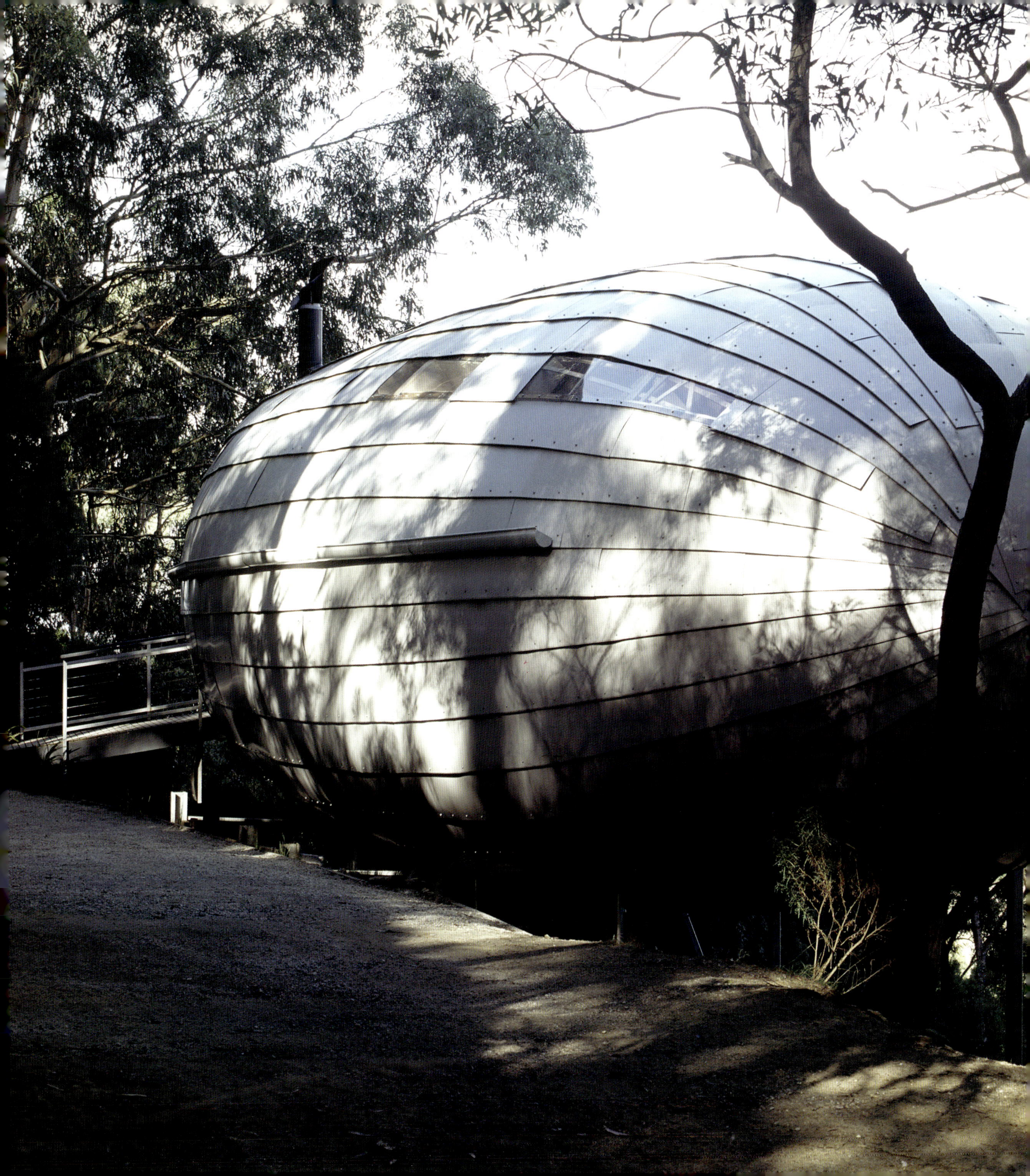

Carl-Viggo Hølmebakk
Mountain Cottage in Sollia

Photographs: C-V. Hølmebakk

Sollia, Norway

The cottage is situated 2953 feet (900 meters) above sea level on a west-facing hillside with a striking view towards the Rondane mountains. The site sits on the back side of a vague elevation in the sloping landscape, which makes the ground slant "backwards", away from the view. The immediate surroundings, with a few pine trees and the ground covered in reindeer moss, makes for choice views.

The main volume of the cottage embraces the elevation, with the rooms organized in a linear sequence to capture the best views. A gravel terrace adapts to the ascending terrain and creates a sheltered outdoor space facing west and the view. On the east side is a two story annex connected to the main building by an entrance porch.

The ground of soil and gravel presented the danger of frost heave, the frost depth in the area being 8.86 feet (2.7 meters). A traditional foundation layout would have effectively destroyed a great deal of the vegetation around the building. In order to avoid this, it became important to come up with a foundation principle that would occupy a smaller portion of the ground area.

The end result was a concrete sustaining wall that holds the gravel between the house and the terrain. This wall also anchors the wooden structure that cantilevers above the ground to the east. In this way the ground's insulating carpet is more or less limited to the size of the building itself, while on the west side the insulation is covered by the gravel terrace.

The cottage has a post and beam skeleton of laminated pine wood. The upper beams have a 1:60 tilt that creates a markedly sloped ceiling in the interior spaces. The structure is exposed in the interiors and towards the terrace. The cantilevered part of the building has a covering of pine heartwood boards.

The interior siding and fittings are pine plywood. The structure of the plywood ceiling generated a geometric pattern of rectangles, painted in 19 different colors. The wooden floors are pine, while the passage area along the terrace is ground concrete. The fireplace and other masonry is concrete brickwork. All exterior wood is treated with tar.

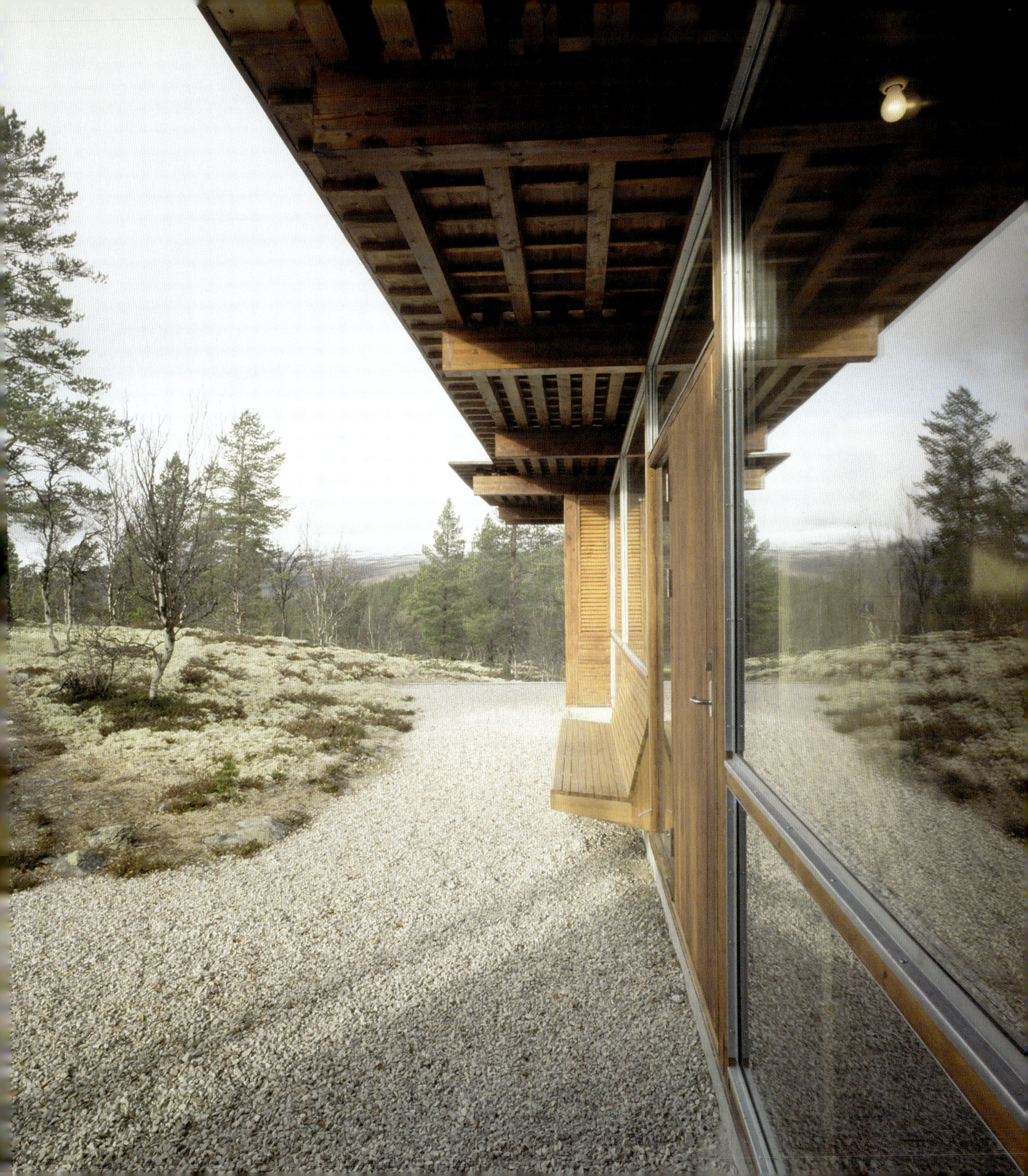

The main volume of the cottage embraces the elevation, with the rooms organized in a linear sequence to capture the best views. On the east side is a two story annex connected to the main building by an entrance porch.

Floor plan

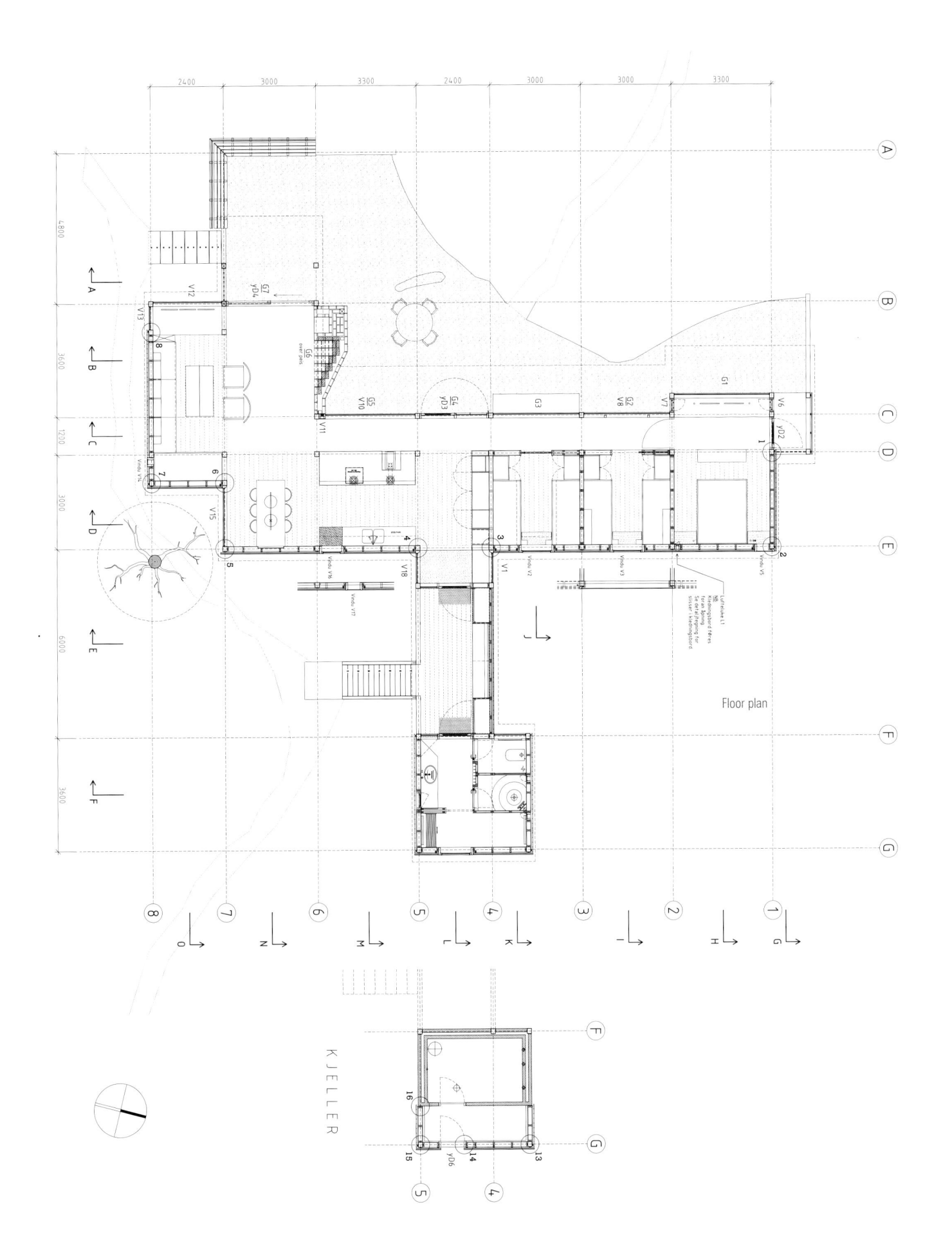

KJELLER

125

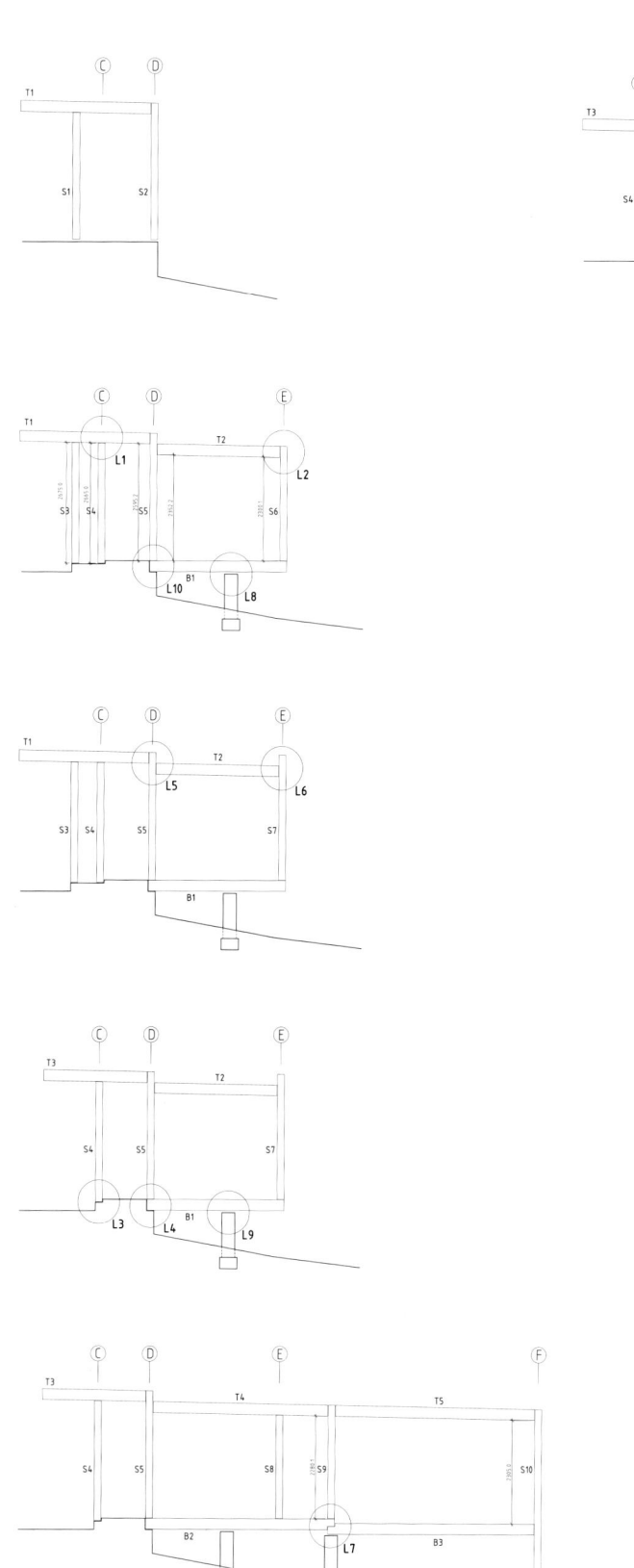

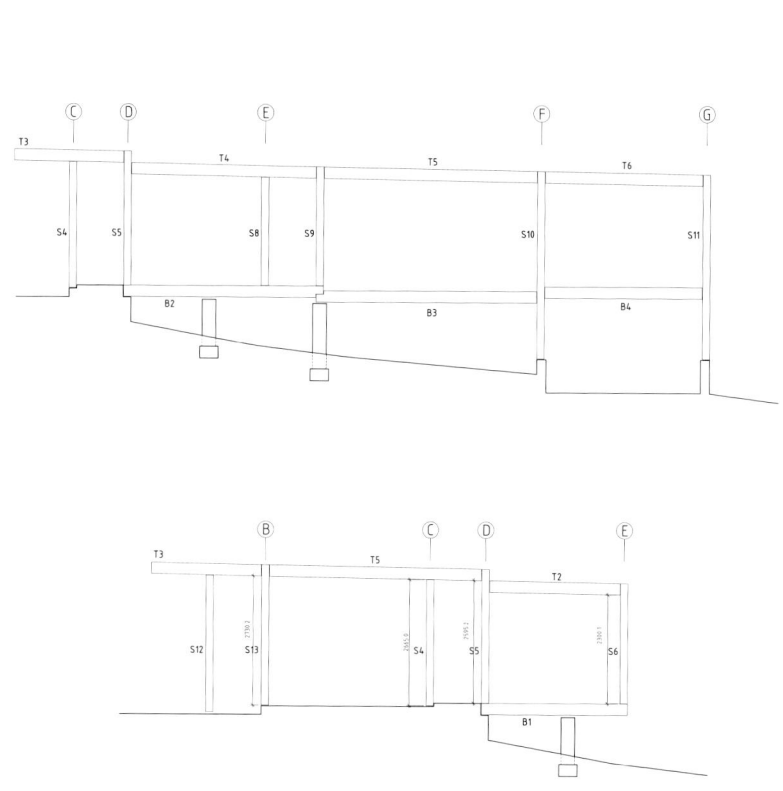

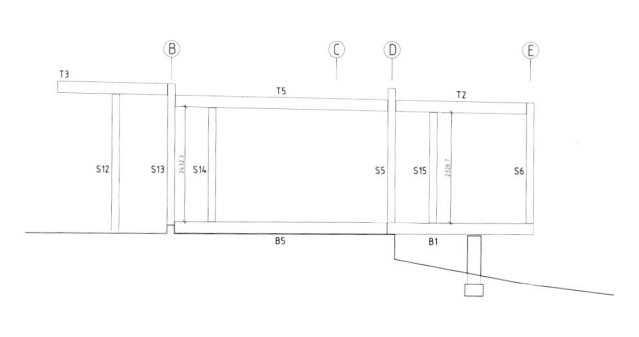

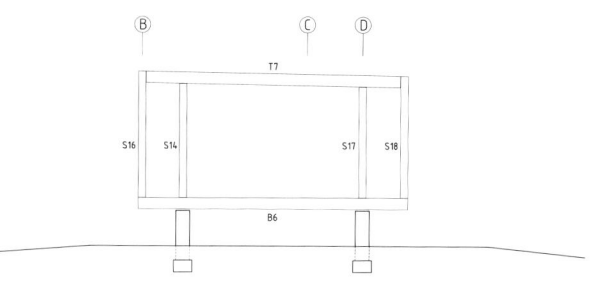

Sections

127

Reflected ceiling plan

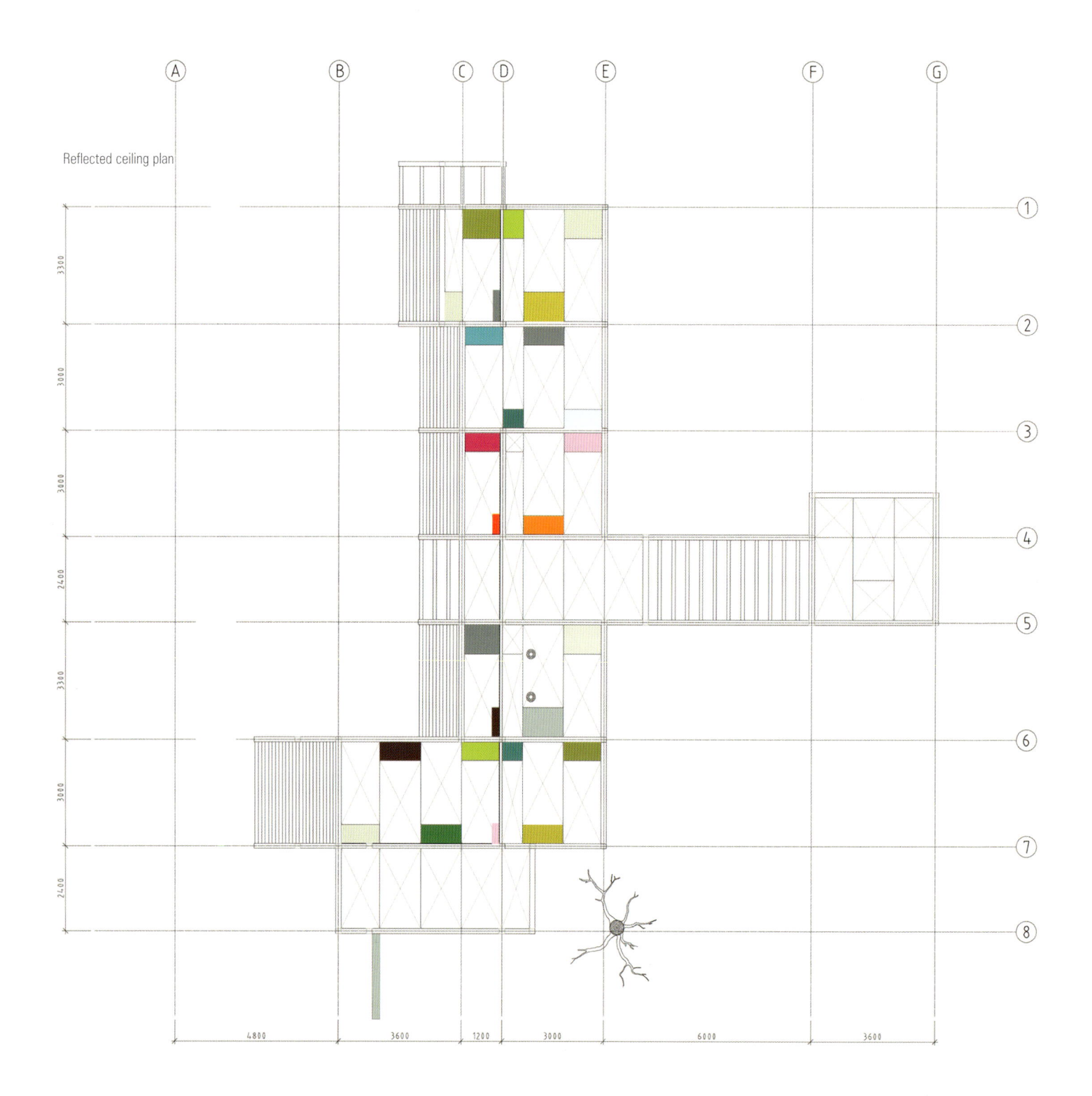

The fireplace and other masonry is concrete brickwork. The interior siding and fittings are pine plywood.

130

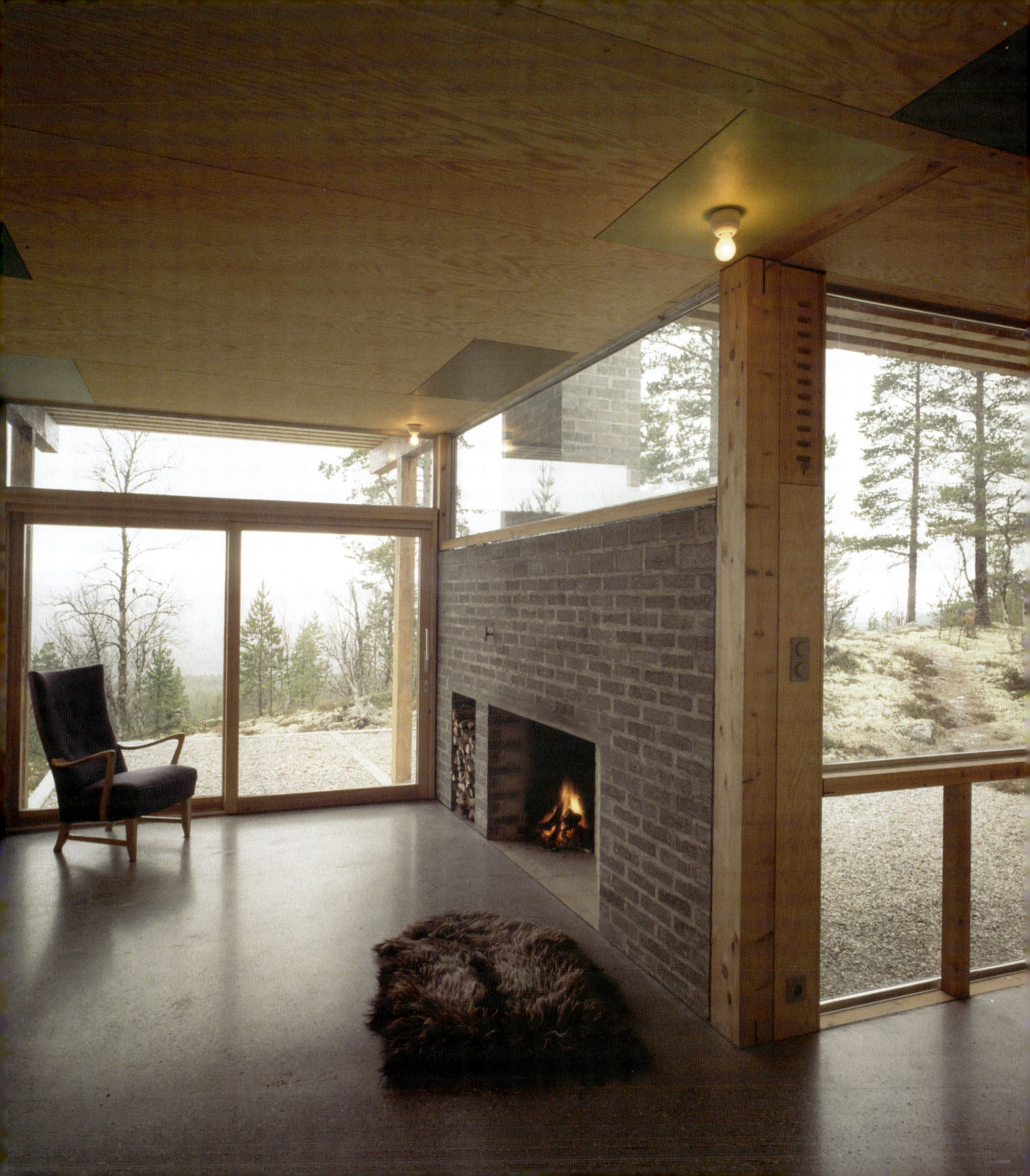

Constructive details

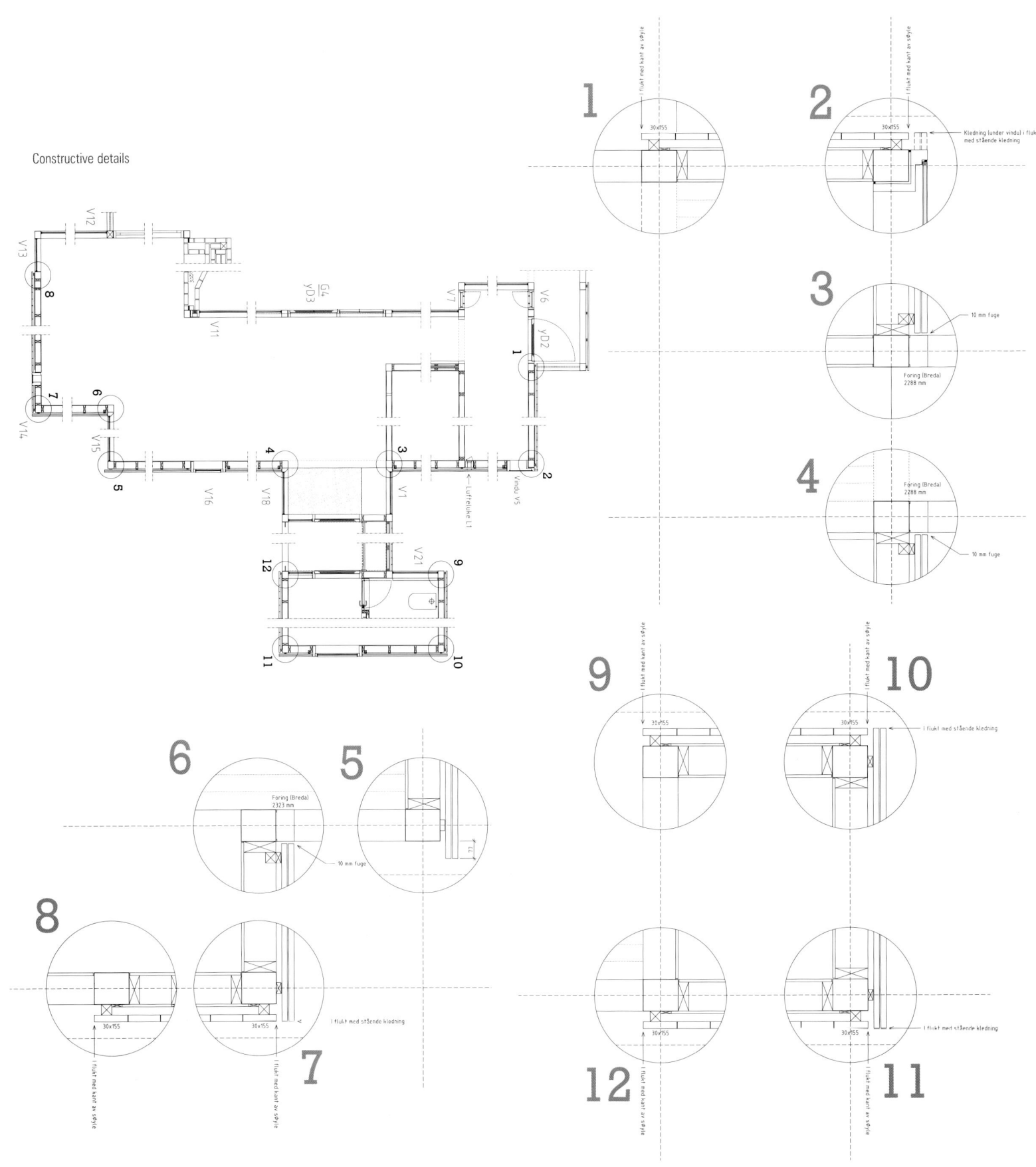

132

133

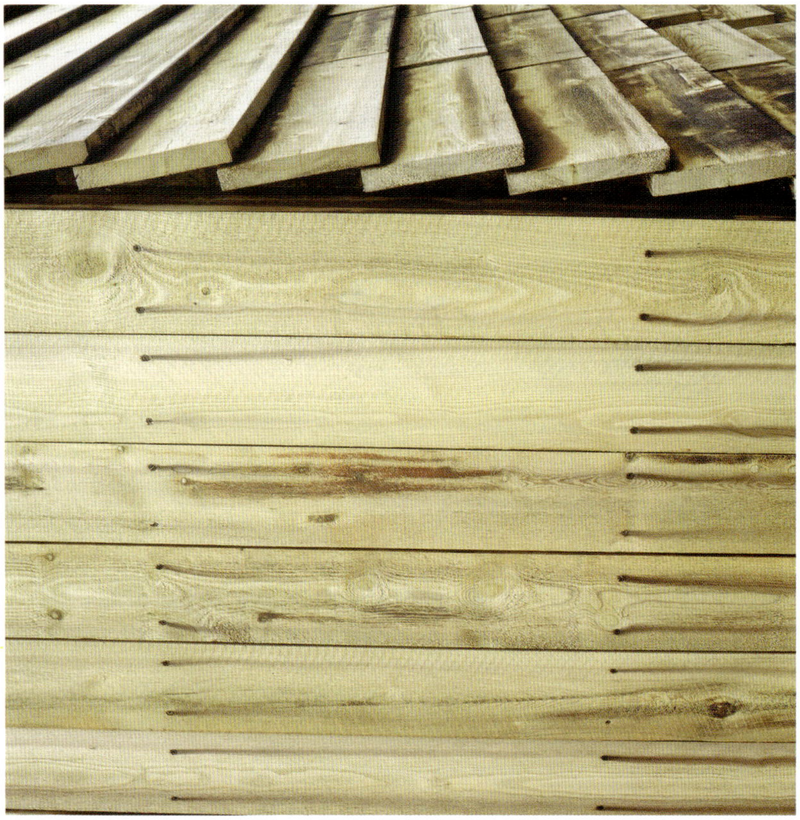

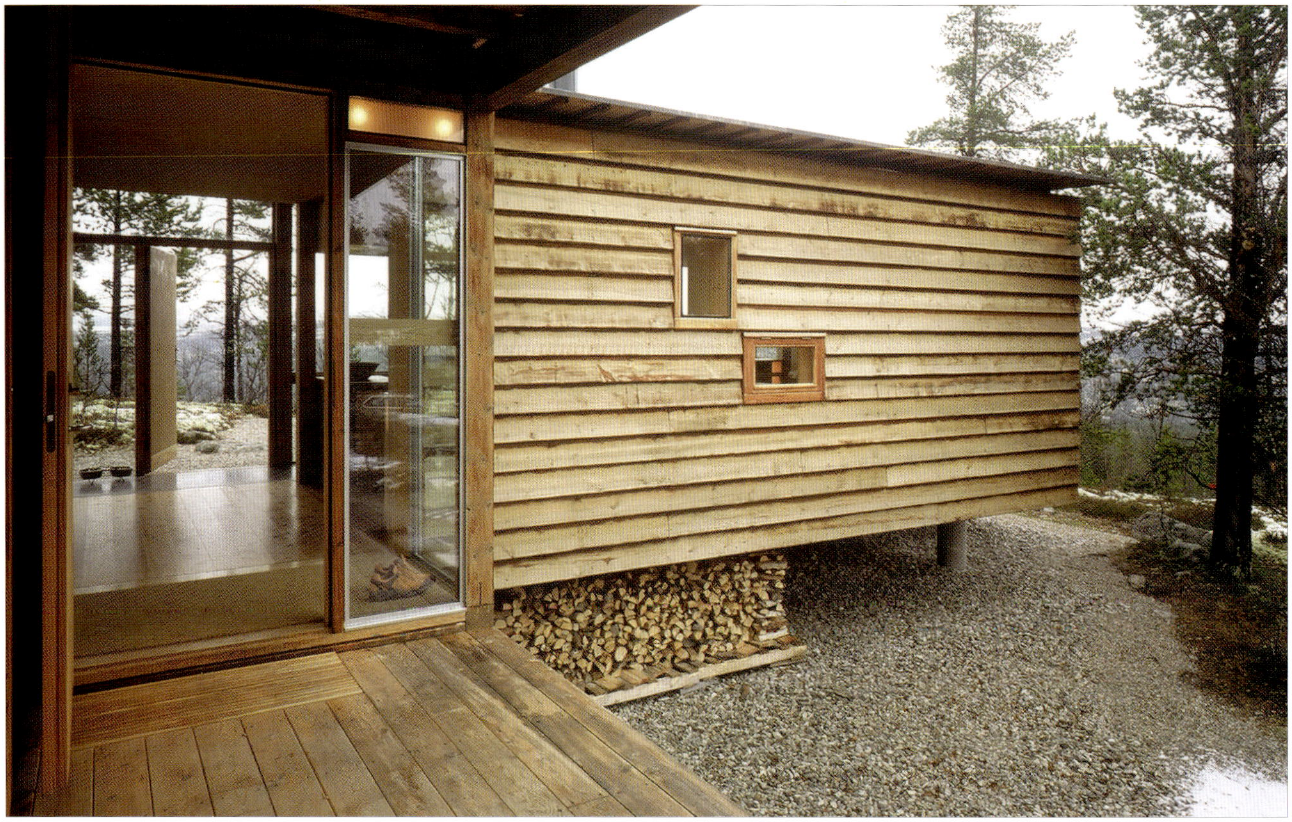

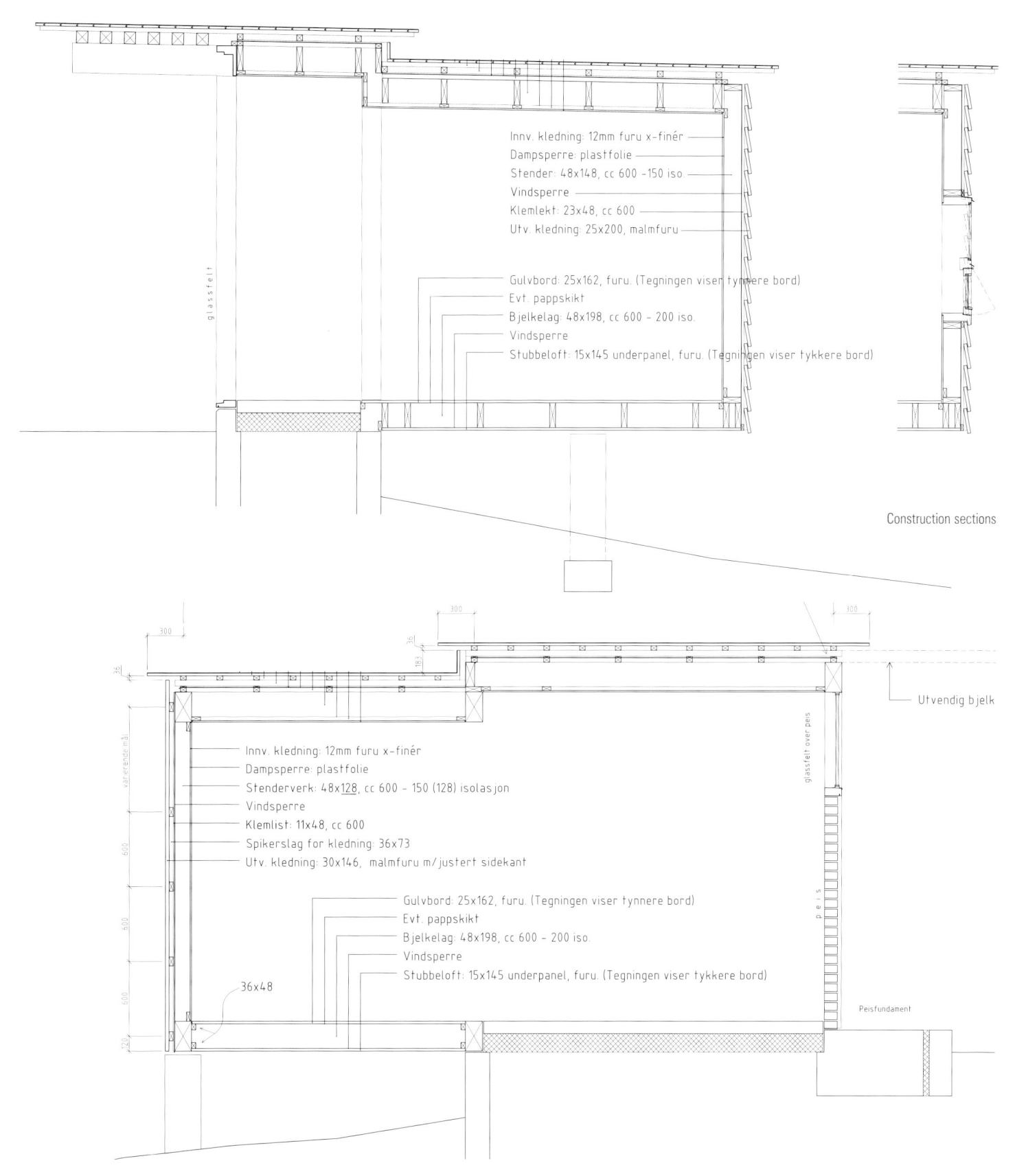

Innv. kledning: 12mm furu x-finér
Dampsperre: plastfolie
Stender: 48x148, cc 600 -150 iso.
Vindsperre
Klemlekt: 23x48, cc 600
Utv. kledning: 25x200, malmfuru

Gulvbord: 25x162, furu. (Tegningen viser tynnere bord)
Evt. pappskikt
Bjelkelag: 48x198, cc 600 - 200 iso.
Vindsperre
Stubbeloft: 15x145 underpanel, furu. (Tegningen viser tykkere bord)

Construction sections

Utvendig bjelk

Innv. kledning: 12mm furu x-finér
Dampsperre: plastfolie
Stenderverk: 48x128, cc 600 - 150 (128) isolasjon
Vindsperre
Klemlist: 11x48, cc 600
Spikerslag for kledning: 36x73
Utv. kledning: 30x146, malmfuru m/justert sidekant

Gulvbord: 25x162, furu. (Tegningen viser tynnere bord)
Evt. pappskikt
Bjelkelag: 48x198, cc 600 - 200 iso.
Vindsperre
Stubbeloft: 15x145 underpanel, furu. (Tegningen viser tykkere bord)

36x48

Peisfundament

Denton & Corker & Marshall
Marshall House

Photographs: John Gollings

Phillip Island, Victoria, Australia

This is a weekend holiday house overlooking a small bay two hours east of Melbourne.

Buried into the dunes, the house is visible from the beach as a low black line - the color of the rocks - with ragged tufts of dune grass above it. It is completely hidden from the landward side. The objective was to maintain a low profile and to have an internal focus to the house, avoiding engagement with the surrounding context.

The house is a long thin concrete box, black inside and out, set along one edge of a large square courtyard contained by three-meter-high black concrete walls with dune berms ramped up to roof level on three sides. On the open ocean elevation, windows are sized and positioned within each room to act as picture frames to the views, and the proportions and locations of the windows are determined by these internal considerations. The courtyard offers protection from winds and is a north facing sun trap in winter.

The house in no-way connotes a residence or domesticity. In its context it lurks like a Stealth bomber, hidden and subversive.

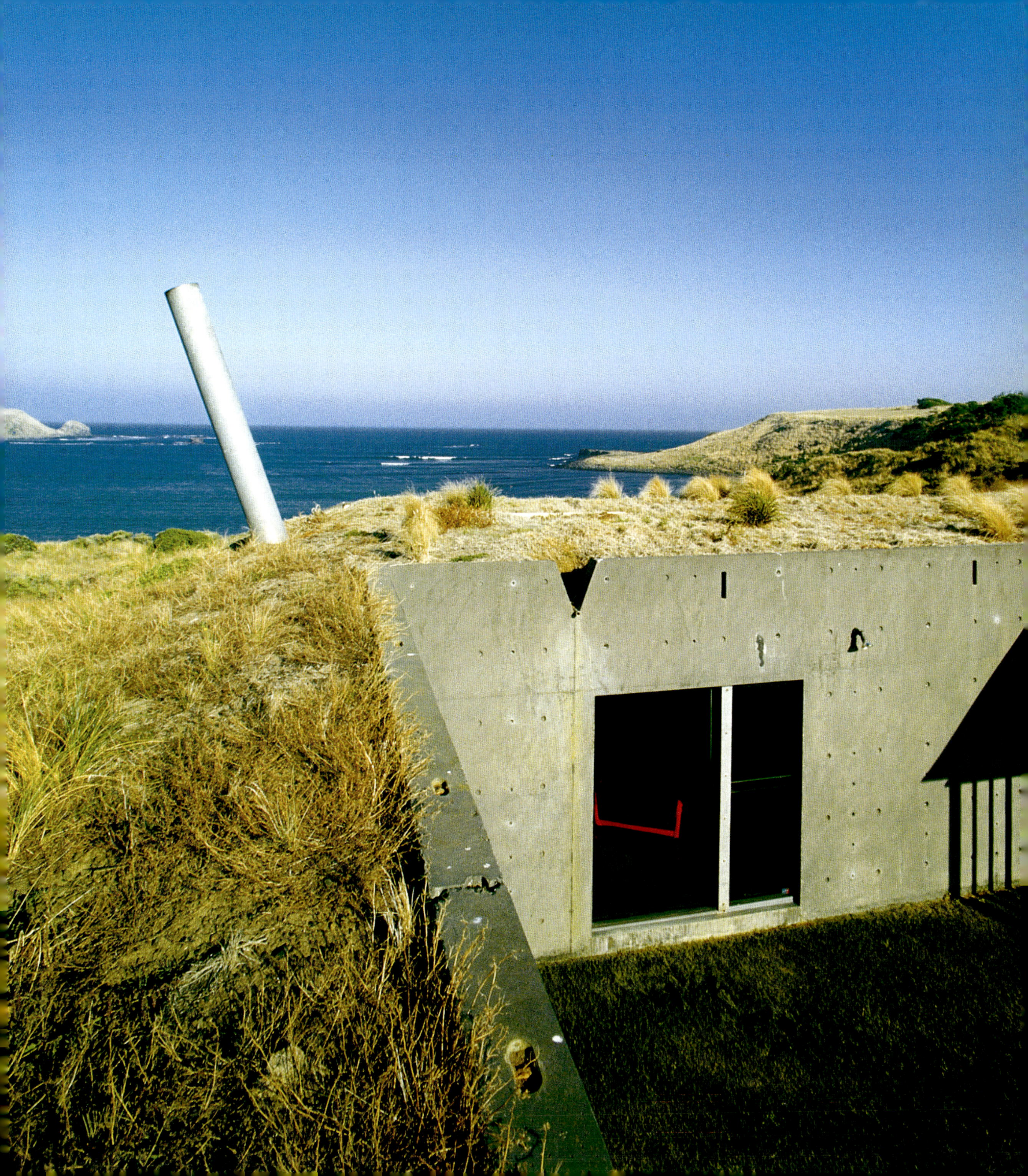

138

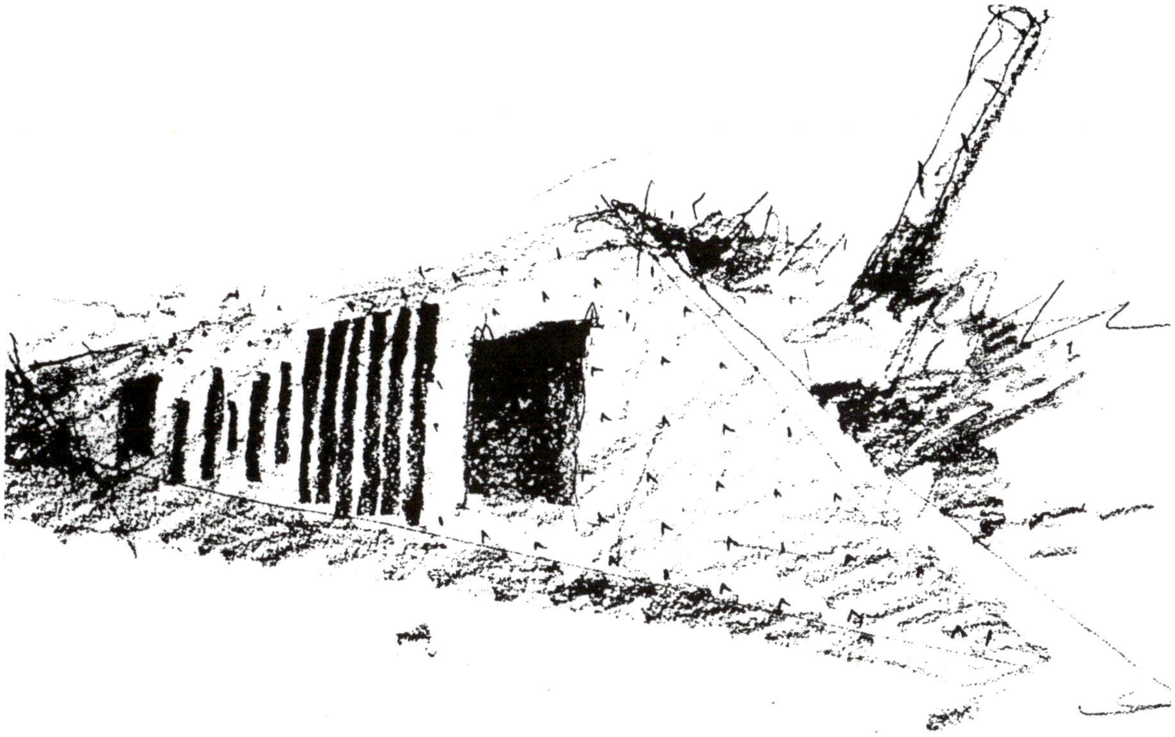

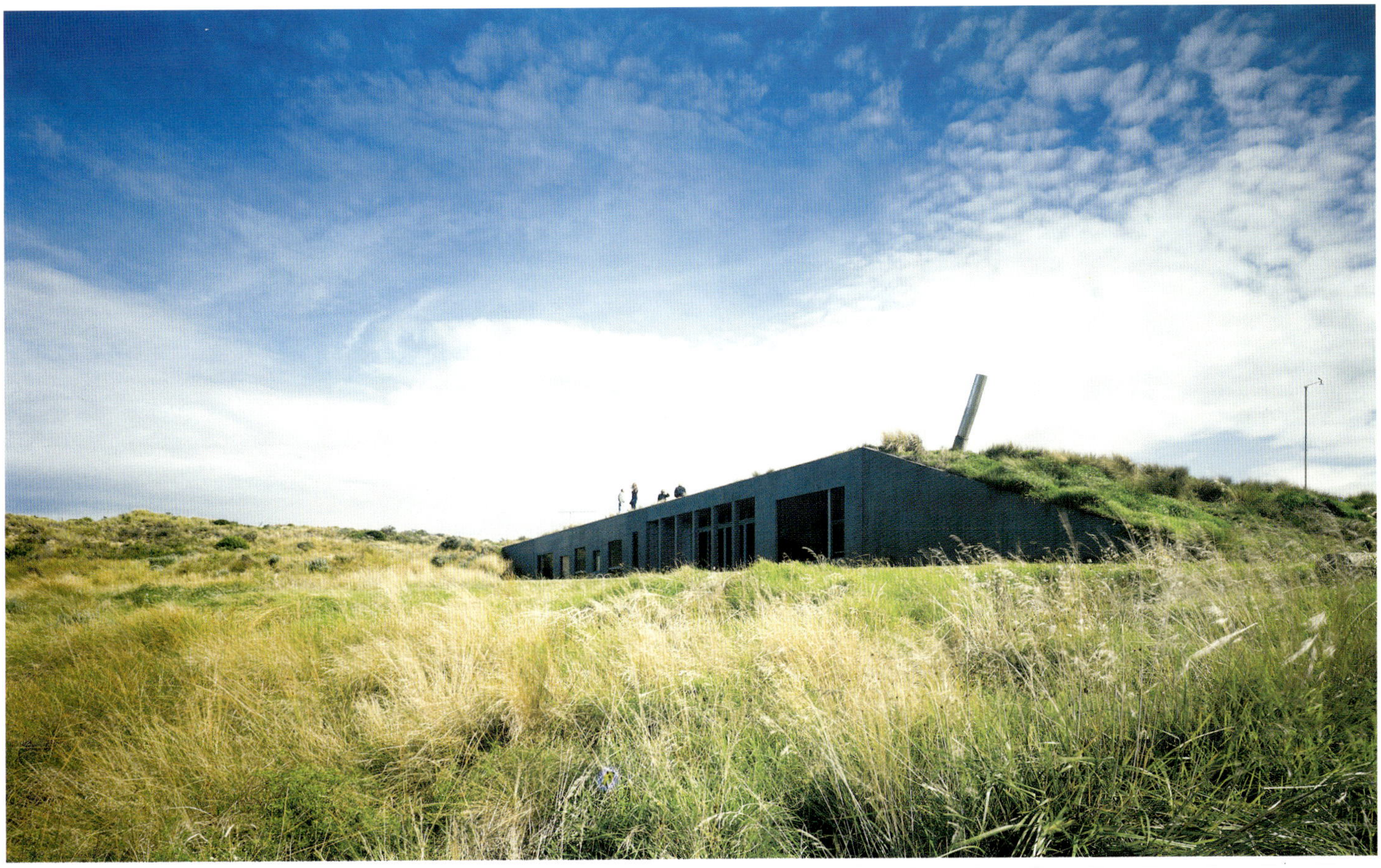

Main elevation

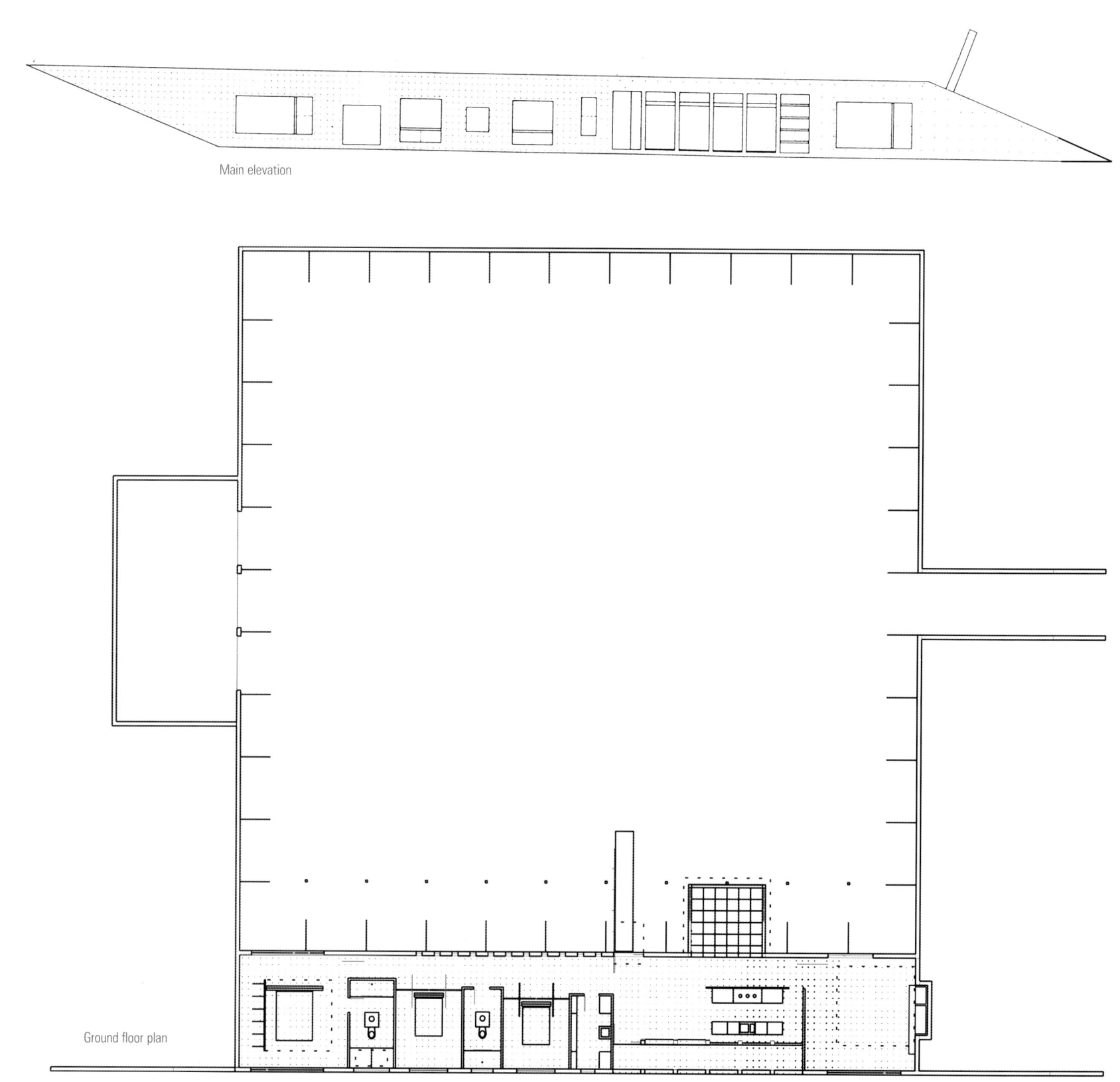

Ground floor plan

Windows are sized and positioned within each room to act as picture frames to the views.

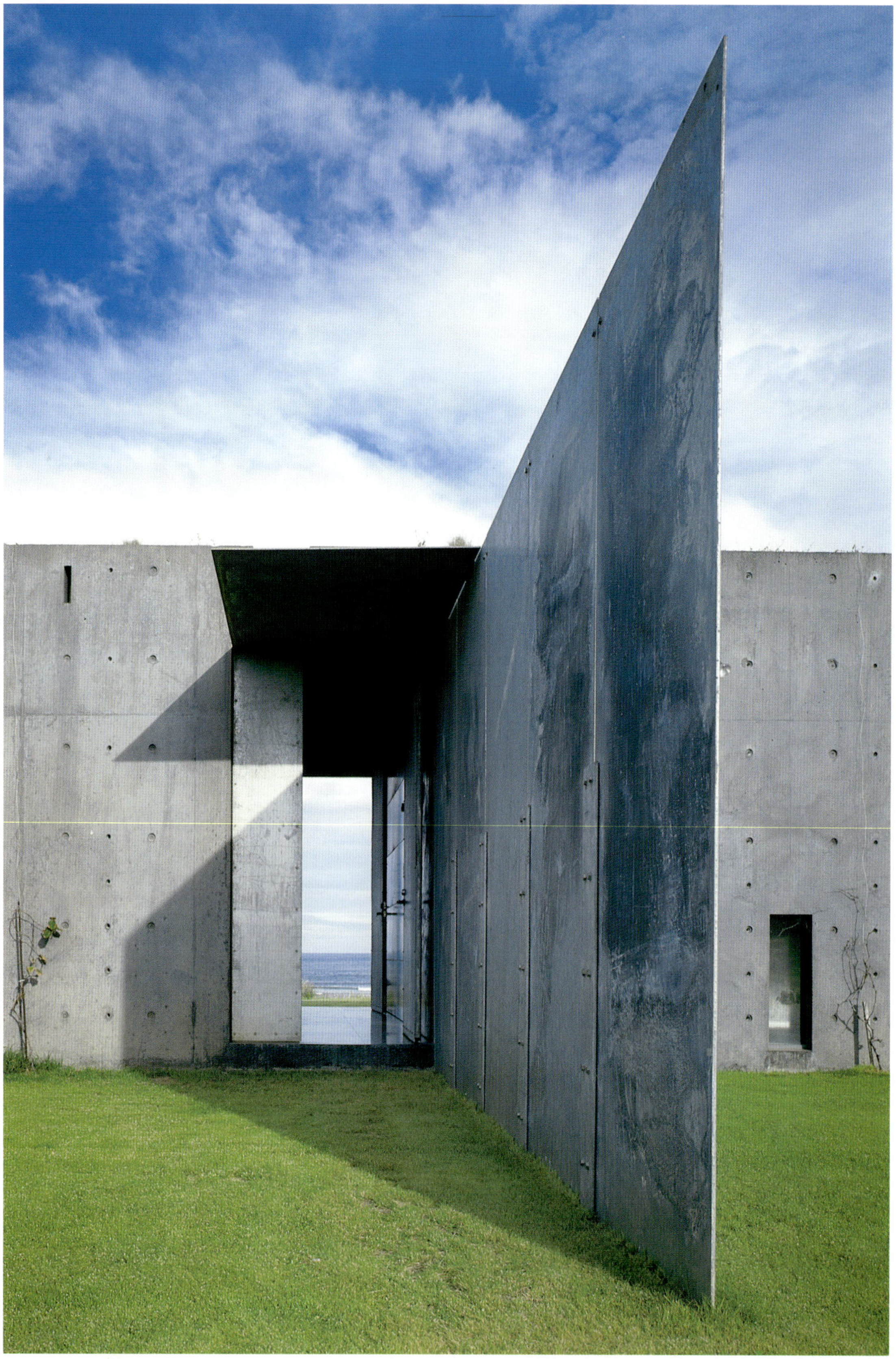

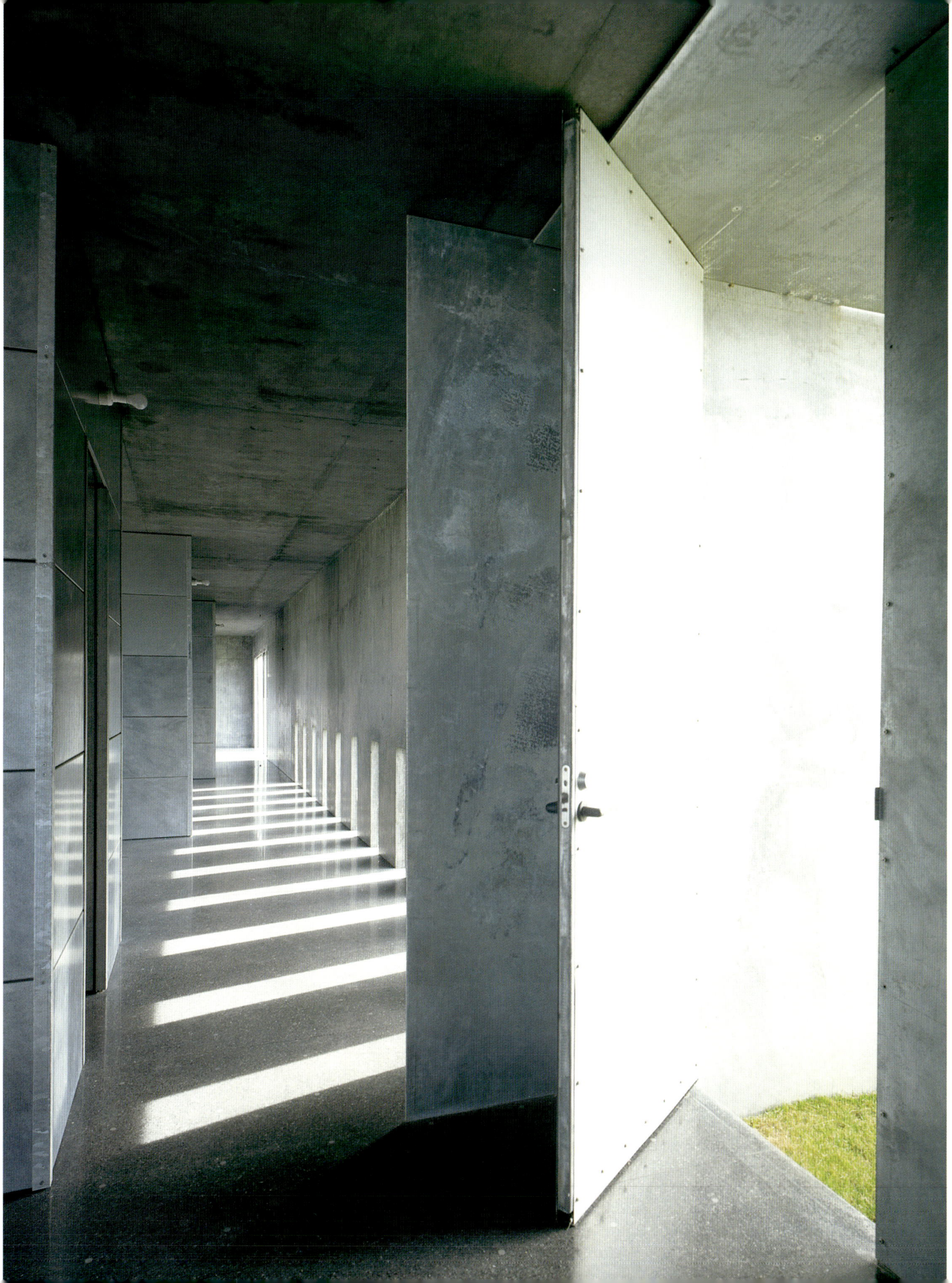

Peter Hulting Architect
Meter Arkitektur
Guest Appearance

Photographs: James Silverman

Gothenburg, Sweden

When Swedish architect Peter Hulting was asked to transform this old farm site into a couple's new home, he immediately saw the potential to create an unpretentious, sensitive space with the ability to connect both to its immediate surroundings and the neighboring open landscape. Specific only in their demands for a concrete floor and clay roof tiles, quality craftsmanship and simplicity were key to the couple's vision of "a house that could age with dignity".

Walking into this small summer house situated on Sweden's west coast peninsula, you are immediately struck by a sense of space that belies its 538 square feet (50 sq m) of floor space. Everything from the furniture to the lighting has been designed to enhance the building's shape and size - from the elongated Japanese-style table and benches, to the long steel-pipe chimney that guides the eye upwards from the open fire to the wooden ceiling.

A combination of wood, concrete and plaster creates a range of tactile surfaces that compare and contrast in equal measure. The smooth concrete floor incorporates the water-carried heating system, while the use of sawed larch tree for the exterior walls and reclaimed clay tiles on the roof allow the building to sit perfectly within this picturesque setting.

In order to maximize on the available space, Hulting opted for an open plan design. By creating a large glass frontage overlooking the south-facing landscape, sliding doors define the inner space when required, while at the same time ensuring the interior of the guesthouse remains cool in the summer.

Creating compact solutions in such a reduced space was central to the design concept; this was achieved, in part, by allowing the dividing walls to work like large pieces of furniture within the main space. Towards one end a wardrobe doubles as a wall divider, separating the sleeping area from the rest of the house. The reverse of this wardrobe doubles as a set of bookshelves at the foot of the bed. There is also space for two loft beds here, while the simple design of Ulf Scherlin's "Birå 4" cupboard ensures that any clutter is neatly stored away out of sight.

To the left of the bedroom, two sliding doors conceal the toilet and shower areas. The floors, tiled in Portuguese stone, offset standard white tiles that have been 'brick-mounted' and finished with a dark grey grout.

The kitchen sits in a semi-recess, cleverly defining its parameters without encroaching on the open-plan design of the overall space. The stainless steel of the kitchen contrasts beautifully with brightly colored handmade Portuguese tiles.

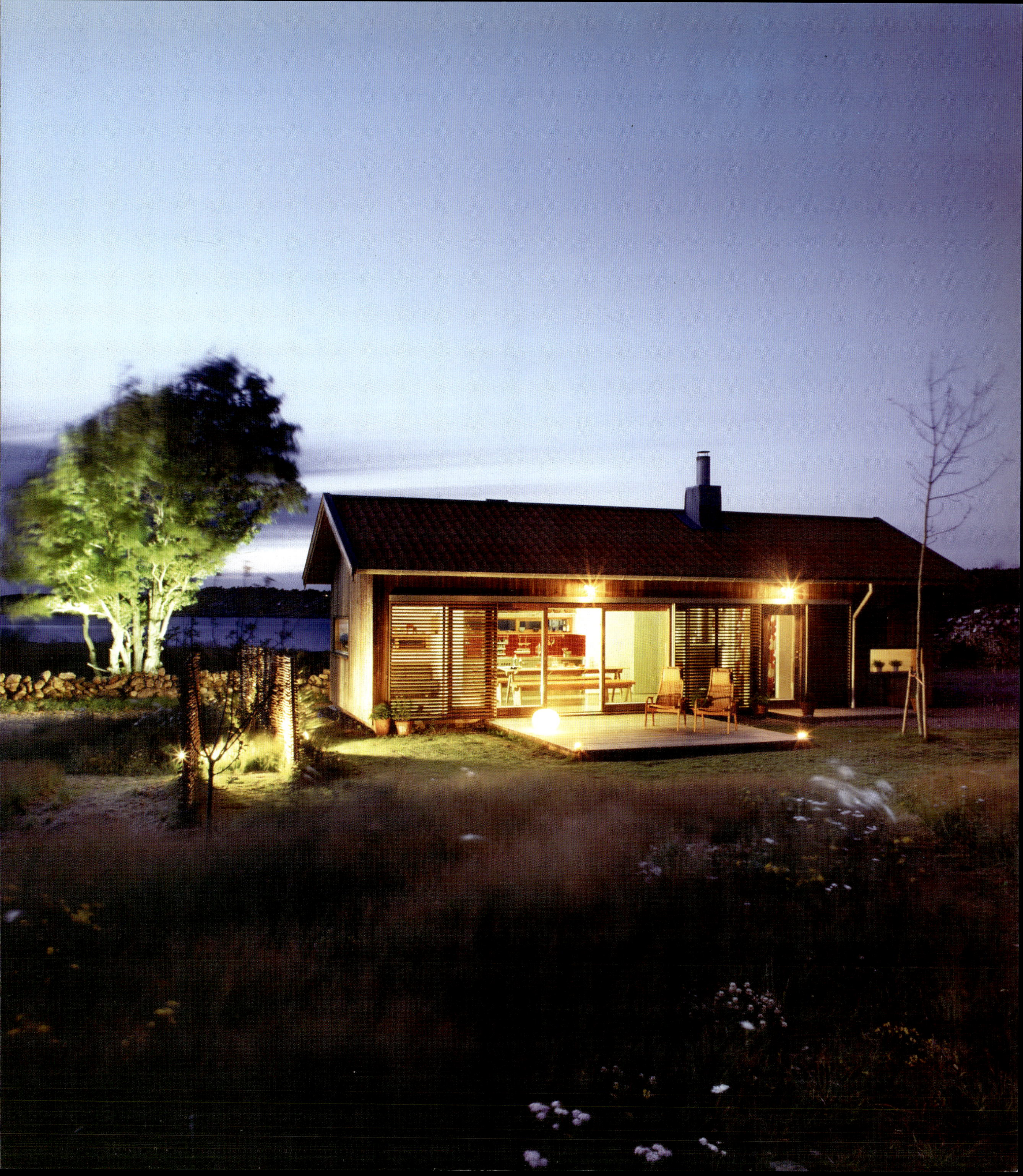

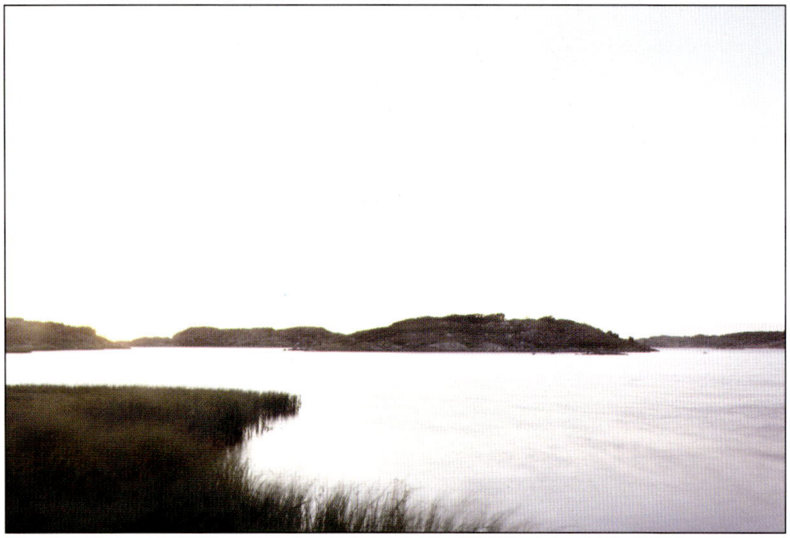

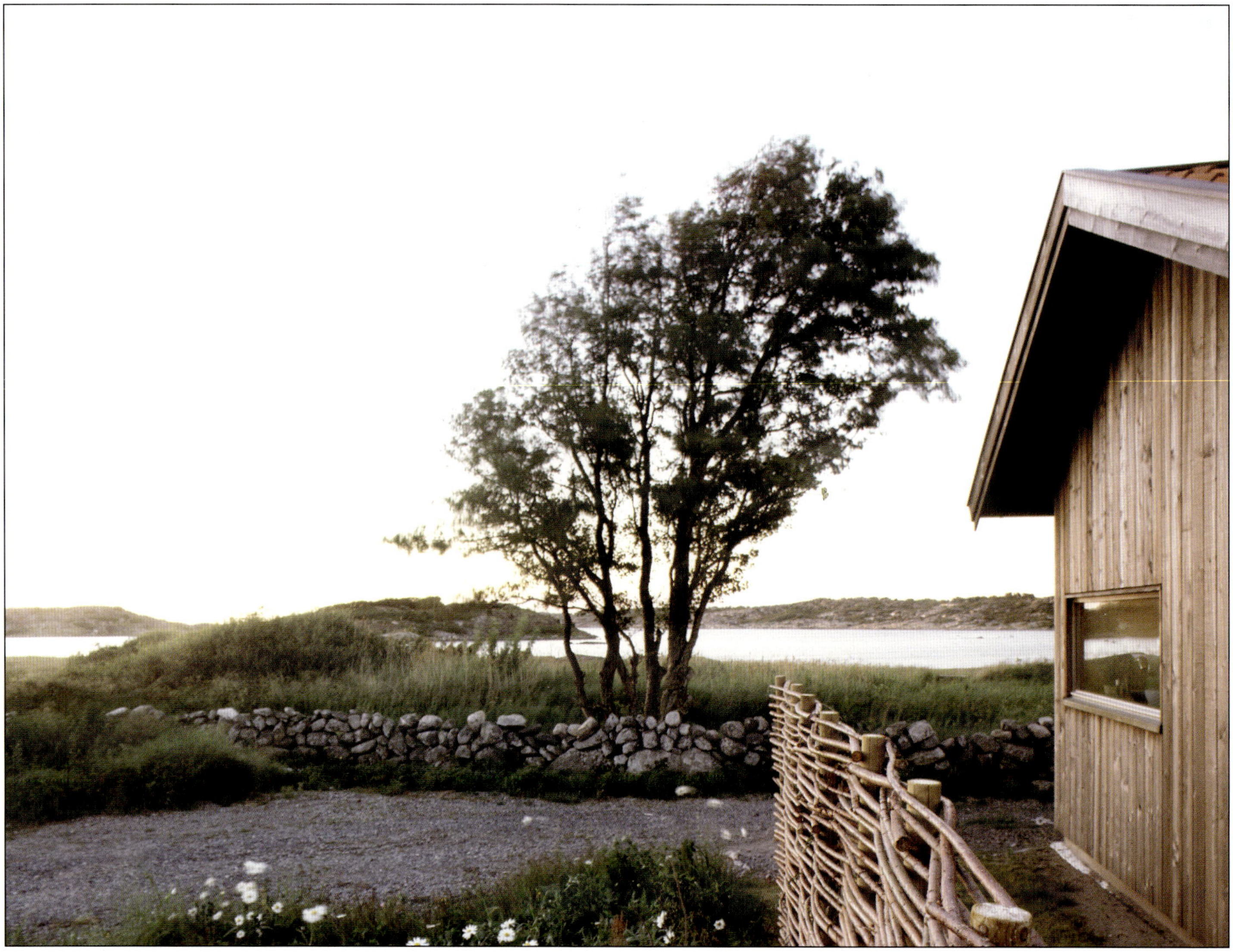

The shape of the dining table and benches add to the sense of space. Large sliding glass doors capitalize on the view and provide easy access to the exterior deck.

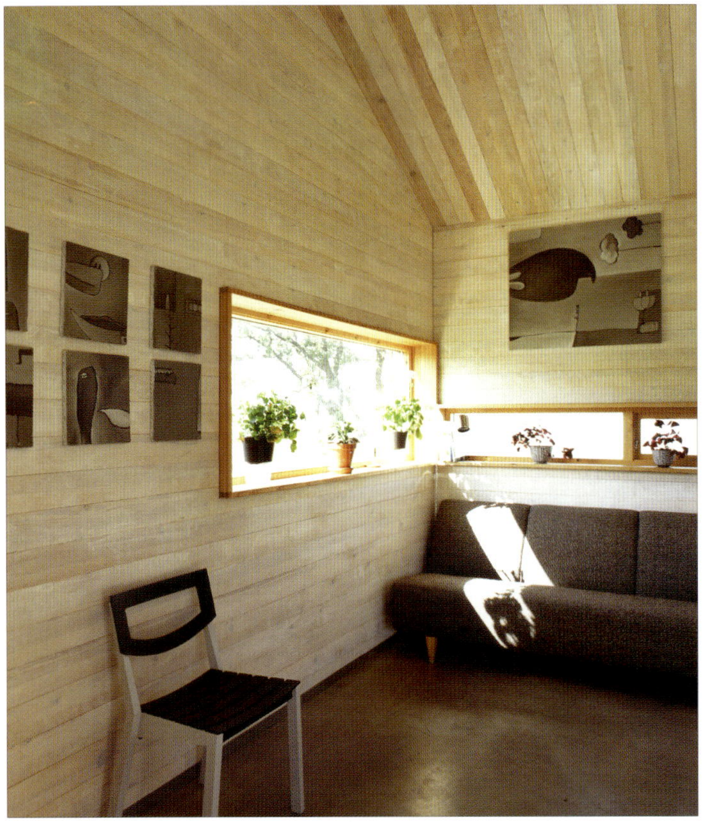

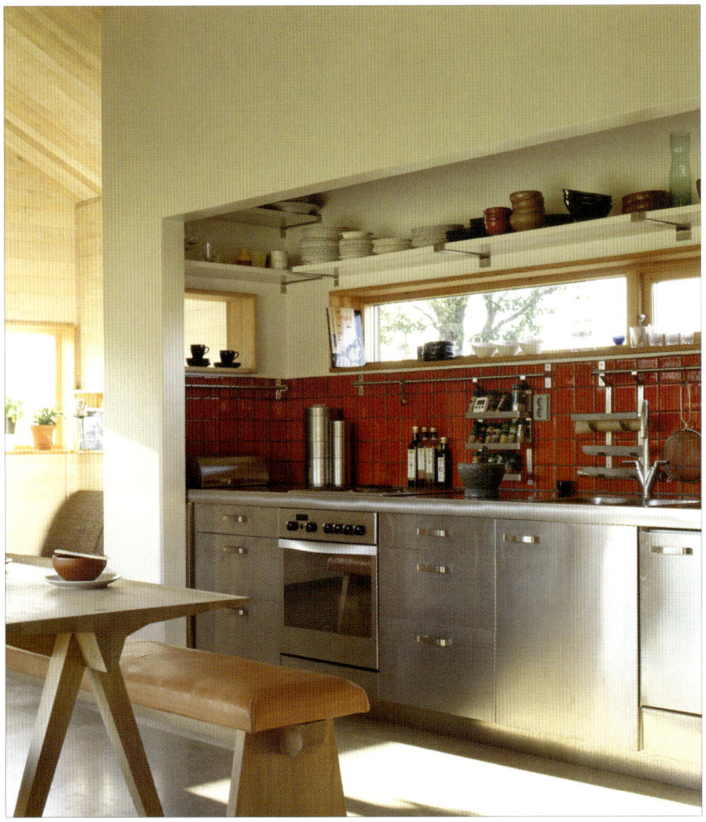

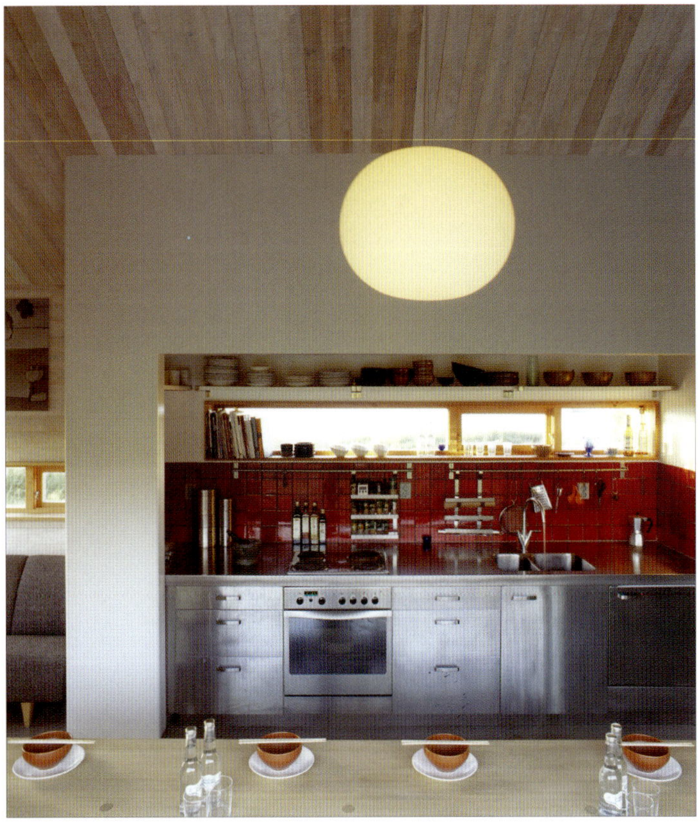

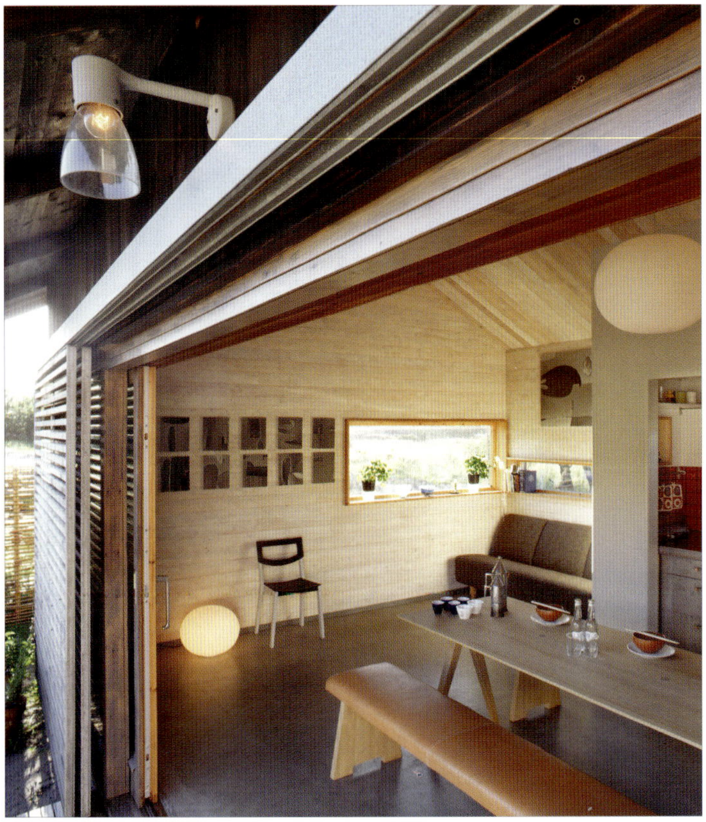

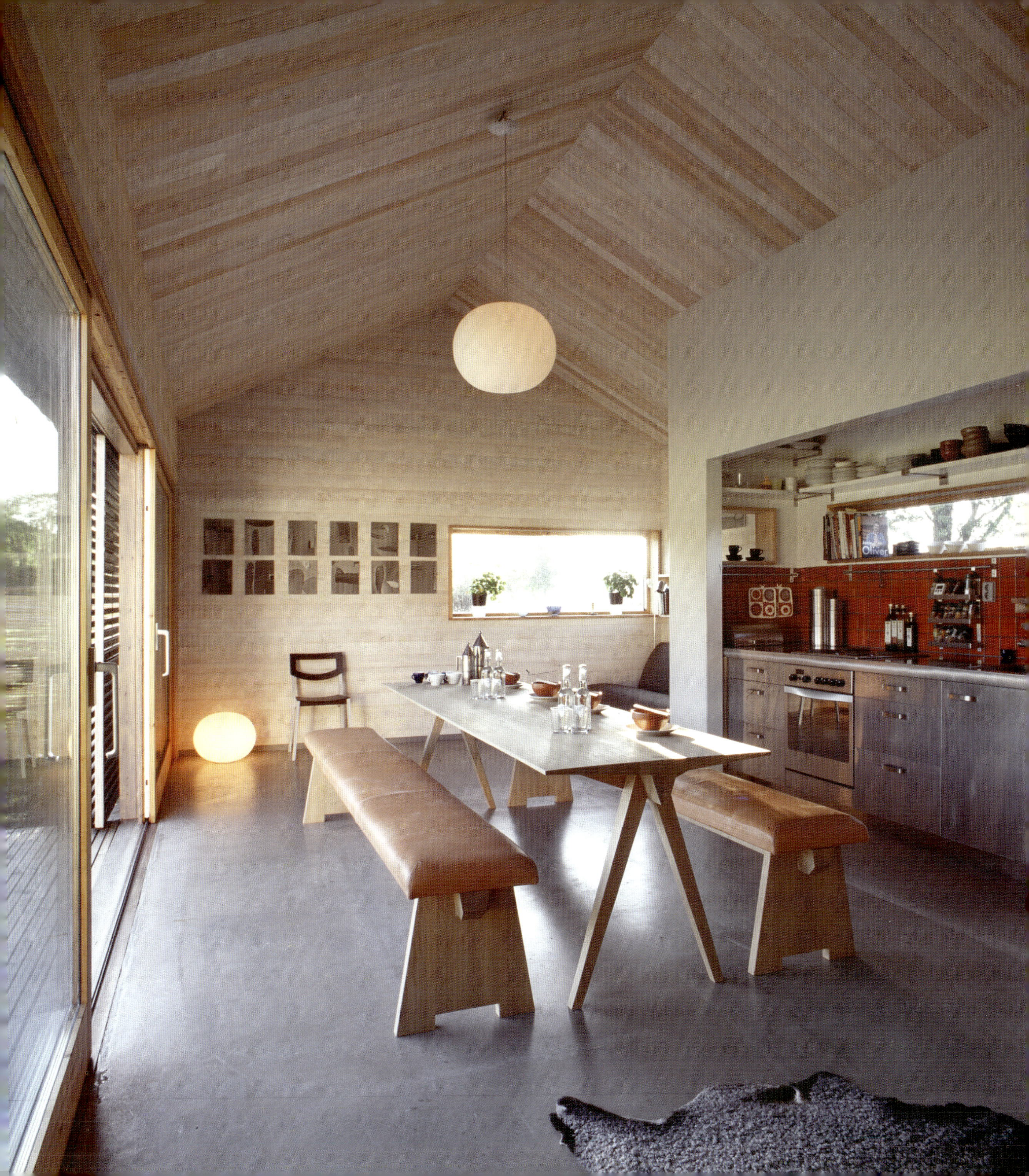
Oliver

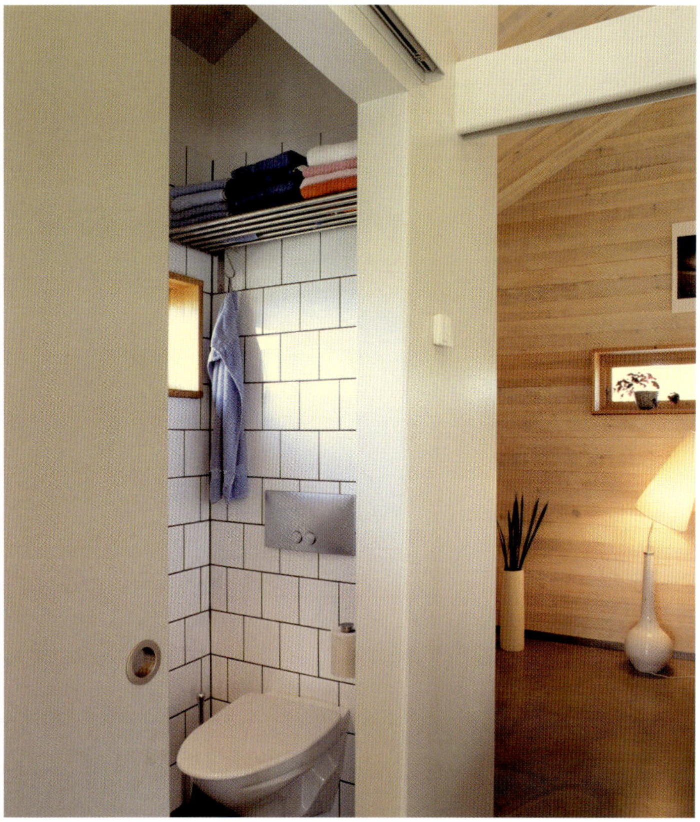
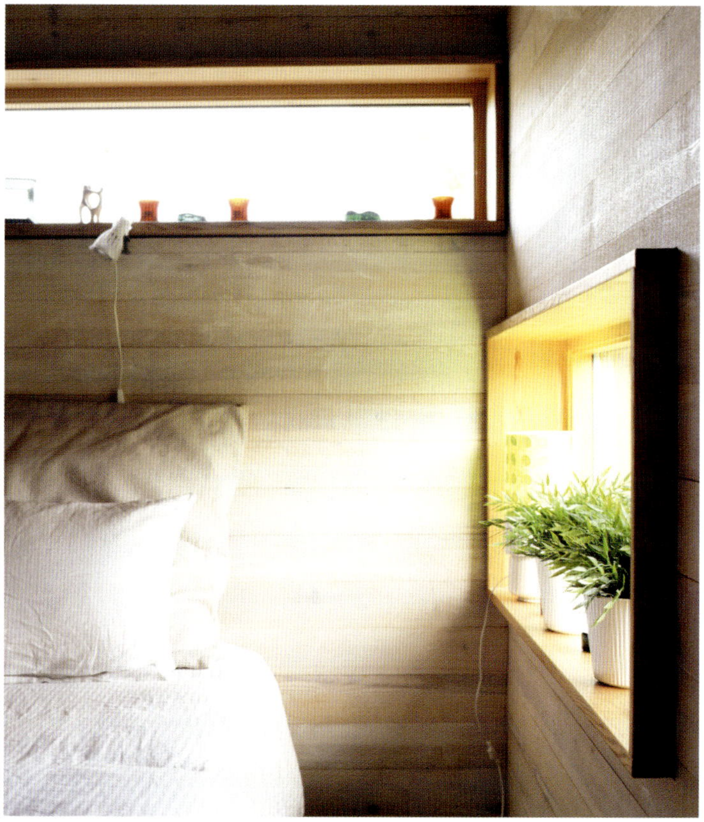
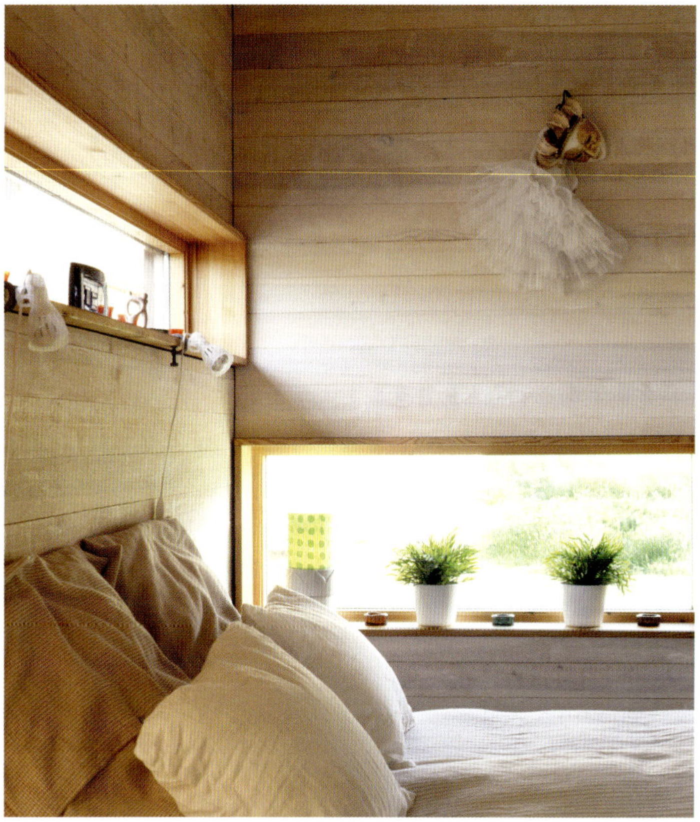
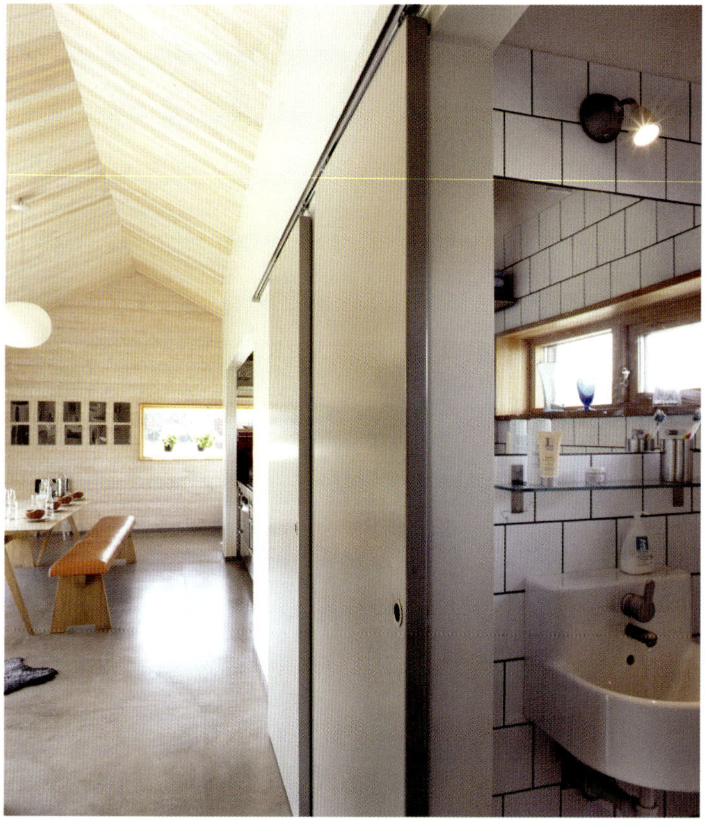

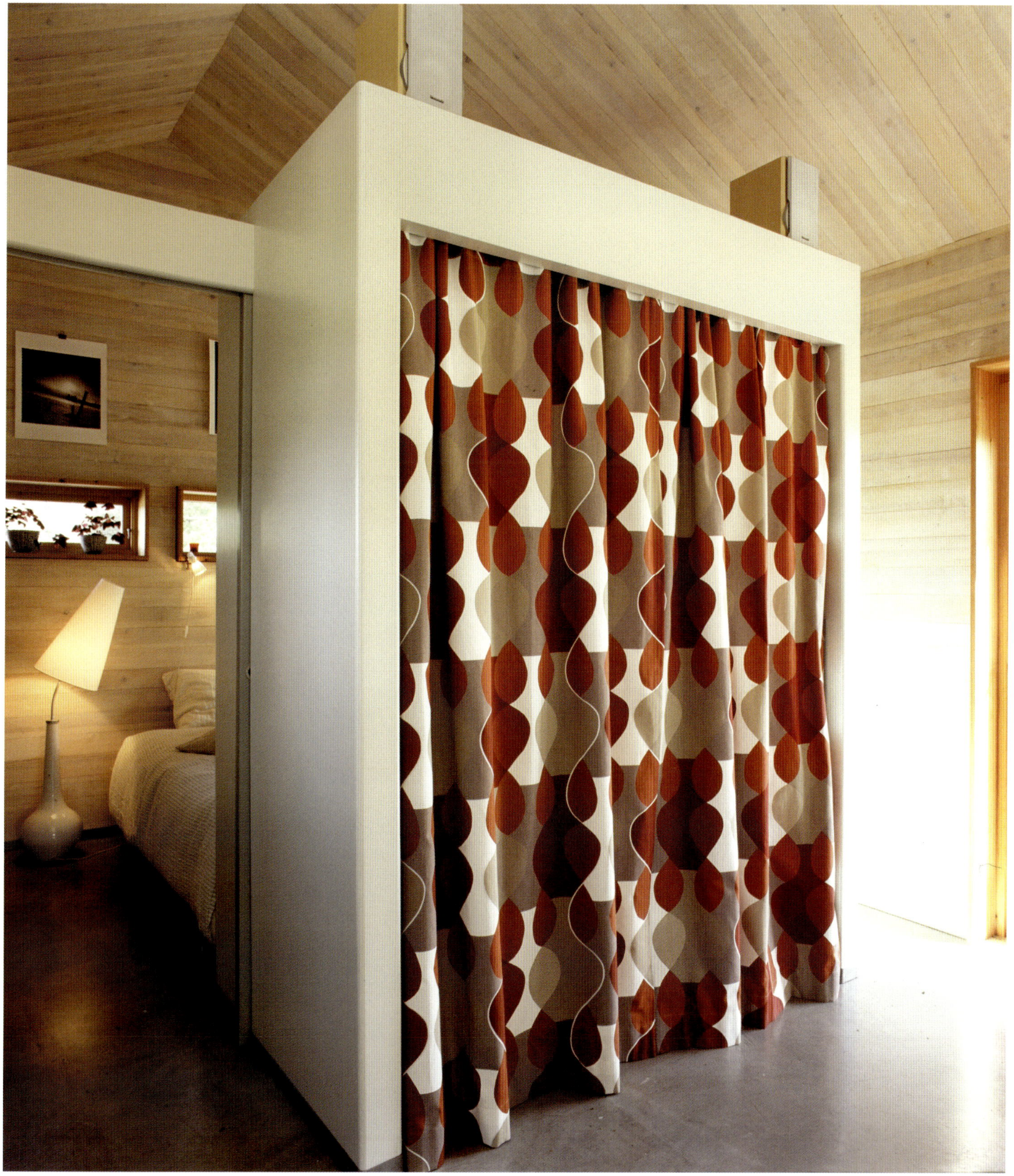

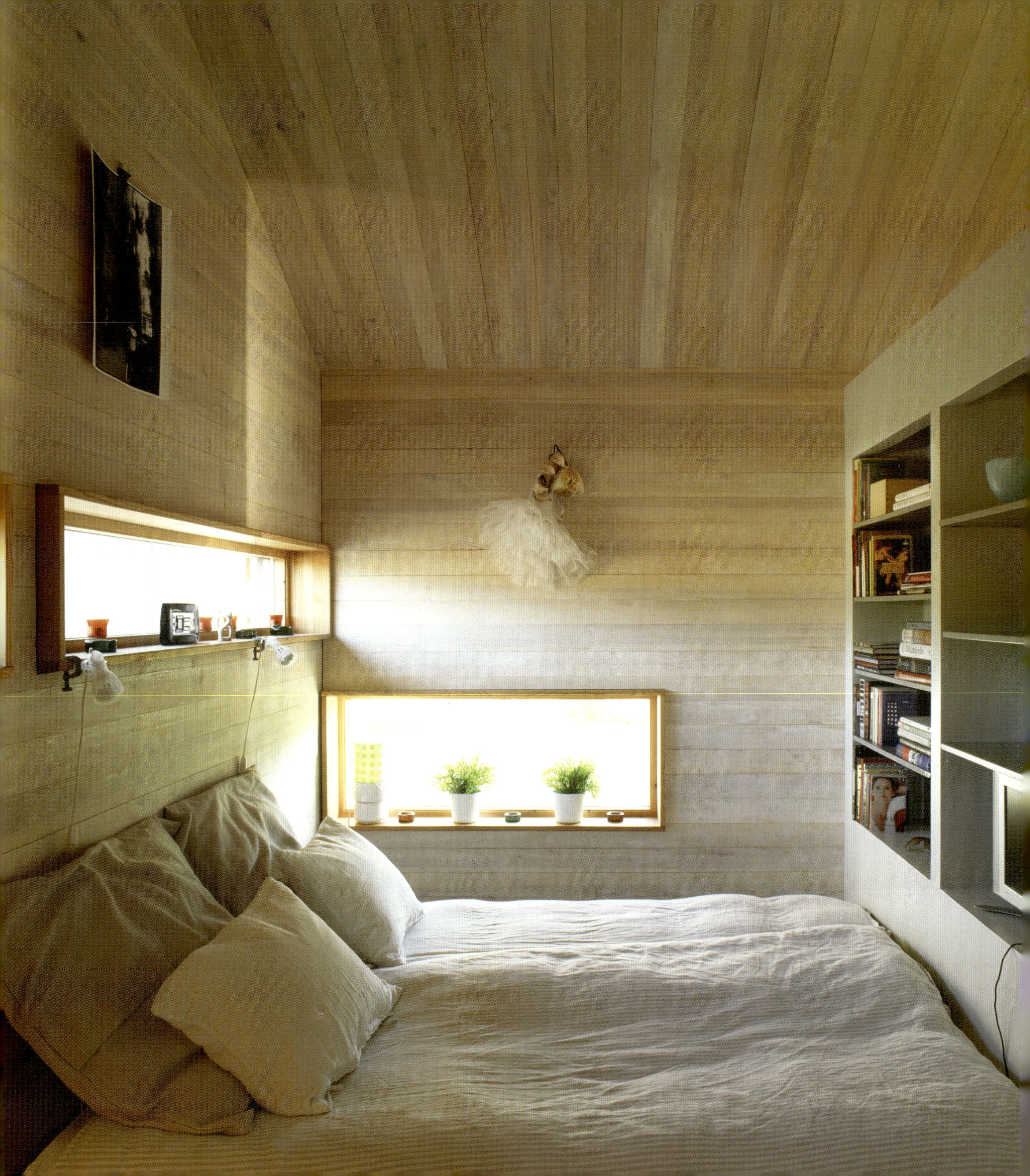

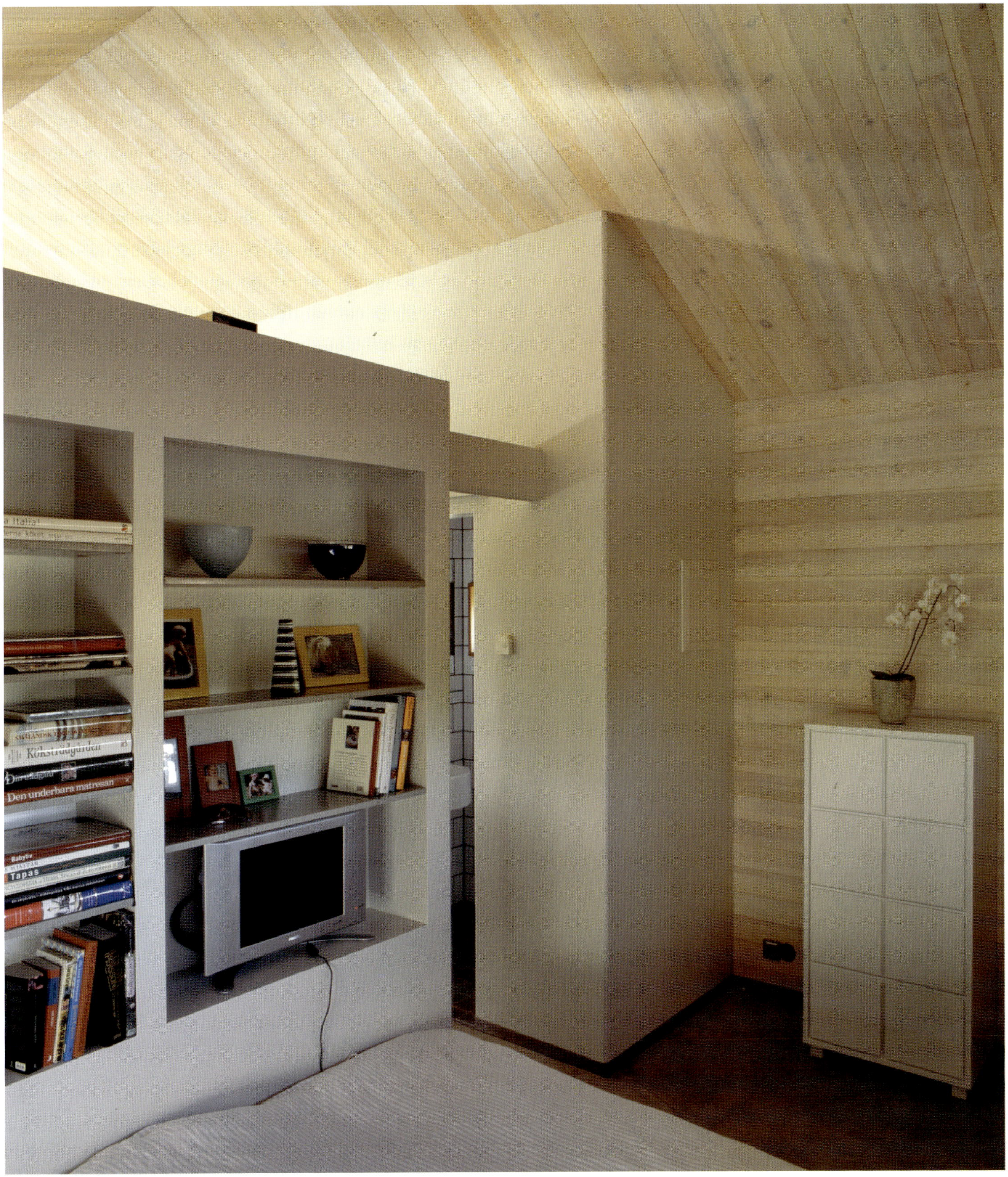
Den underbara matresan
Babyliv
Tapas

Jarmund-Vigsnæs
Villa Bjørnsen / Sund

Photographs: Nils Petter Dale

Nesøya, Norway

This suggestive residence designed by the prestigious Norwegian architects Jarmund & Vigsnaes spans two small hills in an exceptionally gorgeous area of Norway. The dip between the hills naturally forms the ideal setting for a small garden, which can be directly accessed from the house. The wall is penetrated by access points and window openings, revealing the layout oriented toward this front garden.

The simplicity of the Cartesian outer shell is contrasted by a rich and varied section, with a continuous light distribution filtered throughout the longitudinal section of the house.

The interior displays a clear and orderly distribution that allows for a certain degree of flexibility or an adaptation of the spaces via sliding doors that can alternately enlarge or close off the rooms. The garden-facing picture window in the living room floods this area with abundant natural light; likewise on the upper floor, where the TV rooms opens directly onto a terrace.

The interior design and choice of furniture have been meticulously planned, giving particular importance to the use of wood and standard Scandinavian design references, as seen in the chairs by Alvar Aalto.

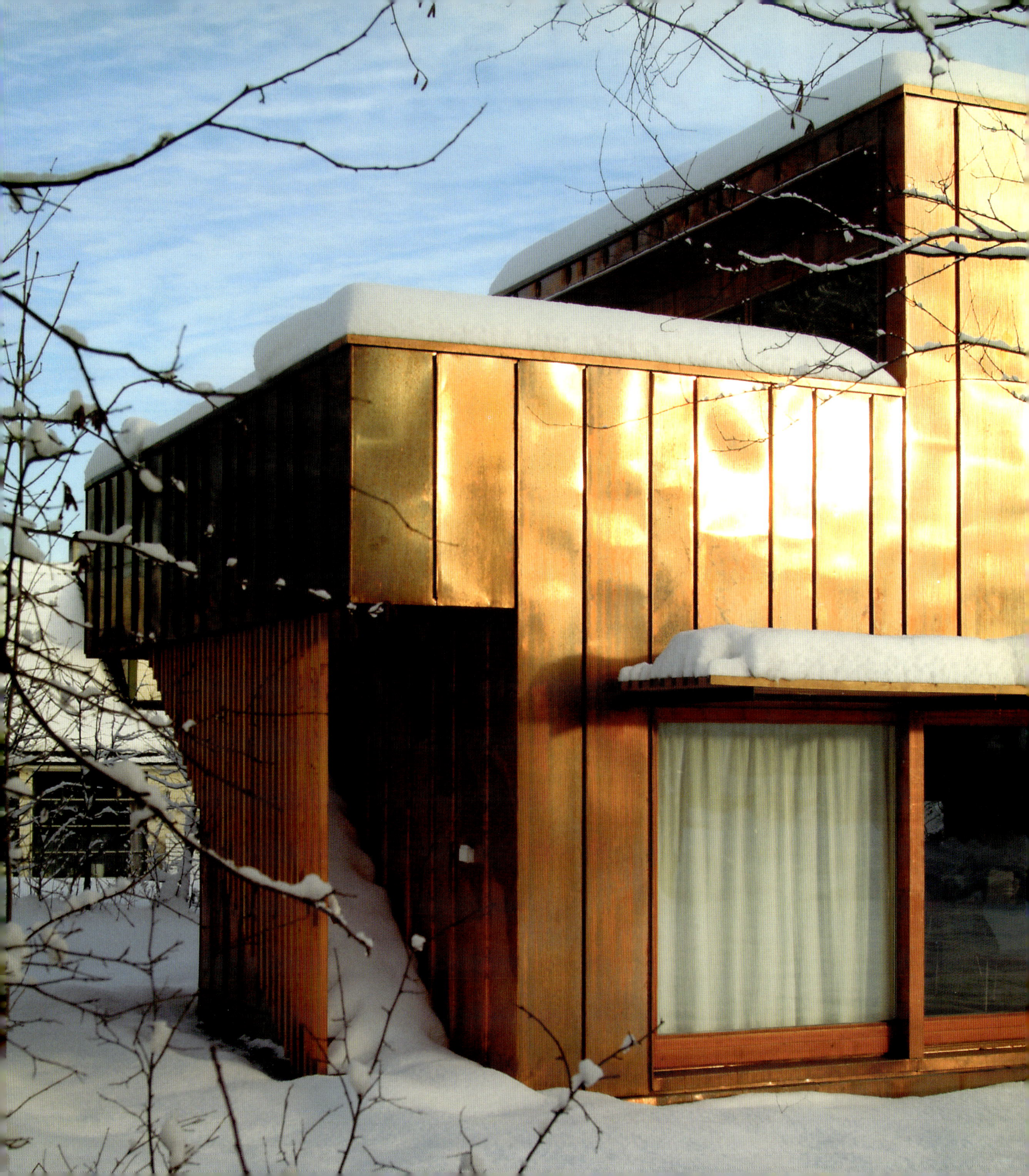

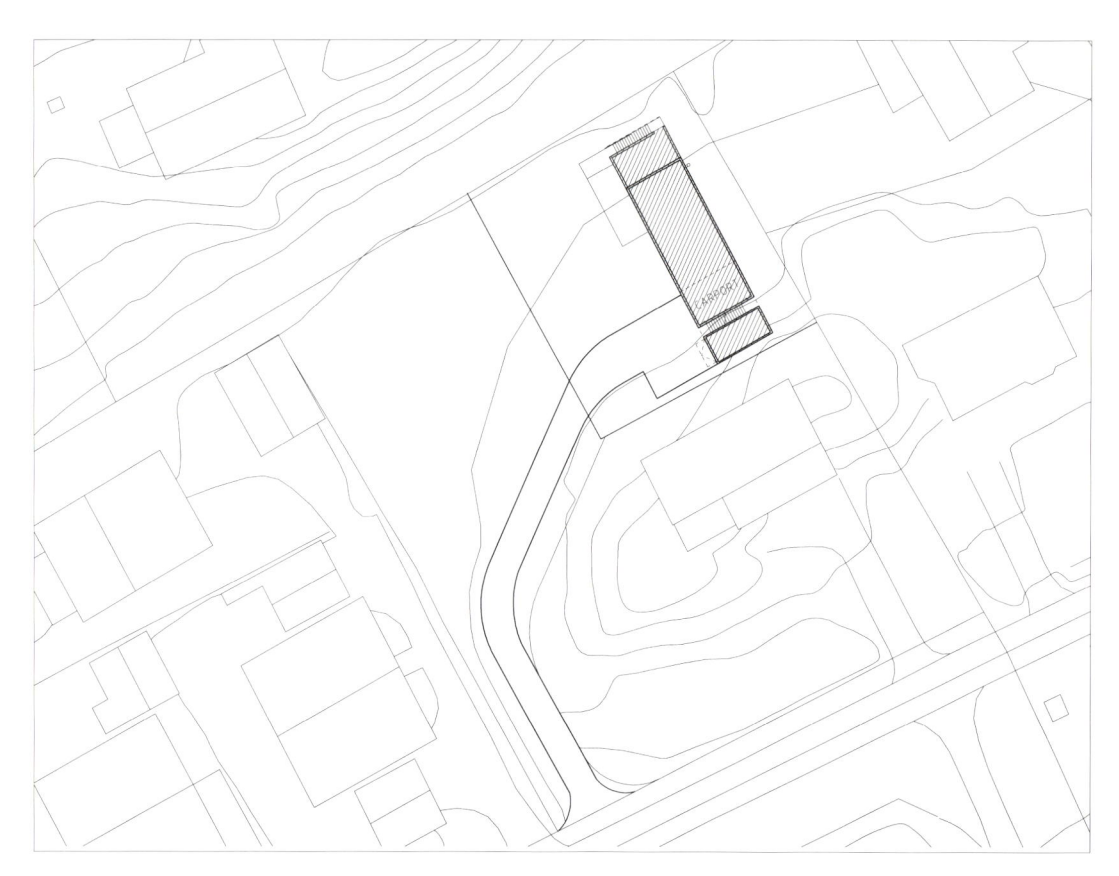

Because of its calculated placement within the site between two low hills, the house naturally delimits a garden, while at the same time ensuring a desirable degree of privacy.

Site plan

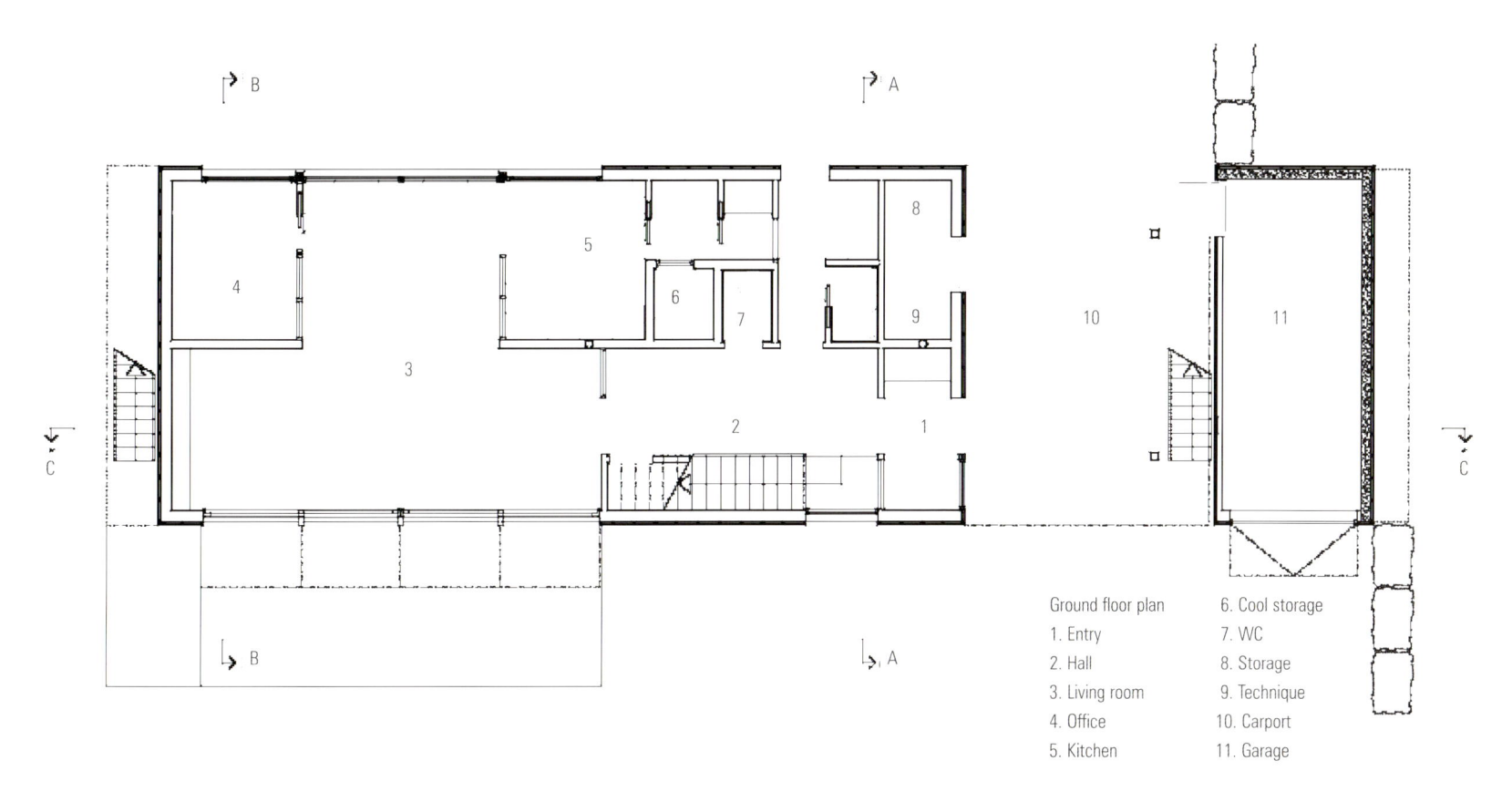

Ground floor plan
1. Entry
2. Hall
3. Living room
4. Office
5. Kitchen
6. Cool storage
7. WC
8. Storage
9. Technique
10. Carport
11. Garage

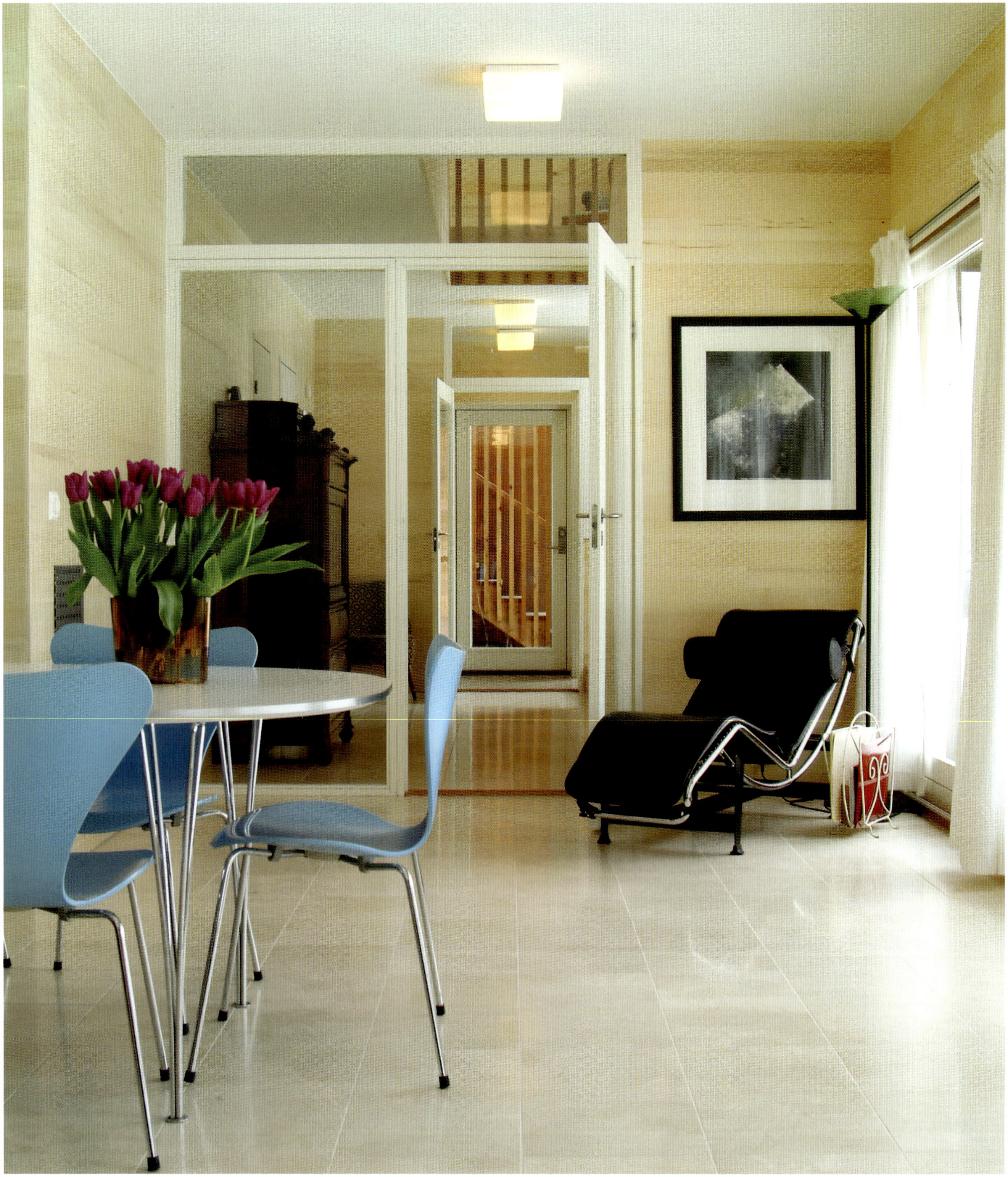

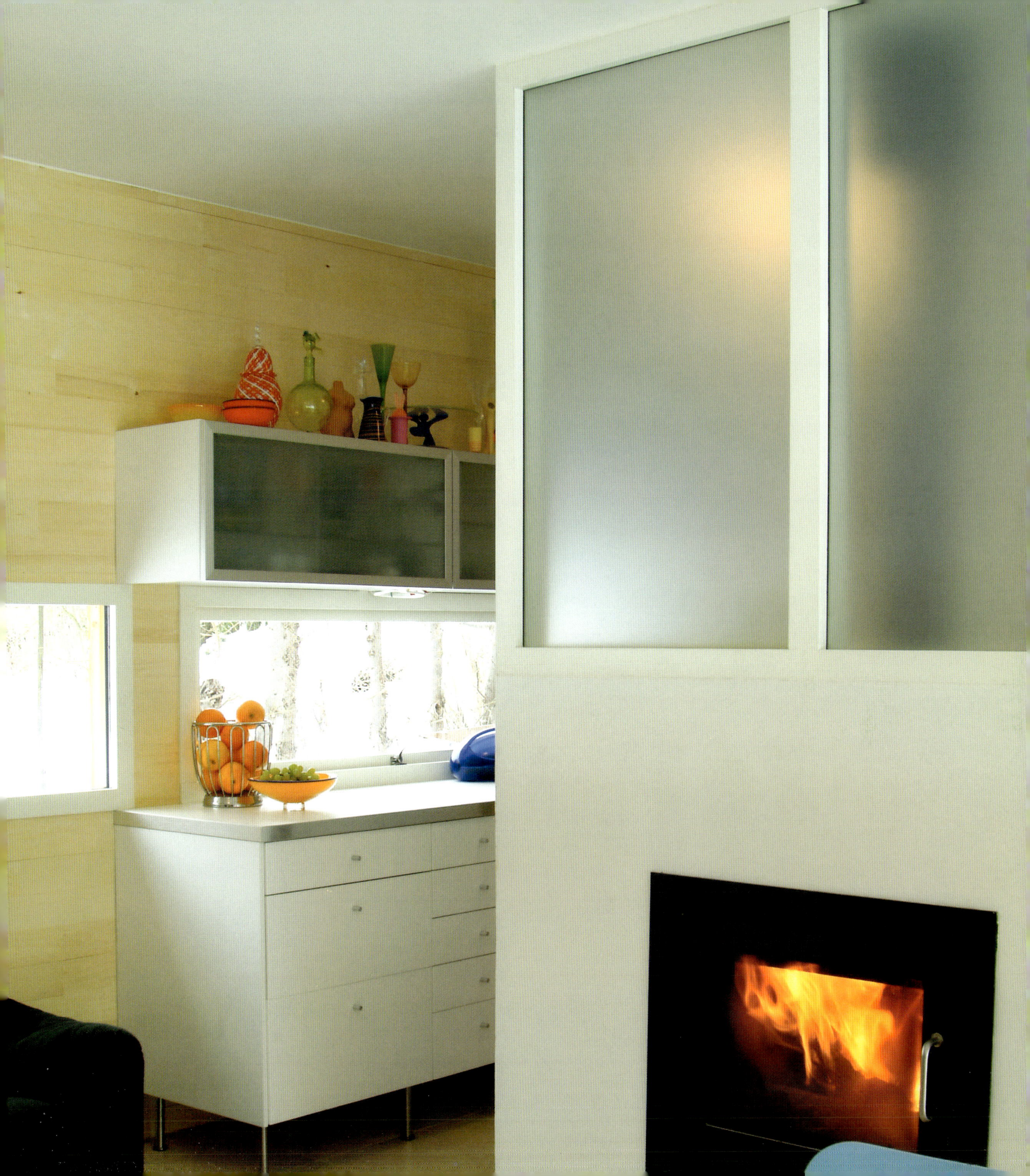

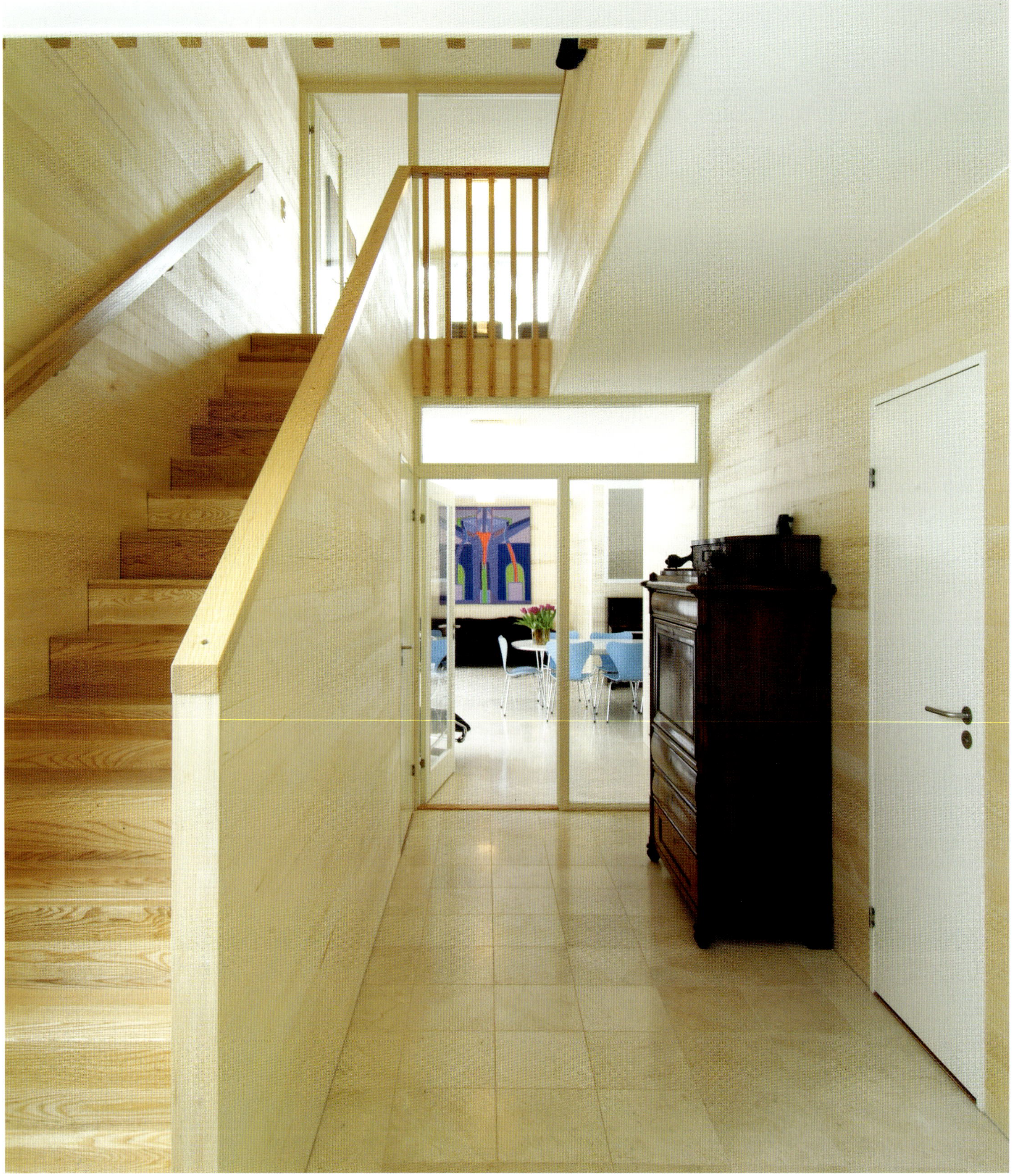

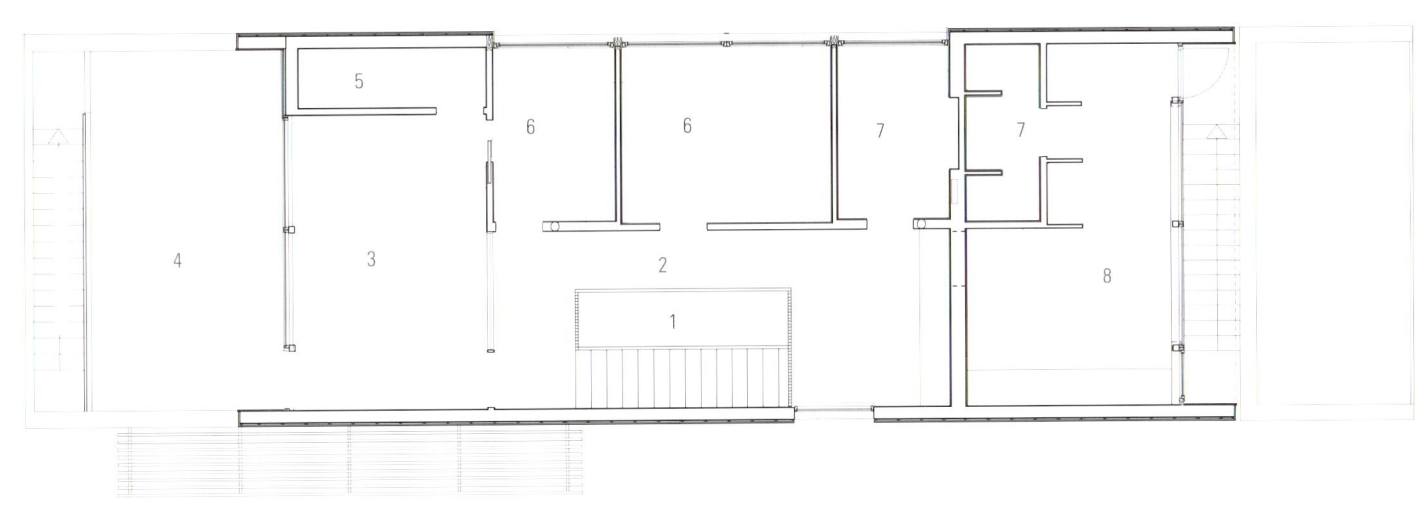

First floor plan
1. Open down
2. Hall
3. TV room
4. Terrace
5. Storage
6. Bedroom
7. Bathroom
8. Studio

Section CC

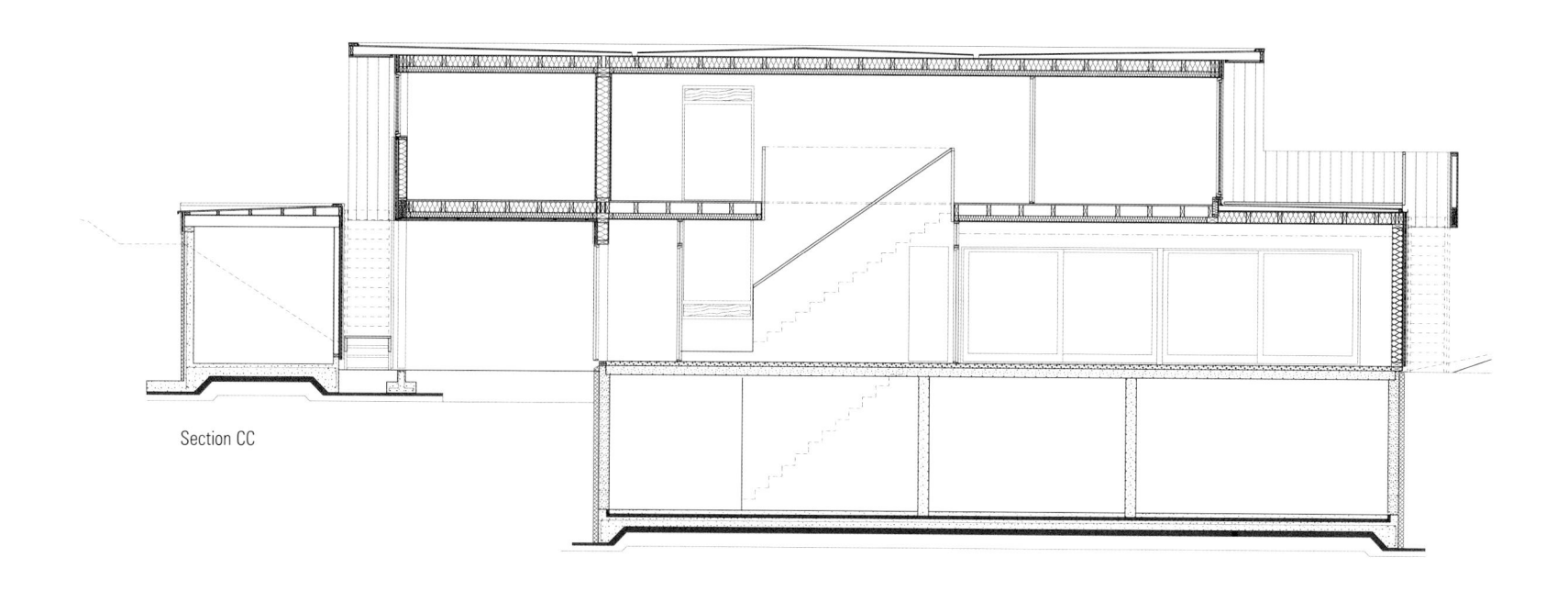

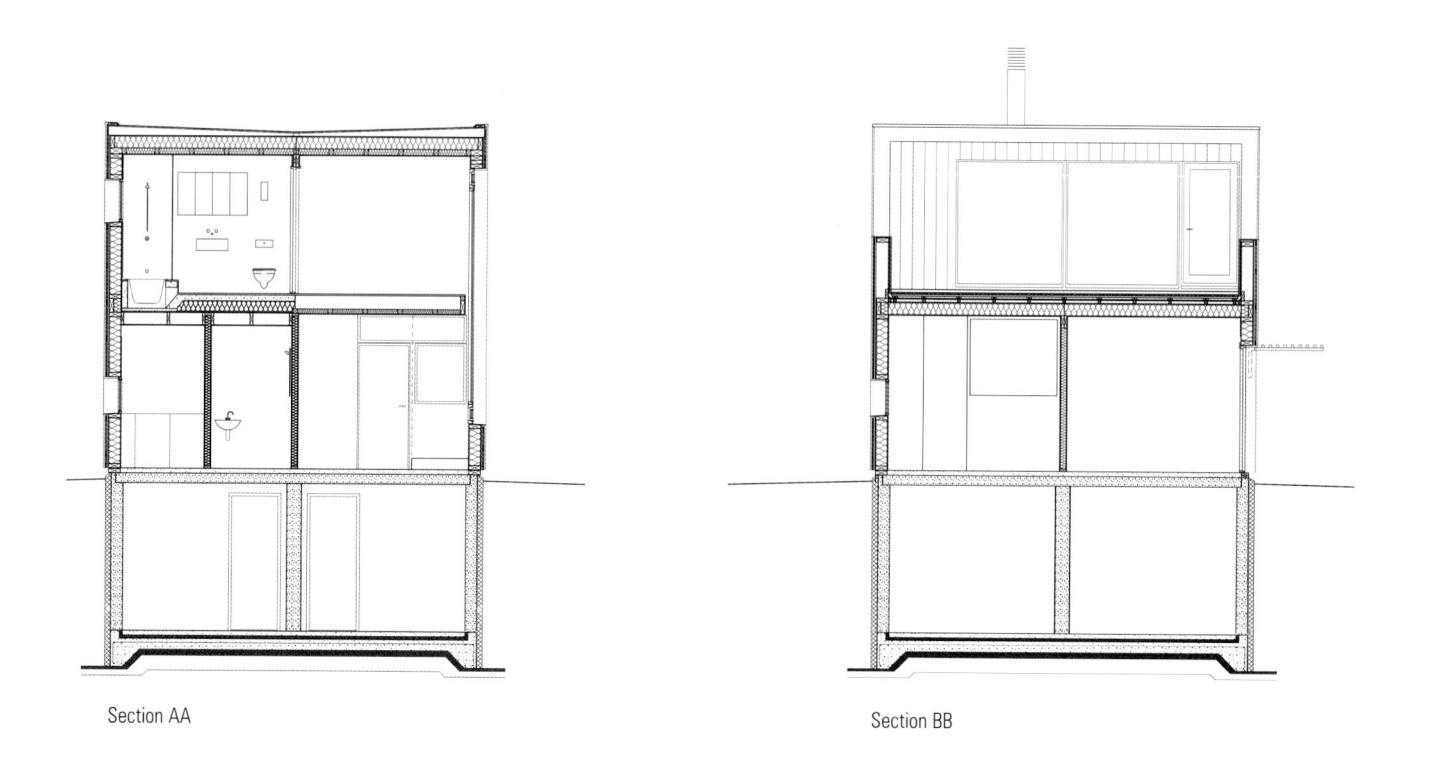

Section AA

Section BB

163

The simplicity of the Cartesian outer shell is contrasted by a rich and varied section, with continuous light filtered throughout the longitudinal section of the house.

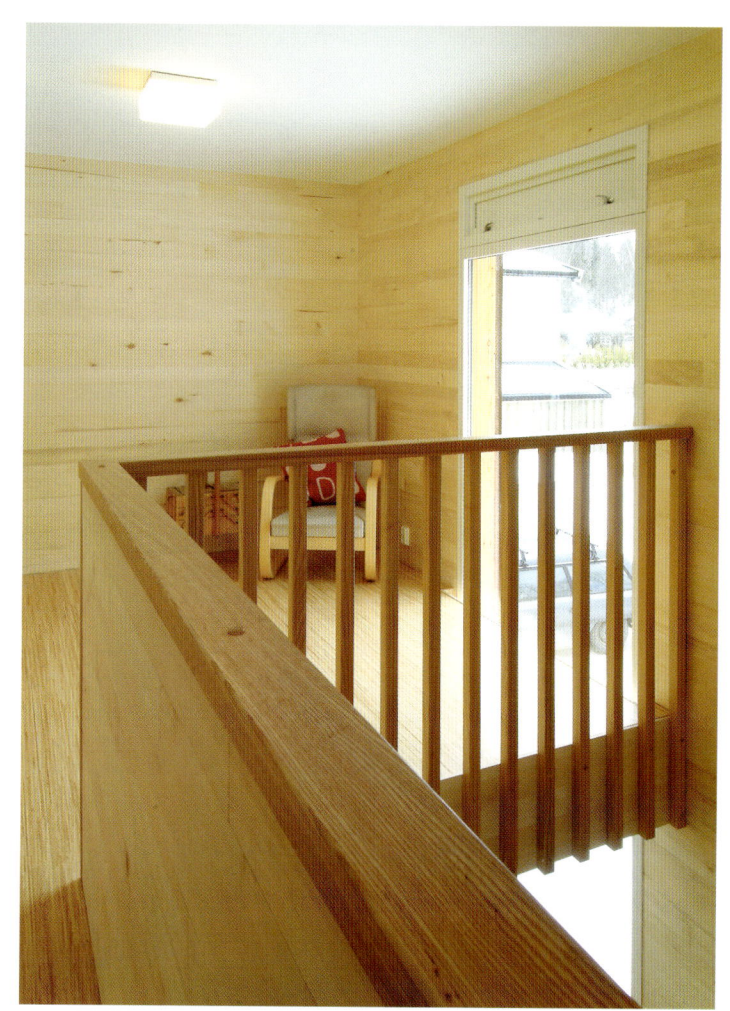

165